Almost White

ALMOST WHITE

Forced Confessions of a Latino in Hollywood

BY
RICK NAJERA

SMILEYBOOKS

Distributed by Hay House, Inc.
Carlsbad, California • New York City
London • Sydney • Johannesburg
Vancouver • Hong Kong • New Delhi

Published in the United States by: SmileyBooks, 250 Park Avenue South, Suite #201, New York, NY 10003 • www.SmileyBooks.com

Distributed in the United States by: Hay House, Inc.: www.hayhouse.com • *Published and distributed in Australia by:* Hay House Australia Pty. Ltd.: www.hayhouse.com.au • *Published and distributed in the United Kingdom by:* Hay House UK, Ltd.: www.hayhouse.co.uk • *Published and distributed in the Republic of South Africa by:* Hay House SA (Pty), Ltd.: www.hayhouse.co.za • *Distributed in Canada by:* Raincoast: www.raincoast. com • *Published and distributed in India by:* Hay House Publishers India: www.hayhouse.co.in

Cover Design: Juan Roberts/Creative Lunacy
Interior Design: Cindy Shaw/CreativeDetails.net

Library of Congress Control Number: 2013943812

Tradepaper ISBN: 978-1-4019-4312-7

SUSTAINABLE
FORESTRY
INITIATIVE
Certified Chain of Custody
Promoting Sustainable Forestry
www.sfiprogram.org
SFI-01268
SFI label applies to the text stock

14 13 12 11   4 3 2 1
1st edition, September 2013
Printed in the United States of America

To my wife, Susie, and our children,
Julian, Sonora, and Kennedy—
your love has made me a better man.

CONTENTS

Author's Note

This is a work of nonfiction.
Conversations have been reconstructed
to the best of my memory.

PROLOGUE: WELCOME TO THE ICU

"Although I lived in comedy, I looked more like a victim in a medical drama. The wound to my head created a dangerous swelling on my brain."

I was bleeding badly. My forehead was pouring blood from a wound over my right eye. I was incoherent from the fever raging throughout my body. They found a blood trail leading from my front room to the living room to under my daughter's bed, as if I had sought refuge there. More blood led to my bedroom, where I finally collapsed.

My house looked more like a crime scene than a home. They found blood outside as well. Where it all began I will never know for sure. What *is* certain is that, after I struck my head, I crawled my way to my bedroom. It was over six hours before my wife and daughter found me. By that time, the wound over my eye bled slowly because I had so little blood left to lose.

Susie, my wife, said I was unresponsive when she dialed 911. I was lucky my wife was Anglo. If she had been Latina, she would have never called 911 until she had thought of a good alibi to tell the police. I joke, mostly because it's how I deal with pain. It's also how I find my way to the truth.

I had pneumonia and I didn't even know it. The pneumonia had left me hallucinating with fever, which must have caused me to have a seizure and fall. I always said I never felt rested with my hectic schedule and now, ironically, I was deep in a coma.

When the paramedics arrived, they assigned me a number three on the official Glasgow Coma Scale (GCS). Why they rate comas in Glasgow is a mystery, but a three on the coma scale is as close to death as one can be. When the ambulance brought me into the ICU, the doctors confirmed my Glasgow "three." Although Susie was hysterical and crying, had I been conscious, I would have been fixated on the GCS. That's just how my mind works. A coma scale named after a city is a concept too enticing to ignore.

Do other cities have coma scales named after them? Why not a Tulsa, Oklahoma Coma Scale (which must be a very deep coma with fried catfish and cars going in a circle)? Why do people in Glasgow rate comas? Was it for bragging rights? *"Ach, Seamus, a three on the Glasgow Coma Scale is nothing. I was a wee two and still could drive myself to the hospital!"*

In reality, there were much more important questions that needed to be answered, such as, was I going to live? And, if I did return to the living, would I have brain damage? It was so sudden, my fall. One moment you're living and the next, you're almost dead. There is no brave final speech as you lie dying on the noble field of battle. Most people die in mundane ways. Like choking on a ham sandwich or an allergic reaction to a bee sting. Or lately, from texting while driving, leaving last texts like "I'M RUNNING A LITTLE LAAAAAAAAAAATE." This is how you die surprised and alone.

Within hours, friends heard of my "collapse" on Facebook. Then it spread to Twitter. I was an Internet sensation. The rumors were flying. Stroke. Heart attack. Some said I had walked in on a robbery. The truth was this: I was dying from a perfect storm of pneumonia and head injury. The pneumonia, coupled with a seizure and a fall, created a gaping wound over my right eye. Days later in the hospital, I had two black and swollen eyes and blistered lips. I looked like someone who lost a battle in a medieval war.

After my MRI, the doctors warned my wife, "Rick may not come back as his normal self." If I had been conscious, I would have told them that was a good thing. Normal is not a word that describes me. Being abnormal is closer to my normal state. Days later they had to tie me down. I had torn the IV line out of my arm in a rage against death.

Ironically, although I lived in comedy, I looked more like a victim in a medical drama. The wound to my head created dangerous swelling on my brain. The doctors gave me blood thinners and put me under so they could buy some time and figure out the cause. The answer was simple. Pressure, pressure, relentless unending pressure! I had been under extreme pressure, overworked, and exhausted. I had been overworked for some time, perhaps all of my life.

I had just finished directing a diversity comedy showcase for CBS, "the most watched network in America," as they like to say. My minority friends joked that it was the "Caucasian Broadcasting System." But every year for the last seven years I wrote and directed this show, and it's had great success. Sixteen network series regulars and two *Saturday Night Live* cast members have come out of the showcase. I had created jobs and careers, all with the support and wisdom of CBS. At the same time, I felt it wasn't successful enough because I didn't do it merely as a civic duty; I also did it for survival. No job, no life. In Hollywood you need to work. CBS had hired me every year to direct this show and teach a master class to these diverse Hollywood hopefuls, and I did.

For seven seasons, I had committed three months at a time to create the show. Every year I wrote, directed, and worked with one of the best casting directors in Hollywood. We were an odd pair—an abrasive, opinionated Jewish casting director, and an abrasive, opinionated Latino writer/director. We must have seemed like the *Driving Miss Daisy* diversity couple. Fern Orenstein started her career casting *Baywatch* and hated Shakespeare and improv. These are not my words, but hers. She is tough but honest. She showed me how the industry thought. But she cared for these showcase actors as irrationally as I did. I have seen her tirelessly try to get them work. So I stand accused of that mad Miss Daisy love for her.

The network loved what we did, so, that year they added more writers and actors, which only increased my workload. I was probably sick then, but I was too busy directing and writing to notice. My undiagnosed pneumonia spiraled out of control, and when pneumonia spirals out of control, it will control you. It will take you by your throat, lift you in the air, and shake you like a terrier with a chew toy. I should have known that I was sick, but I had to keep working. This show meant so much to me. All my life I had dealt with culture and diversity in Hollywood, so I directed the diversity showcase each year because I felt I had to. Hollywood today needs more diversity in front of and behind the camera. This is the inherent pressure every minority in Hollywood feels. In this network showcase, I represented African-Americans, Latinos, Asians, the LGBT community, and so many others. I had the United Nations of comedy on my shoulders. The entire time I was on Broadway, only four casting directors saw me. Over a thousand top executives in Hollywood saw the four performances of the diversity showcase. It was an amazing opportunity for the actors. Every year I gave it my all, and the numerous opportunities that came out of it for the actors in the showcase only encouraged me to give even more.

If I died, all of this would just be part of my obituary. As I was lying on a hospital bed, intubated and sedated, an obituary seemed in order.

In every story, there is a beginning, a middle, and an end. More than anywhere else, in Hollywood, the story commences when you are defined and cast as a "type." I was cast as the "Latino." I always had to fight for my identity because, when you are Latino, to white America you're not black and you're not white. What you are is almost white. Now, lying in the hospital, I was almost dead. They gave me a syringe full of sleep, and I drifted into darkness. Tied to the bed, with IVs in my arms and a tube down my throat, I looked like a man with no future. And with no future, I dreamed of my past.

LITTLE HOUSE
IN THE BARRIO

*"Oh, we don't love tacos.
We just thought you'd be more comfortable eating tacos."*

Being in and out of consciousness for two weeks seems like only a few minutes when you're living on the Island of Limbo. I was on the other side of my consciousness, like a bad neighbor who stays up late and plays his music too loud through paper-thin walls. I had strange glimpses of life—flashes of people and places—but I was strapped still in a warm cocoon of darkness. At least my body was.

The last time I was this close to death I was a child. I must have been in first grade. Back then, you could let your kids walk to the grocery store unescorted. I was holding a bunch of used bottles in my hand to cash in for some candy money. I was at a crosswalk in the street, and a driver in the right-hand lane at the stop sign motioned for me to cross. I shook my head and told *him* to cross. The driver again motioned for me to go. I again shook my head and motioned for *him* to go. Again, he motioned for me to go and I then motioned for him to go. Finally, I went, but so did he, along with a ton of car. I was thrown into the air. My skull and leg were fractured. Then I remember waking up in a hospital my mother crying over my body. It was the first time I ever saw her cry.

I had a normal childhood. Well, at least I don't remember any additional traumas. I was different from the other kids at my school because I was Mexican-American, and most of the children I went to school with were not. You could always spot me in the class photo. I'm not that dark, but, next to the white kids, I looked like I was from the Mayan

1

Yucatan with a bow and arrow in hand. My sister is dark because she has a lot of Native blood in her. I have a lot of Spanish blood in me. I know this because, when I was younger, I made her build me beautiful missions in the backyard. I also stole her gold and gave her chicken pox and measles. Of course, I'm joking. She had no gold. But color is an issue with Latinos. Either you are too dark, or too white, or too indigenous, or too African. It's strange how in school, I was exotic, and in the backyard, I was not.

I was born in a border city and had another border on display inside of me. I was a Mexican hyphen American, and, to me, a hyphen is a border. It's a separation. A fence. A line in the sand. It's a permanent "Do Not Enter" sign in front of a country. Today these hyphens are optional— some people use them and some people don't. But this is the way I grew up and the way America grew up, and it shaped the way we saw each other and the world.

I grew up in a little city called La Mesa, outside San Diego. Why La Mesa? That's a mystery to me. *La mesa* means "the table" in Spanish. Maybe Spanish missionaries brought the first table there to impress the Native indigenous people. Perhaps they chose that name because an indigenous man had a vision of a table while in a small pox–induced fever and died muttering "Laaa meeeessssah, la messsaaaah," hacking a death rattle "Laaa Messssaaaa" and the name just stuck. The city next to La Mesa was El Cajon, "the box." La Mesa was, "the table." Spanish missionaries had very little imagination. Its claim to fame is its little league baseball team, which won the Little League World Series in 1961.

I gave up baseball early when a ball hit me out in left field. It hurt like a searing fireball from the sky. What kind of fun is a game where you have to worry about flying objects coming out of the sky? It was like playing lawn-dart tag. It was strange, because I'm a Latino; I had to survive piñata parties where you blindfold a kid, give him a bat, spin him around in the middle of a bunch of unarmed kids, and let him swing wildly as candy falls from the sky. Children risked their lives for a few pieces of old 99-cent store candy. So I should have been tougher. But it was my first experience in baseball, and I was a fast learner. My actual thought at the time was, *Wow, this is painful. I'm bleeding. I have a tooth on the ground. I'm joining the swim team. PAIN! I hope I don't cry. Uh-oh, too late. I'm crying. I hope no one sees me. Uh-oh, too late. The dugout is laughing at me. Mostly my coach.* My baseball days were over.

Latinos are supposed to be good at baseball. We are also supposed to be good at bullfighting, but that doesn't mean I have to enter the ring. Baseball became popular because all the children of multinational corporations around the world played baseball, exporting it and Coca-Cola to places like the Dominican Republic. Their baseball ambitions were fueled by poverty and the success of Alex Rodriguez—after all, he did get Kate Hudson. Baseball had been *berry, berry* good to him, but baseball was not *berry, berry* good for me.

La Mesa had baseball and an abundance of old transplanted ex-Midwesterners who had moved there to work in the factories that dotted the harbor. Some retirees remembered San Diego as a nice Navy town. The retired officers lived in Point Loma and, if they were enlisted men, well, they lived in La Mesa.

Although I was living in a very white "all-American city" with a Spanish name, I still had the Mexican work ethic. I began working at age eight. I mowed the grass for an old woman who lived down the street from me. She had no nose and she covered the area with a bandage as if no one would notice. I never asked, but I always imagined her nose was bitten off in a bar fight. Maybe in a bear attack. Maybe it fell off from frostbite when she was crossing the mountains into California.

On Sundays, she had me pull out weeds in her backyard. At the end of the day, she would pay me in old silver coins that might have come from a robbery she had committed during the Great Depression. Or maybe it was a settlement from the loss of her nose, a cannery accident, or something worse.

She told me I would make a good gardener. She never got my name right. She called me Ricardo. I told her my name was Rick, but she insisted on calling me Ricardo. I remember her looking at me and saying with her odd-sounding voice, "No, I think your real name is Ricardo. It sounds better for you. Rick is your white name, but I know your real name is Ricardo. Now take that hoe and get them weeds, boy."

I would sing old Mexican spirituals on my blistered knees, attacking "them weeds" under a blazing sun while being called Ricardo. My parents named me Rick because it was simpler to pronounce. "Rick" I told her, looking up from the weeds. I imagined being whipped like Kunta Kinte. "My name is Rick, not Ricardo." "No!" she said again, "Ricardo!" (Insert whip crack here.) Because of her nose I gave her a lot of slack.

The hardest thing for me was not to look at that bandage covering her empty nose. She was a mystery. The city I grew up in was a mystery, too. There was a chicken ranch down the street. You could leave money on the counter and take a dozen eggs, or, in my case, take the money and leave the eggs. I was a pioneer even then, as I was the first person to bring crime to La Mesa. I was also the first child laborer.

People trusted people back then. The owners had what I considered a real Mexican family living on that chicken ranch. They had ten kids. I saw an actual chicken walk through their front room once as if it were a guest. The owner's name ironically was Mr. Man. These Latinos literally worked for the man!

As I grew up, I called my hometown Barrio La Mesa just to give myself some street cred. My father had moved us there from the real barrio of Logan Heights because my mother, a Mexican woman born in Boone, Iowa, thought it was a nice city to raise a family. She was right. We lived in a two-bedroom house with five kids in one bedroom and my parents in the other. We were poor Mexicans compared to the other families that lived around us. Whether our neighbors wanted it or not, mine was one of the first families to bring Mexican culture to La Mesa.

Years earlier, around 1930, my grandfather had created a barrio. Logan Heights, California, was a quiet little white neighborhood. Until my grandfather moved his tall, blue-eyed, light-skinned self there with his very dark-skinned, part Apache wife and all of their children. When the Realtor who sold him the house saw my dark-skinned grandmother and her six children, he asked, "Are you Mexican?" My grandfather replied, "Yes, and it's too late now!"

My grandfather brought cockfights, loud mariachi music, and backyard boxing to Logan Heights. He inspired the "Great White Flight of 1930." Both he and my grandmother came from New Mexico before it was even a state. Before then, my great-grandfather crossed over to the States from Chihuahua, Mexico. He was fleeing Pancho Villa's army and a civil war; he had ten children and feeding them was war enough. Mexicans cross borders. It's what we do. We travel to work.

Look at America today. Atlanta has one million Latino citizens. The South has the biggest growth of Latinos in the United States. "Hotlanta" is hotter now that it has a mix of salsa and grits. New York has one million *Pueblanos* (Mexicans from Puebla, Mexico). The United States is the second-largest Latino nation in the world, and a majority of children born in the U.S. today are Latino. The largest group of Latinos in the U.S. are Mexicans. Why is this happening? Latinos have tenacity, endurance, and faith. Why? Because we are optimists. You have to be an optimist to cross a border, travel into a country where you don't know the language, look for a job, and send the money you earn back home. All with the threat of deportation hanging over your head. That's optimism if ever I've seen it!

My father was an optimist. He went to Vietnam during the Tet Offensive to work on downed helicopters as a civilian contractor, just for the overtime. One of his many *other* jobs was as a door-to-door salesman. He taught me my biggest lesson, one that has helped me more than once in life.

He said, "Son, *mijo*, I was a door-to-door salesman. I knocked on about a hundred doors a day. I always heard a 'no,' but around the hundredth door, I always heard a 'yes.' You got to knock on a lot of doors and hear a lot of 'nos' before you hear that one 'yes.'" So, optimistically, he moved our family to La Mesa to find a better life. My father was looking for that one "yes." We were all willing to work hard for it.

My family had moved to La Mesa because my mother wanted me to have peer pressure from the children of doctors, lawyers, and dentists in order to spur me on to higher education. My mother was also optimistic. Education was very important to her. She had only a high school education. My father was the same. They both dreamed of their children going to college, so they wanted to surround us with children from good families who would pressure us to go to school. They believed in the words of Victor Hugo: "He who opens a school door, closes a prison."

My best friend in a very white La Mesa was a little freckle-faced kid named Nicky. His family seemed like refugees from some *Little House on the Prairie* episode. I imagined that their oxen had died, forcing them to empty their wagon and live in our neighborhood. They would call each other "Brother" and "Sister" and "Ma" and "Pa." I felt like I should be chopping wood and milking a cow whenever I saw them. I'd hear them say things like, "Sister, can you pass me the ketchup?" And, "Oh sure, Brother." And, "These are some mighty good string beans. Are we having apple pie after supper tonight, Ma?" I swore they had a still for moonshine hidden somewhere.

Every Friday night, Nicky would invite me over to have dinner with his family. Right after the dinner prayer, they had a build-your-own-taco ritual. In the middle of the table, they piled their lazy Susan high with big, Anglo, American-type tacos and filled them with overcooked hamburger meat, oily processed cheese, and wilted lettuce. The whole family would spin the lazy Susan from left to right like an industrial assembly line. It was an in-home taco factory; every taco was built on time and with maximum efficiency. We would sit around the table and have tacos we built ourselves and wash them down with Tang or Kool-Aid.

I remember once, on my tenth taco Friday night and after my third taco, I looked to my freckle-faced buddy and said, "Wow, Nicky, your family loves tacos!" He was quiet. Then I asked his mother, "Why do you all love tacos so much?" They all looked at me, smiled, and said, "Oh, we don't love tacos at all, Rick. We just thought you'd be more comfortable eating them."

At first, I shrugged it off, thinking with my eight-year-old mind that they were really ignorant to think that I loved these tacos, because the truth was they were not even *good* tacos. Not at all. They didn't even qualify as true tacos. They were taco-like. It was like someone folded hard clay, fired it, and filled it with lettuce and ketchup. These tacos were more like the ones served in the cafeteria in my elementary school where I worked part-time as a dishwasher in the kitchen. Yes, I wore a hairnet. I was ashamed as the kids threw silverware in my garbage disposal just to hear the grinding sounds of cutlery.

Now that I think about it, I was a gardener and a dishwasher before

I was eight. Why did I get picked for those jobs? The Asian kid in my class got to help the nurse. So, the Asian kid was in the medical field and headed for a scientific career. But I, the Mexican-American kid, was wearing a hairnet and standing in front of a garbage disposal. And now, this all-white family invited me to dinner every Friday night to join them in building tacos that they thought I would be more comfortable eating.

In my eight-year-old mind, I thought there was something wrong, but then I thought, *Maybe these people are really trying hard to be hospitable. In fact, they are trying so hard, they are serving a dish they don't even like. Are they prejudiced and ignorant, or do they really like me?* Still, uneasy and confused, I took a moment and decided that their eating tacos proved to me, beyond all reasonable doubt, that they must really, really like me. They ate bad tacos with me!

Later, I threw a baseball through their window. I'm sure they wondered if I'd done it on purpose, or if it was an accident. I wasn't sure, either. In the end, I always try to choose the nicer explanation for someone's behavior. I hoped Nicky and his family would do the same for me.

A VIRGIN
AND A MOTHER

*"Virgins, whores, long-suffering barrio mothers
and the men who made them that way."*

My mother was a huge influence on me. She pulled me out of the barrio and away from my father's parents. That was her plan. My grandparents were hard-drinking, union-organizing, fighting Mexicans. In fact, two of my cousins later married Cesar Chavez's daughters. In the 1940s, my grandmother tried to organize the tuna canneries in San Diego and was labeled a communist. When someone called her this to her face, she said simply, "I have a son in war. How many stars do you have on your window?" They gave you a star when you had a son overseas.

"America's Finest City" had little appreciation for my Latina grandmother. Born dark, she was said to have had lots of native Apache blood in her. She once dislocated her ankle and put it back in place herself. My father had found her in the backyard pounding on her bone. She was indigenous-Mexican tough. She organized at a time when people got blacklisted for doing so. In skin color and in attitude, she was brown and strong. She looked like those women who traveled with Pancho Villa's army. I never had a sentimental moment with her.

Grandma was not the grandmother on the packet of Abuelita chocolate sold in stores. That grandmother was very white looking, with a hot cup of chocolate in front of her smiling sweet face. My grandmother was more like the Aztecs or Mayans who had invented chocolate—which, in its original state, isn't sweet at all. She was dark chocolate, and skin color still means a lot in Latino and Anglo culture. If you don't believe me, turn on a Spanish telenovela on Univision. It's filled with European blondes speaking Spanish. It looks like American television in the '70s—like the cast of *Charlie's Angels* moved to Mexico.

My father's family was not polite. They were tough, opinionated, angry Mexicans that came from a long line of angry Mexicans. My mother's side was full of hardworking, conservative, nice Midwestern Mexican-Americans. Her side dined on Midwestern food like ham, green beans, and ambrosia salad, all wrapped up in a flour tortilla.

I remember my mother was always working as she seemed to have three or four jobs. She worked as a banquet waitress, so I would get steaks and sometimes smoked oysters, shrimp, or crab, depending on how fancy the party was. I nearly got gout from that diet. I began to look like King Henry VIII.

I loved every stolen moment with my mother. She and my father would leave for work, leaving my brothers, sisters, and me with a dollar or two and the immediately dismissed advice, "Don't buy junk food." The truth was that all food then was junk food. I would eat Chef Boyardee and snacks with names like Strawberry Quik and Space Food Sticks. The only thing quick about Strawberry Quik was the sugar high. I would eat this food and watch TV. Television was my escape.

I never saw Latinos on TV except for Desi Arnaz in *I Love Lucy*. Maybe I'd see a Latino on *The High Chaparral* or in a Western movie. They played the Native indigenous roles along with Italians and Mexicans. My favorite Mexicans, ironically, were Eli Walach in *The Good, the Bad and the Ugly* and Burt Lancaster in *Valdez Is Coming*. Seeing Latinas on television or in movies was even rarer, and, when you saw them, they were portrayed as virgins, whores, or long-suffering barrio mothers. But we all knew that was a lie, because our mothers were all virgins.

Latinos, especially Latino men, love their mothers. They revere their mothers. It's not to say that other cultures don't, but we do it in a different way. We are a mestizo culture, born of the union of Europeans with native blood—the conqueror and the conquered live inside of us. We are a culture created by a singular woman. Women are a mystery, yet to the Latino male, they represent everything. The Latina woman is a virgin and a mother at the same time. How that is possible, we will never know, but it is. That is precisely why Latinas are a mystery.

But to the Mexican psyche, there is an extra layer of historical complexity. A woman can be the supreme creator and also the destroyer, she who aids and comforts the enemy: Malinche. Of course, the jury of history is still out on Malinche. I see her as a complex survivor of a world that was ending and a bridge to new beginning.

Malinche, daughter of a noble Aztec family, was the woman who translated for the Spanish conquistador Hernán Cortéz, conqueror of Mexico, and therefore helped him conquer the Aztecs. As the story goes, she was a dark-skinned Aztec princess who was given to Cortéz as a slave when he landed in Veracruz. Malinche—whose name some say means "the captain's wife" or "from the sea"—began to translate for Cortéz from Mayan to Nahuatl, the Aztec language. They were close, extremely close, as Cortéz fought and argued his way through Mexico, making alliances with natives against the Aztecs.

Imagine if an army landed in Los Angeles and made treaties with every street gang, uniting them to destroy the city. That was what Cortéz did, all with the help of Malinche. She was a survivor, but, in the end, she had no choice. She was given to him. Later she would conquer him. Through their conjugal union, Malinche, aka Doña Marina, and Cortéz created the mestizo race, the half-European and half-indigenous people who populate most of Mexico today. There are other examples of this mix in Latin America as well. Throughout the Caribbean, for example in Cuba and Puerto Rico, the mix of European and African was more common.

Doña Marina, the New World woman, gave birth to a new race. We idolize and worship the women who are the mothers of our race, because they represent motherhood, love, and comfort in our world.

Ten years after Cortéz landed in Mexico, another mother appeared to build a bridge between the old world and the new. The story is this: Early on the morning of December 9, 1531—the Feast of the Immaculate Conception in the Spanish Empire—the peasant Juan Diego was on a slope on the hills of Tepeyac and saw the vision of a girl, 15 or 16 years of age, surrounded by light, speaking to him in Nahuatl, his language. She asked that a church be built on the site, and Juan recognized her as the Virgin

11

Mary. So he went to the Spanish archbishop, Juan de Zumárraga, and the archbishop told him to return to Tepeyac Hill and ask for a miracle. In response, the Virgin healed Juan Diego's uncle. A healing always gets a divine being noticed. Then she sent him back bringing flowers that were out of season because it was December. And not only that—these flowers weren't even from Mexico. They were Castilian roses, Spanish flowers. So Juan Diego took them in his *tilma*, which is kind of a cloak that the peasants wore. When he opened the cloak before the bishop, the flowers fell to the floor, and in their place was the image of the Virgin of Guadalupe on the fabric. And they still have that image today.

What was really interesting about the Virgin of Guadalupe was that she appeared speaking in Nahuatl. And if you look at the image of her, she's darker than any other rendition of the Virgin Mary. She became the Nahuatl goddess, blending the native with the Virgin Mary.

There was a temple of the mother goddess Tonantzin at Tepeyac, too, and that was destroyed for the chapel to the Virgin built on the site. So, the newly converted Native indigenous people would go to the temple to worship, but they were partly worshipping the Virgin Mary as Tonantzin. It was a triumph of adaptation, if you will, of the natives taking their indigenous beliefs and mixing them in with the Spanish beliefs and making a hybrid belief, a hybrid culture. That's why the Virgin of Guadalupe was so important in Mexico—because she really unified the indigenous and the Spanish. She visited Native indigenous people when they were at their worst—when they were totally defeated. And she gave them hope, in the form of a bridge between indigenous and Spanish culture, creating the mestizo culture. The Virgin of Guadalupe became our ultimate mother and healer—she was our bridge of peace.

My own mother and my father both worked multiple jobs so their children could live in an strong middle-class neighborhood. I was a latchkey kid. My friends had mothers who stayed home, made such inventions as pizzas (tomato sauce and cheese on top of an English muffin), baked cookies, were involved in the PTA, and went on annual vacations. All of this was foreign to me.

My mother was a waitress and she actually liked it. She had come to

California to work in the lemon orchards and packing plants in Santa Barbara during the war. Her brother had joined the Air Force and her future husband, my father, was fighting over in the Pacific. I didn't even exist at that time, but my mother imagined me. I was part of the family she dreamed of in her head. Maybe Malinche dreamed the same thoughts when she slept with Cortéz; not of destroying and conquering Mexico, but rather about having a loving family. A family that would be all hers. A family that would not gift its daughter into slavery. Maybe she dreamed of giving birth to a nation as my mother dreamed of giving birth to a doctor or a politician. It's in every woman's soul to be the guardian of the family.

Women are born with a strange ability to bear pain and sorrow. My mother loved her life, but she had known real sorrow. When I was a child she showed me a picture of her brother Joe. It was a black-and-white photo that she had stored in an old box. He was dark haired, serious, and handsome. There was writing on the photo: "Love, Joe." She held it tenderly and told me, "Your uncle Joe would have loved San Diego. It was always so cold in Iowa."

I asked her why she had come to California from Boone, Iowa, and she told me, "When I came to California, it was during the war. I loved California. I told the train conductor that I was an Indian princess. And he said he'd look after his important guest. I was on my first adventure. Your grandmother didn't speak much English and we were poor, so she was more scared when I left home than she was when your uncle Joe went off to war. Joe joined the Air Force. I went to California to work there. Back then there were a lot of jobs in California because the men were at war. I was just 16." She became very quiet.

I see moments like this in my life as screenplays.

RICK stands near his MOTHER who is by her dresser in the bedroom. The room is decorated like a warm, inviting, comfortable cocoon. There are family pictures on the wall. An old cardboard box lies open on top of her bed. She puts the black-and-white photo down gently as if it was not an old faded photo but her own brother himself . . .

MOTHER

This photo is so old. Look how handsome my brother was. You know how he died?

RICK

Sure, I remember. My uncle Joe died in World War II.

MOTHER

Yes, that's right, but your cousin Danny did some research. He met a man that wrote about the prisoner-of-war camp in the Philippines. That man was put in the same POW camp as your uncle. He and your uncle Joe alone survived the Bataan Death March. That's when the Japanese marched most of the prisoners from one end of the island to the other. They called it a death march because so many prisoners died. They brought my brother Joe to a POW camp. There were Japanese planes near the camp. He knew how to fly because he was in the Air Force, and he wanted to steal one so he could escape. At least that's what he told one of the survivors. Danny had read about a man who had memorized almost every man's name in the camp, except Joe's. Maybe he didn't remember my brother because his last name was hard to pronounce—Uballe.

But when your cousin Danny went to his book signing he asked, "Do you remember a young man named Joe Uballe from Iowa?" The man looked up, surprised to hear that name again, and his face lit up. He remembered Joe at that exact moment. The man told Danny that Joe was a brave young man. He dreamed of stealing a Japanese plane and flying away from the prison camp. Joe was only seventeen at the time. Seventeen.

RICK

I wish I could have met him.

MOTHER

So do I. The Red Cross told your grandmother that they were going to liberate the POW camp where Joe was. She was so happy that her boy would soon be back in her arms. She thought he was too young to go to war, but he wanted to go anyway. He was an American and he felt it was his duty.

RICK

He sounds like he was a good guy.

MOTHER

But then a week later, a telegram arrived telling us that Joe was killed before they could liberate the camp. The Japanese POW commander had ordered his men to toss all the American prisoners in a pit and light it on fire. A witness said one of the American soldiers in the pit actually got out and pulled a Japanese soldier back in with him.

RICK

Was it Uncle Joe?

MOTHER

I don't know.

She pauses for a moment.

I always wondered if it was Joe or if he was looking up and thinking of flying away from all the pain. He was so pure and good and they killed him. After your grandmother heard that Joe was killed, she had a nervous breakdown.

She turns and looks away, trying hard to hide her pain.

Well, Rick, after that war I met your father. He was still skinny from fighting in the Pacific. I met him in front of Horton Plaza in San Diego. I was 17 and he was maybe twentysomething. He told me he was going to look after me. He thought I was just a naïve girl from the country, but I knew I would marry him. We did get married and we had you and four other children. I worry about you kids with all the things going on nowadays, but back then it was bad, too. During World War II, we thought the world was ending, and, for some it did. It did for my brother. My mother never got over his death. For me, I found a little life. I found hope by marrying your dad and having a family. I had you later in life, after your brothers and sisters were older. I moved us out of the barrio to La Mesa so that you would become something great, have a family, and get a good job. Maybe you will work at the post office. Those jobs are always secure.

RICK

Was I an accident?

MOTHER

Yes, you were. (she laughs) The whole world is an accident according to some people, (confidently) but I say there are no accidents. There is a plan, although we may not see it. I moved us to La Mesa so that you would have children of doctors and lawyers surrounding you, so you would want to be like them. That was no accident. That was a plan.

I think back on that day, look at the world and my mom, and realize there's no such thing as a secure job anymore. Nowadays, government jobs at the post office are endangered because of the digital age. Saturday mail delivery missed the chopping block in 2013 but it's only a matter of time. I think of all the pain my uncle Joe must have felt when he left to go to war, alone and only 17. I think of how alone he must have felt so far away from home.

I used to feel alone when I left San Diego to work in Hollywood. Sometimes 100 miles away felt like 100,000 miles, because I had to explain myself to executives who would ask me to write about the Latino experience. Show us the "pain of the barrio," they'd say. I'd tell them that there is no pain in the barrio. The barrio is just your neighborhood. It's your family and friends. The pain comes when you leave the barrio. I think that's why I related to my uncle Joe. He'd left the barrio and so had I.

La Mesa was a very white-bread Southwestern town 15 miles from the Mexican border, where television stations signed off in Spanish and played the Mexican national anthem. I lived on the border—the Mexican border—along with all of its contradictions and ironies. The La Mesa townspeople would always ask me questions. I seemed to be a foreigner in my little town, so I began to explain the only way I knew how. I told stories.

I had been quiet as a young child and seldom spoke. My teacher even sent a note to my parents asking them to talk to me about speaking more. I was just very shy, but the teacher decided I was S-L-O-W. She mistook my shyness for stupidity. As a result, I flunked kindergarten, or was "held back" as they called it. "Held back" sounded better, like I was almost ready to go, but not quite. "Hold on, little buddy. Why don't you wait another year in kindergarten . . . let me hold you back." The term *flunked* was too politically incorrect to use.

Because I was S-L-O-W, I was sent to a special class. One day a teacher said to me, "Why don't you tell me any story and I'll write it down." So, I made up a story called "The Colored Boy" about a boy with skin made up of so many colors that no one could understand him, but no one could be prejudiced toward him either. This boy meets another boy who is colored, too. He invites him to his planet where skin color doesn't matter because different colors are considered beautiful. In fact, color is a thing of honor. The more colorful and different you are, the better. The boy lives on a planet where diversity is cool.

I don't know how or why I came up with that story, but that was the first story I ever wrote. I remember how the teacher wrote it down, read it back to me. Using cardboard and cloth and sewing needle, she stitched my paperback book together. This one teacher noticed me, a kid flunked out of kindergarten. She taught me the power of writing. The attention I got from writing began to change me from a shy child to a child with a voice.

It's amazing to me when I think about it now that I was talking about race and color when I was six years old. I understood that we all constantly changed colors and things just like the "colored boy." And I guarantee you that no white kid in my school thought the same way. I wish color had not been an issue—but it was.

Eventually, I talked more and more and then was told that I asked too many questions and talked too much. So, in a strange way, flunking kindergarten me helped me to become me. I was the colored boy. A teacher taught me my most important lesson at that time: that I had a story to tell, and if I had a story to tell I could find an audience that would want to listen, and if that audience wanted to listen to my stories I must be important. She gave me the confidence to tell my stories.

School was always a strange place for me. I would get lost and bored. I had a different view of the world. One day when I was in the fifth grade my teacher came to school dressed in colorful East Indian clothes. She made chapati, Indian flat bread. I looked at it. "Hey, those are tortillas," I said. "No," she corrected, "they are chapatis." I continued trying to convince her that they were tortillas. "Look," she said, "we're learning about India." I wouldn't give it up. "But Mexico is only 15 miles away," I told her. "And they make the same thing, but they call them tortillas, not *chapatis*." She sent me out of the classroom. I stood in the hallway, indignantly eating my chapati, thinking it would be much better with guacamole and melted cheese and salsa. *Why am I learning about India and not Mexico?* I wondered. I never got the answer.

I never did learn about Mexico at the school in La Mesa. Years later, the situation is worse for Latinos. In fact, in Arizona, Mexican-American studies have been outlawed. Maybe they were banned so teachers could spend more time teaching students about India. Maybe the teachers will dress in Indian clothing and cook chapatis, and somewhere in Arizona, a Mexican-American child will mistake it for a tortilla.

When my mother told me the story about my uncle Joe dying for America, it reminded me that Latinos have given their lives for this country, even though Latinos are seldom recognized for their efforts in our wars or seen on screen giving their lives for this country. Our histories are fragile and easy to forget. When I write about brave Latino men like my uncle Joe, and remember strong Latina women like my mother, I keep their memories alive and remind the world that there are many other Latinos—they are just never seen on TV.

THE
COCKFIGHT

*"The cockfight is life or death. There is only one who will survive.
But in the end grilled, baked, or deep-fried, no chicken gets out alive."*

My last name has a Latin sound. It should, it's Latin, but somehow when Anglo girls pronounce my name it sounds exotic. Especially when pronounced with that all-American accent of the blonde girls that I knew growing up. Girls with names like McMillan or Yule or Campbell. Blonde girls that smelled of soap and freshly washed hair. Most of the girls in my neighborhood were Anglo; all-American girls who made me cookies and played house with me. Practically the only Latino girl in my neighborhood was my sister.

We lived in a really small house. I'm sure my neighbors used to look at our small house crammed with a large Mexican family and say, "Too many damned Mexicans!" When I would wait for the bathroom in the morning, I used to mutter the same thing—"Too many damned Mexicans!" My parents had moved there to get away from all the Mexicans we called relatives.

There are millions of Latinos in America. I don't know them all and, personally, I'm glad. Facebook relationships take too much time, and, with social media, I'm too busy to talk in person.

When I was a child, though, I assumed every Mexican I met was related to me because many were. I love being Latino. I just thought there were too many of us. Not just Latinos. There were too many of everybody. It seemed we were all being squeezed together.

I first felt that way when I realized I had four other siblings and we were growing up in a two-bedroom house in La Mesa with two really stressed adults. With my people, when it comes to math, we are great at multiplication—we have multiplied all over this country. We love family and we think the more, the better. I think the loneliest man in the world is not the Maytag repairman, but a fertility clinic doctor in a Latino neighborhood.

I lived in a white world because of my mother. She was the Malinche that moved us out of the hood. She was looking for a better life. I think every generation looks for a better life for their children. I have lived in both worlds and between both worlds. As a kid, I hung out with a little girl named Betty Johnson. She was a nice girl, yet painfully shy. I liked her because she made me pizza on an English muffin with cheese and tomato sauce. She was my American dream. She had three square meals every day and was served lunch regularly at noon. Consistency is the way to a man's heart.

Betty Johnson had a good American name. In all fairness, I was named Rick, but after that came my last name. Najera. Najera sounded like an Arabic war cry. And when pronounced with a *j* rather than an *h* it sounded Japanese. Najera. It always sounded foreign, and growing up only 15 miles from Mexico, I was always made to feel that way. People looked at me and questioned my loyalty. I was a potential spy for Mexico. But Betty's last name was Johnson. Her *J* letter did not phonetically turn into an *h* sound. Her *J* was a solid and loyal *J*. My *j* was sneaky and lazy, crossing borders trying to be an *h* when it wasn't. Who could trust my *j*? My foreign name was dangerous.

"On Cinco de Mayo, we attack." If I were a spy, I would pass the word out to my Latino brethren. "We catch the gringos by attacking on Super Bowl Sunday or during the final episode of *American Idol*. They won't know what hit them." Then again, they could catch us off guard by counterattacking during the World Cup.

In truth, Mexican spies don't exist. We have no James Bond. Our James Bond wouldn't be called Double-O-Seven. He'd be called Double-O-Julio and have to work a second job. A Mexican spy would have had a horrible time in a James Bond tuxedo. Put a Mexican in a tuxedo and he looks like a waiter. No way around it. A Mexican James Bond in a tuxedo would end up taking drink orders. "One margarita shaken, not stirred. Coming right up." Latinos deal with the identity cocktail. We have to explain our history and ourselves way too much. I had to explain myself every time I said my name.

People ask, "You're Rick? It's not Ricardo?" as if I'm trying to hide my Latino identity. My parents named me Rick because they liked the directness of that name. I have met other Latinos with more "ethnic" names, like Cuatemoc or some other Aztec name. Puerto Ricans with names like Usnavi, named after ships that their parents had seen in the harbor of Puerto Rico, which actually say "U.S. Navy." Cubans named out of gratitude after people who had helped them reach the mainland—such as Manuelito Immigration Attorney Greenburg-Garcia.

Our names reflect our journey. I have a Mexican friend named Jimmy Shaw. Shaw is an Irish name, a reflection of the Irish who came to Mexico in the 19th century. We are a strange mix of contradictions, but everyone wants to belong and to be understood.

I wanted my family to be understood, so that's why I started writing and telling stories. Maybe it's because my father told such great stories to me. He would go to movie theaters, see a film by himself because one ticket was cheaper, come home, and act out the movie for me. He was an amazing storyteller. Years later, I would see the same film and it never seemed as vibrant, funny, dramatic, or suspenseful as the film my father had described. I remember how he loved the story of *Man of La Mancha* and his impossible dream. My father had fought windmills all his life.

My grandparents were old Mexico. I spent time with them when I was young and in the barrio of Logan Heights. My grandfather and grandmother were less affectionate and much tougher on me. They were disciplinarians bent on my survival. I came from a generation of infinite possibilities. They lived in a world of limited opportunities. They lived in a world where the goal was to get a good job and provide for your family as soon as possible.

My grandmother never liked my mother much. We Latinos, especially Mexicans, have an old saying: "She had Mexican Alzheimer's. They forget everything but a grudge." She held a grudge against my mother.

She resented the fact that my very light-skinned, Midwestern, Mexican-American mother had moved us out of the barrio to La Mesa. But my grandfather wanted me to keep my identity strong among the white children of La Mesa. My grandfather would never let me forget who I was—Rick Najera, not Ricardo—or where I came from. That's why he took me to my first cockfight. There is nothing more Mexican than a cockfight.

I could see the lights of Tijuana from San Diego. My grandfather had a place there. It was his own ranchero, or little ranch, where he raised fighting cocks. Anglo people always wince at the concept, but fighting roosters and bulls are a part of our Latino heritage. We come from a military tradition, born of feathers and fury. The bulls were just an interesting way of getting our meat tenderized. The cockfight is life or death. There is only one who will survive. But in the end grilled, baked, or deep-fried, no chicken gets out alive.

My grandfather was named Chon, short for *concepción,* or "birth" in English. I was the grandson of Birth. He was born in San Andrés, Chihuahua, Mexico, before the revolution. He was a boxer and a baker with catcher's mitts for hands from kneading bread. Chon worked in Weber's Bakery, home of Weber's white bread. During the Great Depression, Chon had to stop baking bread at home in his beehive oven for the neighbors because he was becoming competition for Weber's Bakery. My grandfather never said much, but he did a lot.

One day my grandfather took me to Tijuana, a place where he ruled and felt more at home. I was a child, and he drove me across the border. Tijuana, with its dust and dirt, reminded him of his ranch in Alamogordo, New Mexico, where he lived after his family left Chihuahua. His family ranched a hostile but beautiful land. Legend was, my great-grandfather left Mexico when Pancho Villa's men did an impromptu survey and inventory of his ranch. It was like a Mexican IRS audit, but not as fun as an American one. Here I was, years later, going to Tijuana, to a rancho in the hills.

All Mexican-Americans are born on one side of a hyphen. I like to say the border is something we share, but in San Diego, that was not the case. In San Diego, a border is something we enforce.

24

I was six years old when I took that trip to Tijuana with my grandfather; I had never been before. He watched me closely as I watched the ancient fight, a battle between two opposing worlds, each one crashing into the other in order to get breeding rights to pass on their genes. He was trying to see what I saw. The loser was going to be lunch, but was it cruelty or a natural competition, one that each year would better the roosters' and chickens' strength?

I watched with a strange fascination. I knew this was important but I had no idea of why. I felt I was watching something ancient. My grandfather had arranged this rite of passage, I later came to think, to see if we shared a common bond. My grandfather wanted me to understand him. He wanted to see if he was in my blood. His father had shared this with him, and his father before him. This was a primordial cultural dance of life and death.

After my grandfather died, I found a book with strange names and birth dates. I thought it was his *otra,* his "other woman." No, it was the birth date of the roosters he loved and raised. My grandfather loved his roosters and his family. To him, being Mexican was his identity, unfettered and without question. At times, though, he would question my identity. He wondered what kind of Mexican I was, if I was one at all.

I used to tell a story about the first time I realized I was Mexican. I told my mother I was going to play with the Mexicans down the street. She said, "You are Mexican, so you can stay home and play with yourself." Then I went down to the schoolyard and a kid named Bradley was there. He grabbed my basketball out of my hand and pushed me to the ground. I got up and said, "You took my ball." He said, "It's my ball now, wetback." I had never heard the term before. It didn't sound like a bad word. Quarterback, halfback, wetback. Just to play it safe, I kicked his ass.

After beating Bradley up, from the corner of my eye, I saw the schoolyard teacher running up to me. "Why did you hit Bradley?" she asked. At this point, Bradley was crying. Arrogance is lost quickly when your nose is bleeding. He was a bad crier, all high-pitched, blowing snot bubbles, face full of tears. "Because he called me a wetback," I replied. She looked at me strangely, not getting that this light-skinned, brown-eyed child in this very American school on Lemon Avenue in California was a Mexican-American. She asked naturally and almost sweetly, "Are you Mexican?" I said, "Yes." She looked down at me and said simply, "Well then, you are a wetback, so why'd you hit Bradley?"

At the time I was confused. I got angry years later when I realized what had happened. I was confused as a child by identity because I was American and proud of that fact. My family had earned that right with their blood and work. I was proud to be Mexican as they were; that is the double sword of identity in America. In the United States you can't deny your heritage, but you can't celebrate it too much either.

Bradley and the "wetback" is a true story. Most comedy is the truth delivered with timing. Fifteen miles from the border on a playground, my identity began to be shaped.

This is where I began, on the border between two cultures, always being asked to choose. Sometimes I felt as alien as the colored boy that I first wrote of in kindergarten. Now, looking back, I realized the colored boy was me.

THE
BORDER

"Every Latino has a border still inside of them.
That's what we must cross before we feel we truly belong."

The so-called U.S. and Mexico "border" is actually more of a barrier than a border. It is the desert that forms the natural obstruction between the U.S. and Mexico. The border wall itself is not that strong. It seems to slide into the sea and disappear into the horizon just like the sun. Where it extends out into the surf, there are signs in Spanish warning the undocumented to swim around it or risk getting caught up in a riptide.

That corrugated fence between America and Mexico is made from steel landing strips from a forgotten war. On the Mexican side, there are crosses symbolizing the immigrants who have died crossing the wall in an attempt to find work. On the American side, there's nothing. Just a small plaque on the ground that reminds people that on one side is Mexico, and, on the other, the United States.

As a child, I remember once watching the sunset at the border wall. Two dolphins jumped out of the water right in front of the fence, with the setting sun as their backdrop. It was a magnificent sight. They did a perfect acrobatic leap right there in front of that fence, red with rust, as if to mock all fences, borders, and walls. The dolphins were alive and free and had swum in that sea for thousands of years, and they will continue to swim thousands of years after that fence has crumbled into the sea. Their jump was perfect and in unison, just like the dolphins I saw at SeaWorld, but their acrobatic show was not for tourists or for a fat herring reward. It was purely out of the joy of being free.

27

On the Mexican side of the fence, there was a family playing in the sea; a few undocumented workers looking over the fence, sizing up the odds and getting ready to cross; and a family with a photo album talking to another family on the other side of the fence. On the American side, a lone border patrol agent sat in a squad car looking on with binoculars. I looked around to see if anyone else had seen the dolphins jumping out of the water. Judging by the nonchalant stares, no one had. I was the only person who had seen the strange sight. Often, I feel I am life's only witness—the one who sees what other people miss.

I have talked to those wanting to cross. Many had no shoelaces, as border patrol agents had confiscated them when they had them put on suicide watch. They were waiting for the sun to set before attempting to cross the border from Mexico, to look for work. If they made it and crossed deserts and oceans and survived robbers and cartels, they *might* get a job in the city of those distant lights. They might find a job with tips and a meal or two for free, so they would have more money to send home.

In fact, the money Mexicans in the United States send home to Mexico is the country's third-biggest source of income. Oil is first and tourism is second. Mexico is America's third-largest trading partner—larger than Japan, Germany, and England combined. I repeat, Mexico is our third-largest trading partner, and almost ties with China for the second spot. We, as Americans, are linked to Mexico far more than to Europe. Why do we not realize that? The 11 million undocumented people in the shadows are a huge market that can help our economy far more than it can hurt it. Latinos are an opportunity, not a problem.

Mexico is far more important for our future than any other country, and the Latinos here in the United States are far more important for the future of the United States than the English, French, or Germans could ever be. Why are we not seeing that? My answer is that the media keeps relegating us Latinos to troublesome footnotes in the media landscape. They donate a CNN special every once in a while and a Latino sitcom every 10 to 20 years; a few biopics like *Selena* or *La Bamba,* or now possibly *The Jenni Rivera Story.* According to Hill + Knowlton, the media only devotes one percent of the news stories to Latinos.

When politicos give lip service calling for diversity and Latino rights, they remind us that whoever gives them the votes or the money is their real constituency. Even though American politics is the best politics that money can buy, we may not get the advocacy necessary to fight for Latinos. Recently, many politicians have complained that Latinos are "The Sleeping Giant"—that we have not come to the polls as effectively as they had hoped. It's because we still have not been invigorated and activated. The reason there was a huge surge for Barack Obama by Latinos in 2012 was because many felt he might not get elected, and the alternative was Mitt Romney.

I know many Republican pundits were convinced Obama won because he "played" to the minorities and offered them "gifts." And they're right. In 2012, the Republicans "played" to older white males and offered them "gifts," too. For the first time, *they* were the minority. Republicans have not reached out to Latinos in the past, but now they have no choice. Republicans should court the Latino vote. But Marco Rubio does not count.

Traditionally, Latinos have viewed democratic elections with a skeptical eye. There is an old joke in Mexico that goes like this: One day, an American politician showed a Mexican politician an American computer system and said, "This is the best computerized voting system in the world. Within 24 hours, we know who has won the election." The Mexican politician smiled. "That's nothing. We know who won the election before the people even vote." In many ways American politics is not much better, as it takes millions to get elected.

The Latino on the street level sees American politics as belonging to the person who can buy the votes. Millions are spent on elections, but very little is spent on Latinos. At least it seems that way to us. The Center for Responsive Politics estimated that $6 billion was spent on the 2012 presidential election. That's a lot of ads and messages. However, many Latinos believe that expectations have not been met before or after that election. Promises made have not been fulfilled. What Latinos see is that the government spent billions . . . bailing out the banks.

Where are the billions for Latino homeowners? Where are the bailouts for them? Many of us wondered why it took so long for President

Obama to push the DREAM Act, a bill that would help undocumented students who have lived in the United States for years get an education. "DREAMers" are children of undocumented workers who were brought to this country when they were children. Many of my fellow Latinos and I wondered why Obama executed an executive order so late in the game, when he could have worked on immigration reform his first year in office as he promised. Latinos who are documented and born here still believe that the *undocumented* among us *are* part of our family.

We wondered why, during an election year, Cesar Chavez was getting a national monument. Because politicians knew that to the Latino culture, he was our hero, revered for decades before he was recognized with a national monument. Latinos like myself see both sides as cynically using us as political pawns without truly caring about us. Many believe that the Democrats and Republicans worry more for their respective political parties than the people—especially those who can't form Super PACs (committees that raise unlimited sums of money for or against ballot initiatives, legislation, or candidates). And we may be right.

I think of these things because I am the product of a strange geography. I was born in San Diego, not in Mexico. There is a joke told in San Diego that goes like this: "What's the nicest neighborhood in Tijuana? San Diego!" According to the tourist board, San Diego is "America's Finest City." And they paid big money for that slogan.

I'm Mexican-American, and in San Diego, there were only Americans. Nobody in San Diego liked the concept of hyphens. If you said you were Mexican-American, people would look at you and say, "Why add *Mexican?* Why not just say American, not Mexican-American? Forget that side of your name, son, and jump in the pure American cultural swimming pool. The water is fine. Just don't pee in the pool, son." That was what my high school coach would tell me nearly every day when he had such a hard time pronouncing my name at roll call. "Madoff?" "Here." "O'Bryan?" "Here." "Naj-. . . . Naj-or . . . Na-ha-ro . . . Nohera. God damn it, you know who I'm calling," he would say with a red face.

"Here," I would quickly answer. Coach was a thick, burly jock with a flattop and a whistle. He looked like a big baby in shorts. He would call me "Brother Rick" like we were soul brothers, even though he was white and I was Mexican-American. I was the closest thing to a black person he could find. That's how white the school was. We would hang out in the quad and he would philosophize.

"Brother Rick," he would say, "geography defines people. The Swiss people are defined by time, precision, and accuracy. Why? Because of geography. In northern climates, time is everything. They needed precise measurements to plan planting and harvesting, and to avoid that dreaded snowstorm or occasional little ice age that would come up to freeze their asses off. You are defined by geography, but if you're in a southern climate close to the equator, you can lose that fear of weather. You can fish and tan and eat mangoes that drop easily from trees. You can enjoy life and life is good. It's fun in the sun. In fact, it was the Taino natives of Puerto Rico that invented barbecue. They were having a barbecue in the Caribbean back before Columbus sailed over and spoiled their little party.

"Then there is Mexico," he continued. "You are Mexican-American, and that will make things tougher for you. You will excel in sports, but not in basketball." Years later, a Latino basketball player named Eduardo Najera would contradict that last statement.

"Your people are not tall," Coach would continue. "You need to take up track or anything defined by running, because your people can run, jump, and move."

He was right about geography. My geography did define me. I saw the United States in my parents' rearview mirror when I went to Mexico, and I could get there in 15 minutes from my house. Growing up in San Diego, you are always conscious of the border.

According to the Minutemen, that nice little citizen's group, San Diego is the front line of a Latin invasion. They would drive cars to the border to shine lights on it as Mexicans put mirrors up to shine those same lights back at them. You would have to choose a side in this light war. You were either holding a mirror or shining a light. But both sides with all these mirrors and lights didn't illuminate the real problem—*borders never work*. The Great Wall of China didn't work to keep the Mongolians out. Even after the wall was built, within 50 years, there was a Mongolian emperor on the throne. The Maginot Line in France didn't work against the Germans. The Berlin Wall didn't work against democracy.

When you live near a border, you realize that barriers don't work—this is indisputably clear. There is a saying in Mexico—"Poor Mexico. So far from God, and too close to the United States." Poor Tijuana, even farther from God.

Tijuana is now a lot worse off than I remember. First came NAFTA (North American Free Trade Agreement), an economic invasion; then 9/11, which closed the border; and then came the drug wars. Because the United States loves drugs. The United States is a country founded on addiction. America's first cash crop was tobacco. Now we are addicted to caffeine, and there's a Starbucks on every corner. Ironically, in a recent study, when Americans were asked to best describe Mexico, many said, "Drugs." But it's America's appetite for drugs that has caused the drug wars. You can't have a drug dealer without a drug user.

Mexico is now mimicking this addictive behavior. Cheap drugs are flooding into the poor neighborhoods on the border. Addiction used to be a rich, social phenomenon. That was until drugs became cheaper. Now, the poor can join the misery pool and take a couple of laps. When I was a kid, there were no heads hanging from bridges in Tijuana, only piñatas. This is what addiction has done to all of us on both sides of the border.

Mexico, oh Mexico. I would see its lights and believe everyone there was just a Mexican. No hyphen in their identity. In San Diego, we had our one true Mexican. His name was Don Diego. Sir Don Diego was named after a fictional Spanish landowner during our Spanish hacienda days, not the Don Diego portrayed in *The Mask of Zorro*. The Don Diego of my childhood memory was an actor. Don Diego was the mascot of the Del Mar Fair, a nice man in an elegant *charro* outfit who would ride around in a golf cart waving happily even though his land was taken over by tourists with red faces and plenty of sunblock. I could smell the tequila every time he passed by me in that cart, with a blonde Miss Del Mar Fairground by his side. He was Hollywood made-up history.

I was in high school, beginning to think about life and discovering things about my history not taught in school. Coach was great for that at the time because I was on the swim team, and I liked hanging out with him. I think he liked me because to him I was the underdog. When I ran for vice president of the student body, he even wore my T-shirt. They made him take it off because he could not support a particular candidate, like he was some sort of special interest group that would sway the vote. He was the first Super PAC.

Although I lost my bid for office in high school, I appreciated the support. The guy I ran against had more money to spend on posters and ads; I just wore a T-shirt that said "Vote for Me." On top of that, the messaging for his campaign was better than mine. His campaign manager spread vicious rumors about me. There were no campaign finance rules then, but he enlisted a formidable special interest group to fund his campaign—his parents.

In school, I loved history. If you read history, you will learn that most politicians lose more elections than they win. Abraham Lincoln lost twice in his bid for the U.S. Senate. I lost the Grossmont High School student body vice presidency just once. I quit politics faster than George Washington could chop down a cherry tree. There was definitely more in store for me than politics.

I began to truly grow when I went to drama class. I had been diagnosed with dyslexia, and reading was difficult for me, but somehow I could memorize words and act. The first play I was in, I was cast as Sherlock Holmes. I loved playing the British detective. Acting gave me the chance to explore other lives and to be other people. I began to express myself and imagine what I could be. In high school, a counselor once asked me what I wanted to be. "An actor," I replied. He chuckled and said, "Don't you mean a waiter?"

I didn't care. I was already beginning to dream of other places I could be. Like most of my peers, I didn't want to be in high school. But like none of my peers, I wanted to perform Shakespeare.

SHAKESPEARE
AND ME

"Shakespeare's characters had cockfights,
were lusty and loved life. Just like Mexicans."

I wanted to act for one reason: my father. I adored him. He had a huge spirit. He was the kind of man who was so much bigger than life. He had served in the Pacific during World War II, and had gone to Vietnam. He looked like a movie star to me, and he had the heart and soul of an artist. And I really think I became an actor for him. My brother was born with a cleft palate and spoke with the help of a speech therapist. That was tough for my father because he loved speeches. He joined Toastmasters International so he could speak better.

When my dad would take me out for our special times together, we would go to the movies. I remember he took me to see a British film when I was around ten—*Cromwell*. I sat in this beautiful theater and saw the red curtains open up to this great world with great speeches, and men inspiring other men to do great things just through the power of their spoken words. The people on the screen spoke very eloquently. Richard Harris threw the gauntlet down and spoke about education and justice. He talked about great ideas, great things. My father leaned over to me and said, "See that, Rick? If you could speak as beautiful as that, I'd be so proud of you." It was his Toastmasters training talking. When you are a pots-and-pans salesman like my father was, you need to speak. My father valued speech profoundly, and I began to as well.

Coming from a large family, I *had* to think of a gimmick to get any attention; my parents had five kids, and we lived in a two-bedroom house. My gimmick? Shakespeare. I memorized it and began to perform for my parents and my grandfather and my neighborhood, reciting sonnets and soliloquies.

In high school, my life was easy and my goals were simple. I had a vision, but no plan. When I read *The Great Gatsby* by F. Scott Fitzgerald, I was fascinated by Gatsby's character because, in the end, he was a self-made man. In the part where his best friend tries to understand the "Great Gatsby," he discovers Gatsby's journal after he is dead. The Great Gatsby had written down his goals, so I started to write mine. I knew I wanted to act.

When I finished high school, my parents' advice was to join the Marines or the post office. I tried the Marines and passed all the tests. The recruiter said I was approved for the officer training program, so I almost enlisted. But I knew that theater wanted me more.

My father encouraged me to go to college. He was worried that I would end up without an education. He had finished high school, but my grandfather only finished the fourth grade. At that time, most Latinos thought of education as out of their reach. My father felt it was in mine, so he said simply, "Go to college because you can." I knew it was him talking to his younger self. He wished that someone had the foresight to push him to go to school.

So, in 1977, I made a plan to go to college. I didn't want to go for the knowledge, but for the access. I thought if I was going to act in Hollywood, I'd need to go to a Hollywood school. In my first try at academia, I decided I wanted to go to the University of Southern California. I was accepted into the BFA program there, but then I realized that I needed financial aid. So, I went to MEChA, the *Movimiento Estudiantil Chicano de Aztlán* club on campus. There I met a very dark Chicano wearing a brown beret. I told him of my need for financial assistance. He looked at me, and, after a moment, said, "I have a real problem with you. Look at you, all *güero* (light Latino), and speaking bad Spanish. I don't think you have felt enough prejudice and suffering to be a part of *Movimiento Estudiantil Chicano de Azzzztláánnnnnnnnnn.*"

I looked at him and said simply "Hey, Xochimilco, does right now count?" That was the end of me and USC.

My father tried to help me. I saw him, a dignified and proud man, write a letter to the university, asking for aid, admitting all of his financial faults. I remember him writing that letter for me on our porch steps, trying to get me a scholarship to USC. He did for me what I would never have done for myself—he begged. And that's a dad.

But no scholarship came through. Instead, I landed in Grossmont Community College in San Diego, which saved me about $200,000. I was student body president during my two-year stint there. And I wrote down my next goal: to act. I was haunted by acting. I loved acting. No matter how far I traveled away from it, I always ended up returning. All I wanted to do was act. Not to "make it" or be famous—just to act.

Every weekend I took a bus to Balboa Park to attend Junior Theater. Every day I practiced memorizing Shakespeare on that bus. One day, I auditioned for the Old Globe Theatre with a soliloquy I'd memorized. I was cast. Just like that, I became a Shakespearean actor, which seems as old an occupation today as a New England whaler. It changed my life. It made me believe that I could be anything I dreamed I could be. I could be an Italian guy named Romeo who was in love with a girl he met at a dance and wooed on a balcony. But I still needed to sag my tights in order to look tougher. "These are tights, not panty hose," I explained to my family. "There's a big difference." To the average Latino, wearing tights was not cool. It was like being a folkloric dancer. So I began to act. It was that simple. The Old Globe changed my world. It was the beginning of my story.

I joined the Old Globe touring company, traveled to schools, and played Shakespeare to kids not much older than me. I saw so many Latino kids looking at me, and felt that we all were on the other side. Because I wasn't much older than they were, I recognized that their lives and their stories were the same as mine.

Many had never seen a play, let alone a Latino in one. I saw the hunger in their eyes. I loved how words moved them. They mostly yelled at us and made fun of us, but they also admired us. If anything, they admired our bravery.

I had said yes to an audition, and got into the touring company. I said yes to reading Shakespeare until his words became a part of my vocabulary, and I became a part of his world.

Saying yes was the beginning of my life. My mother said yes to a date. My father then said yes to a marriage, and I was born. And I said yes to life. I know it may sound cliché to be so positive, but to say no is far more common than you think. Saying no is much easier; it stops every action. Saying yes starts the journey. No stops it. It's as simple as that.

I loved Shakespeare. Reading Shakespeare changed my life. I loved Shakespeare because I related to him. How? Easy. I related to Shakespeare's time. Elizabethan England was a mixed-up culture of passion and confidence, and, as Latinos say, *y que*—attitude. (*Y que* means "So what," or "And what are you going to do about it?" *Y que* was a challenge and statement all at the same time.) My grandfather raised fighting cocks. Shakespeare's characters had cockfights, were lusty, and loved life, just like Mexicans. They were also barbaric and poetic at times, just like how I saw my Latino world.

I played every classical role you could imagine. Then I had an unforeseen problem. They found out I was Mexican, and casting began to change. There were no Mexicans in Shakespeare. Just kings and knights and princesses and Caesars.

After junior college, in 1979, I applied to San Diego State to continue my education. I studied acting there for two years. In the theater, I could be anything my imagination would allow. I went from Sherlock Holmes to musicals. There were no borders in the acting world, and I loved it.

This time in my life was like an actor's apprenticeship. I was performing at all the theaters in San Diego, and there were some really good ones. In 1981 I took a job at San Diego Repertory Theater in *Working,* the musical based on the Studs Terkel book, playing numerous characters, from a Mexican field worker to a '60s radical. The show would run for two years.

That same year, I heard of an audition for a project with some of the alumni of the famed Second City of Chicago. I was excited. These kings of comedy were having auditions for some local actors to join their company for a PBS special on mental health, which would be shot at San Diego State. I wanted to audition even though I was totally inexperienced with improv comedy.

I asked a few actors I knew about the technique, and they said simply, "Rick, improv is based on saying yes. If you say yes and agree, you will keep the scene alive. So, always just say yes."

Okay, easy enough, so if I'm in a scene and someone says, "I'm captain of this ship," I say, "Aye, aye, Captain. Yes, you are. All hands on deck. The captain's talking. Listen up!" And if the actor playing the captain does not say "No, I'm not the captain," but agrees, the scene continues. If I say, "Look, Captain, a pirate ship," and the other actor says, "Yes, I see it. What a huge pirate ship she is. Why, she's the biggest one I've ever seen, and it looks like she's heading straight toward us!" then the scene works. But if I say, "Look, there's a pirate ship," and the other actor says, "No, there isn't," we're stuck in a negative limbo. There must be an agreement to the "Yes." It's a suspension of disbelief until the stage belief takes over and becomes the reality.

All of the true greats of sketch comedy were at the audition. Names only real sketch people knew. Severn Darden, Avery Schreiber, and the original Second City members. Following that simple rule I'd been given, when they asked me if I knew improv, I said, "Yes."

I got the job. They hired two unknown local actors. A very talented black woman named Whoopi Goldberg and me.

I learned a lot from Whoopi. She was working on her show, which would later go to Broadway. She originally had a two-person show, but one day her partner didn't show up. So, she just did her own material. That's how she became a solo artist. She said yes to going solo, and her show was born.

As cast mates, Whoopi and I discovered that the way to stay on the show was to write. You could write your sketches and continue to act, or just act and be dismissed. I wanted to continue to act, so I began to write. Whoopi wrote, too. We even wrote together.

I'd never met anyone like her. I loved how she spoke her mind. She took on politics, she took on social change. But she didn't try to be anything other than who and what she was, and that was inspiring to me.

She was just Whoopi, and it was working for her.

She told me that she wrote of her experiences and told me to write mine. She taught me survival. She would write, act, produce. She did whatever it took.

One day I told her I was going to go to Hollywood to act. "Rick," Whoopi said, "you should write." I resisted her advice. "No, Whoopi. I'm an actor."

"Never let yourself be a liar," she told me. "You just gotta say yes."

After *Working,* in 1982, I applied to ACT, the American Conservatory Theater, in San Francisco. Leaving my family and friends, I studied for nearly three years on a full scholarship. There, in the whitest environment you can imagine, in a very traditional acting program, I studied Standard American Speech, but realized there was no one speaking accent-free speech. And there's no place called Standard America.

When I completed the ACT professional program, I was ready to head back to San Diego and my family. Then fate intervened, and I was cast in a production of *Uncle Vanya,* basically to move sets. The show toured to Hollywood, and with two weeks of union pay in my pocket, I bought an old car and decided to stay. Hollywood was an undiscovered world for me to conquer. But I had no Malinche like Cortéz did as my guide. I only had my father's advice—*"Rick, you have to hear a lot of 'nos' before you hear that one 'yes.'"*

ICU:
The Intensive Comedy Unit

"Do you know how to get a man up from a coma?"

I didn't know where I was at first, but I had a bright light in my face. I'm told that I looked really bad. Blackened eyes. A gash over my head. On a resuscitator. A few of my friends believed I would live, but apparently most people thought I was going to die, even my pastor. I was starting to come to in the ICU.

Unbeknownst to me, members of the church, as well as many friends, rushed to my bedside. Lupe Ontiveros called me. Lupe was a great actress, having performed in such films as *Selena* and *As Good as It Gets*. According to Lupe, she played more than 300 roles as a maid throughout her career.

While I was in darkness, she left me a most touching message, which I kept on my phone. She said, "Rick, I heard about your unfortunate situation. I'm praying for you. We all are. We will get through this together." Her words connected me to my Latino community in Hollywood. To me, Lupe was the biggest symbol of that community.

As I was coming to, my wife Susie grabbed my hand and said, "Rick, if you can hear me, squeeze my hand." I was beginning to come back to life. My face was swollen and my black-and-blue eyes were closed shut. My lips were blistered from the fever. I looked like a human mess. She begged again, "Rick, if you can hear me squeeze, my hand." She felt me squeeze her hand and said it was the greatest feeling in her life. At least I had some life force left in me, even if it was only a squeeze of my hand. The human touch was what I needed. And so did she.

My children couldn't visit me. I was glad they didn't see me like this. Even wounded and in the ICU ward, I was their champion and provider. I was like an injured lion in one of those nature shows where everyone wonders if the pride will survive. Nature is not so much cruel as it is logical. If you are wounded in the jungle, you become an item on the menu. No feelings, just cold hard facts. Only the strong survive, and I was a wounded lion with hyenas hot on my scent.

I woke up very slowly, regaining a little more consciousness every time someone came into my room. Every time a nurse entered, she or he would give me a shot. I was coming to, and every time I did, a nurse would give me a needle full of sleep (sedatives) or morphine to take away the pain, or some other drug to help with my fever. They moved me around like I was more a piece of meat than a man. As I began to feel more alive and awake and landed back in my body, I became fully aware of the pain. It hurt like hell.

I began to grasp that my recovery would be hard, and that I could relapse at any moment. My head was fragile. My second chance found me, and I said "Yes!" Yes to getting out of bed. Yes to recovering. I was alive, and, even if some thought I was going to die, I knew I was not. I knew I was getting better. Finally, they took the breathing tube out of my throat.

When I regained full consciousness, there was only a nurse in my room. She was as surprised as I was. I looked at her and said, "Do you know how to get a man up from a coma?" She looked perplexed—not at the question, but that I could speak. I paused for a moment. "Give him Viagra. That will get him up." I'd startled her with a dirty joke. Then I went back to sleep.

By the time my wife came into the room, I was out. The nurse told her what I said, and Susie knew then that I was coming back. She stayed by my side to see if I would wake again. She squeezed my hand. Next, she said, "People are asking about you. They are so worried. Sofia Vergara's manager called." She said it was the first time she saw me open my eyes. "Sofia Vergara?" I asked. My wife knew that I had worked with Sofia on a TV pilot years earlier. Her manager and I were good friends. More and more people from my Hollywood life were calling the ICU and rallying for my recovery. I continued to drift up and down on the Glasgow Coma Scale and in and out of consciousness.

Friends and family began to keep vigil at my bedside. My wife had been keeping people informed of my progress on CaringBridge, a Facebook-type site for people with health issues. People were praying for me. I had been battling Hollywood for years, and it was touching to know that my community was genuinely worried about losing me.

I remembered a young man that I met at one of my shows in Chicago. After the performance, a group of friends and fans came to my house in Wicker Park. This man seemed distant and quiet, so I asked him what was wrong. "Nothing now," he said, "but tomorrow morning I report to prison to serve five years." He was about to lose his freedom, and wanted to savor every second of it he had left. Now, people were savoring me. All of the things I'd done that had bothered people became endearing, charming quirks. The threat of death recast the scene; suddenly, I was respected and revered.

Memory is a very odd and fragile thing. I was beginning to get mine back. But I had forgotten random things. I even joked that I only forgot people that I did not like or I owed money to. The doctor laughed and said some memory loss was common as a result of a coma.

I had gone through hard times in Hollywood. I had tried to forget those lost, hard years, but now the memories reemerged—short, incomplete threads. I forgot the night I collapsed. The fever had left me with some memory loss and a huge hospital bill. I drifted off to sleep again, but not before an old agent called to see how I was. He reminded me of my early years in Hollywood. I was tired, and thinking of those years only made me feel more exhausted.

I was slowly recovering my memory in that hospital bed. I was not able to move or stand, but I could remember.

FADE IN:
HOLLYWOOD

*"Desi Arnaz was a
radical cultural propagandist."*

I am always reminded of my Latino history because I grew up in California right next to Mexico. At one time, California *was* Mexico, and Californians fear that it may one day be Mexico again. But in truth, they should fear not. Because the one thing that America is good at is making Americans. In Los Angeles, I saw my history every day. And you need to know your history to understand yourself.

We are all linked to a larger history, whatever our story is. I read about World War II and the March of Bataan, but it only became real to me when I saw the tears in my mother's eyes as she spoke of her brother Joe. My father had fought in World War II, so the war he described to me in great detail was real to me. There were carriers in the bay in San Diego that we could see to remind us of the wars America fought.

In Hollywood, I was reminded of another history—the history of Hollywood itself. I remember I saw Alan Hale, Jr., the actor who played the Skipper on *Gilligan's Island,* greeting customers at his restaurant, The Lobster Barrel. It was sad and strange all at the same time. I saw where Desi Arnaz built his studio. It was just down the street from where I lived. The Hollywood sign was in the hills above my apartment.

There had been a few Latinos living in our neighborhood in La Mesa. But in Hollywood, there were more, and they were real Mexicans. How do I define real Mexicans? They loved *banda* music and Vicente Fernandez. They had his birthday tattooed on their bodies. Even their children did. They loved the taste of *chile* that would burn lesser men's hearts out. They had big moustaches and so did their men. I felt like an almost-Mexican next to them.

When I was growing up in San Diego, we had grunion runs on dark midnight beaches lit by a thousand campfires and the moon and stars above. Grunions were these little schools of fish that spawned on the beach. Most San Diegans had tried to spawn on these shores at night as well. I tried with some blonde girls with names like Terry, Julie, and Shauna while the songs of the Beach Boys played on the radio. Now I tried to forget all that. I was living in Hollywood—dingy, dirty, and full of its own history—and I was a Latino actor. I had to adjust and play roles written for Latino actors by non-Latino writers who knew nothing about Latinos.

There are more than 53 million of us here, yet we are invisible. You don't see us much on television, and, when you do, we're hidden behind a stereotype—pushing a lawn mower, running from the police. On English language television, Latinos reflect a servant or criminal class. If you think there are stereotypes on English television, it's even worse on Spanish television. There Latinos are blond, blue-eyed Europeans. Because Spanish television reinforces the conquest, they tend to cast leading roles with European-type Latinos. When I was a child, I never saw Latinos on television except on an occasional *I Love Lucy* episode. I'd imagine Desiderio Alberto Arnaz y de Acha III, aka Desi Arnaz, singing songs of love, like "Babalu," with conga in hand, dreaming of getting his red-haired woman, his Lucy. The words, of course, are far from the truth. Desi was a radical cultural propagandist.

> *Que mi negra me quiera*
> *Que tenga dinero*
> *Y que no se muera*
> *Ay! Yo le quiero pedi a Babalu 'na negra muy santa*
> *Como tu que no tenga otro Negro*
> *Pa' que no se fuera.*

Little did America realize that a hot-blooded Cuban man was singing about an African witch doctor (read shaman), and how to get a thick, black woman with big Angelina Jolie–type lips by praising a West African god of the earth with rum and alcohol. *Wait a minute. Desi seemed so sweet!* People never really read the fine print. Desi was a huge star back then, when Latinos were less populous and, therefore, more exotic and less threatening. Now they are just threatening to conservative America.

All this was in my past at this point. I was in Hollywood and the '80s were in full swing. AIDS was identified as an incurable disease. Reagan was President, and the Soviet Union was starting to crumble. They found the *Titanic,* and the *Challenger* exploded.

The world of acting had roles for me, but they were for an actor who had nothing to do with me. I was being offered gangbangers, revolutionaries, and busboy roles. The nice-guy roles like Desi's were gone. Who I was just didn't fit Hollywood. I was a classically trained Latino actor. Some people told me to just say I was an "actor," not a "Latino" actor, but I couldn't shed my identity that easily.

Then I got my first call to audition for a role since my time in San Francisco. It was an audition to play a revolutionary from the Biscayne Islands, which was somewhere off an imaginary Latin country. The casting director gave me my lines and I read them: "Monica, please help me. My name is Juan from the Biscayne Islands." Of course, there was no actual place, but the casting director stopped me and said, "Hold on, Rick or Ricardo." I hesitated. "It's Rick," I said. "You are giving me a Mexican accent," he replied. "I need an El Salvadorian accent. That's where I think the Biscayne Islands are." I paused for a second and said, "Oh, yes, an El Salvadorian accent." With a pause and a dramatic take, I did the exact same accent as before. The casting director looked at me and smiled. "Now that is a perfect El Salvadorian accent!" I got the role.

From Shakespeare to *General Hospital,* playing a revolutionary house boy living in a boathouse on Monica Quartermaine's huge estate. I was in Hollywood.

Being Latino was never an issue until I came to Hollywood. In Hollywood, my culture roots became the number one issue. Suddenly, being Mexican-American defined me. I was always an instant Spanish lesson. "It's 'na-HAIR-ra,' not 'na-JAIR-ra.' The *j* is not pronounced at all. The *j* is an *h* sound, like in La Jolla."

I remember an agent asking me to change my last name to Rivers. I would have been Rick Rivers, not Rick Najera. Rivers sounded good. Rivers were free and roaming, and sometimes could be tamed with a dam to provide power. I was told that Najera sounded too harsh, not like Sanchez or Garcia.

It wasn't a bad idea, changing my name, but Najera is unique. It originates from Andalusia, Spain—the Moorish and Jewish area where people have fought wars over religion, identity, and land for centuries. In the land of Hollywood, I was fighting a war, too. It may not have been a life-or-death struggle; no one would kill or maim me. They would actually do worse. They wouldn't employ me. It was a slower, harsher death, invisible to the eye. Just like my undiagnosed pneumonia that landed me in the hospital.

I'd never been in a gang. I was never a cholo, a street thug. A casting director once asked me, "Ricardo, have you ever been in a gang? The producers really want someone who's from the streets. Have you ever been in a gang?" I paused. "No," I said. "I tried, but I failed the written test. Plus, I lacked hand-eye coordination. It's not easy doing gang signs with one hand and shooting with the other. And, my name is Rick." She kicked me out of her office.

When I got a call to audition for *Falcon Crest,* I figured it wouldn't be a gang-type role. "It's in Napa Valley," my agent said. "There are no gangs in the Napa Valley." *You're right,* I thought. *What would I be, the Cabernet Sauvignon?* So I showed up for the audition in a suit. My first line was, "You'd better not come in my hood anymore." They cut me off and said, "No, thanks." I said, "Wait, do you want me to read it again?" "No, that's it. Thank you."

Then my agent called three weeks later and said he wanted me to audition again. At this point my bank account was near nothing, so I agreed. This time I put on dark makeup and wore ripped jeans, a bandanna, the whole bit. I said, "Don't come to my valley ever again." The same director didn't recognize me. He said, "Oh my gosh, you're so gangy. You're perfect."

To go from a classical actor trained at the American Conservatory The-ater to Paco the gangbanger was, to me, the hardest thing. I wasn't doing the roles my father was proud to have me do. I was playing roles written by other people who didn't understand the culture and were going for the lowest common denominator. I was playing roles that my family would look at and say, "We got you out of the barrio to be more than that. Now you're playing roles about people in the barrio, and they're not even written by people who are Latino."

Now I was living in Hollywood auditioning for the role of Gangbanger #3, and I wondered, *Did Desi ever do roles like this?*

I auditioned for a role on *Fame,* but I lost that spot to Janet Jackson, they decided to go for a woman. Then I auditioned for *La Bamba.* I lost that one to Lou Diamond Phillips. It was the mid-'80s in Hollywood. Los Angeles, like the rest of America, was plagued with a crack epidemic. In 1988, I landed my first film, a low budget, cocaine-filled, drug-smuggling drama called *Red Surf.* It starred Gene Simmons from the band Kiss and George Clooney. My role: a Cuban drug lord named Calavera ("Skull"). Once I was a drug lord, Hollywood considered me a Latino. I would go on to play every lowlife scum imaginable, but in retrospect that particu-lar part bothered me the most. Latino lowlife scum.

Apparently, a Cuban drug lord was the biggest kind of drug lord you could be—much better than a Mexican drug lord, my agent told me. "Everyone is a drug lord in Mexico, Rick. A Cuban drug lord is rare. They wear white suits, dance salsa, sip Cuban coffee, and smoke big Cuban cigars. They are classier." It sounded logical to me. "It's a bigger role, Rick. Your Cuban drug lord is more evil. You have a basement full of pit bulls that you feed your enemies to. You even kill a man with a knife." He sold me on that script.

It was the first film for all of us. George and Gene played surfer drug dealers. It was the Beach Boys versus the Barrio Boys. The night before shooting began, we were toasting to the film with tequila. We were all excited. I remember George had a pet potbellied pig and a great house. I naïvely asked him, "George, what do your parents do? This is a great house." He looked at me, smiled, and said, "This isn't my parents' house.

It's my house." I paused. "Oh," I replied, then asked, "What do you do?" George laughed. "The same thing you do. I'm an actor. I just ask for more money."

At the height of the L.A. crack epidemic, we were shooting on location one day in Compton with no real security. Our detail consisted of one retired motorcycle cop and a wimpy fight choreographer who could make it look like he was kicking your ass, but he really wasn't. That was it.

I was outside the house as they were filming inside. Suddenly, I heard gunshots. The sound surprised me. My gun was with me, not on set, and we weren't supposed to film me shooting my gun filled with blanks until later that afternoon. Why was I hearing gunshots? Then, in the corner of my eye, I saw a guy shuffle by, holding his arm. It was bleeding, and he was terrified. Another guy holding a raised gun in his hand was chasing him. The guy with the gun saw me and pointed it at me. Everything seemed to move in slow motion, just like a movie special effect, and I wasn't even filming. I just happened to be where I shouldn't be, playing a character that wasn't me. The gunman saw that my gun was holstered. I could see in his eyes what he must have been thinking: *Okay, who is this Mexican drug lord and what is he doing in my motherfucking hood?*

Our eyes locked for a second. *I'm a Cuban drug lord, not Mexican!* I screamed in my head. Realizing that I wasn't from his neighborhood, he turned and started shooting at the guy he had been chasing. Finally, the retired motorcycle cop sauntered over. "What's going on?" he asked. "The guy over there is running and shooting someone!" I said. "Oh, that happens all the time in this neighborhood," he said coldly, and walked casually away.

It was surreal. I was an actor playing ghetto in the real ghetto. My character was a drug lord and I had just witnessed a scene from the real drug world. The retired police officer's calm bothered me. No one seemed to care. Then, Gene Simmons, holding an AK-47 with a round of blanks inside, walked over and asked, "What's going on?" I explained to him what had just happened. He smiled. "I'm from Israel. We see that all the time." It seemed the irony was apparent only to me. The policeman and the rocker simply wondered what time lunch would be served.

What you are in Hollywood sometimes matters more than *who* you are. Culture is really important, and to Hollywood, culture equals race. In America, race is defined in a major way by Hollywood. If there is inequality in Hollywood, it is advanced by the distorted images that Hollywood creates and promotes.

In 1988, I worked on a film called *Little Nikita* with Sidney Poitier. We'd have lunch together on set. I remember a scene where I had to act scared as I looked down the barrel of a gun in a bad guy's hand. The scene was being shot in a strange position. My eye line was up, not down, and I needed someone to get on a ladder in order to get my eye line right. So, to help me believe that I was looking at a gun in someone's hand, Sidney got on a ladder and held a gun.

One time at lunch, race came up in conversation. Sidney knew I was Mexican-American. He looked at me and said, "You might be bothered by the amount of time you will end up spending just explaining to people who you are."

I noticed a sadness in his eyes. He had lived through a time of turmoil, prejudice, and hate that I could never imagine. The lesson I learned from him that day was that if you are an actor who is black or brown or Asian, you may get tired of explaining who you are, but you better be prepared to do it. You better know who you are and what tribe you have chosen. It's a struggle, but if I could be half the actor and gentleman that Sidney Poitier was, I'd make my tribe proud.

That's why I began to study my history, to understand who I am and where I came from. That's why history has been so important to me. It gives me a steady compass to navigate with in my life.

I liked working with Sidney Poitier. That job was my first big studio role. Most of my scenes were cut from the film, but I had the opportunity to hang out with and learn from a legend for a few weeks. I met a great actor and a great man, a man who had an extraordinary work ethic and genuinely cared about the people he worked with. Sidney engaged his peers as equals. He was the classiest man I have ever met.

51

LATINOS CHOOSE THEIR TRIBE

"Rick, you're not one of those Latinos."

We don't choose our family. We choose our tribe. Latinos who are more European might pass as American, devoid of culture or questions about culture and identity, but eventually begin to feel the pressure and guilt for being so white, or *güero*. It's not us, but the random lottery of genes. Sometimes when you are lighter you might blend in, but you inevitably betray yourself. In my case, I outed myself by defending my darker brother and sisters. How many times did I surprise someone after a particularly ignorant racial comment with, "Hey, I'm Latino, too!" only to hear, "Rick, you're not one of those Latinos." I'm then forced to choose how I relate to or acknowledge people.

Any minority who might pass for white must choose which side of the racial divide they're on. Now more and more Americans are mixed with different ethnicities and a myriad of flavors. Americans are no longer one culture, but many.

Consider the multiracial President Barack Hussein Obama. President Obama is a combination of African and European ancestry crashing on the shores of America. He was raised by white grandparents who instilled in him a love for this country. It's the other Americans in this country who try to negate his American experience.

When he won the presidency for his second term, I was really hoping he'd come up to the podium, get on the microphone, and say, "Okay, I really was born in Africa and I'm a Muslim." The heads of Tea Party members would have collectively exploded. But that was just me.

Why do I say that Latinos choose their culture? It's simple. Because our culture is very complex. How do we define culture? We are defined by how we look and how we talk. Communication, both literal and symbolic.

Some Latinos speak Spanish. Some are primarily English speakers. Some speak no Spanish at all. So not all Latinos can be defined easily or simply by the language they speak; we speak many different dialects and languages. Spain has many official and unofficial languages: Aranese, Catalan, Basque, Galician. And that's little Spain. Ten percent of Mexico does not speak Spanish. In Mexico, they speak more than 80 different indigenous languages in addition to Spanish.

Our culture is also defined by space. We're tactile people. We give *abrazos* (hugs) out very easily, although not all of us do in the same way or as easily. Caribbean Latinos tend to be even more tactile. They always hug and kiss, even more than Mexican Latinos. Blame it on the warm weather and rum. I'm sure no cultural anthropologist would observe things the way I do, but, every time I've been to Puerto Rico, rum seems to break the ice.

Latinos are defined by family as well. Some Latinos are more matriarchal, like Puerto Ricans, or more patriarchal, like Mexicans. Latinos are defined by our "biological variation." We come in all shades and colors because we are racially mixed. How did we get that way? I believe it's because we are very tactile as a people. Hugging led to other things, and our wandering Latino nature inspired us to see the world and impregnate it. Thus, Latinos are a very mixed culture. Color is a never-ending question for Latinos, because we come in every shade. Being "almost white" does not mean that I'm lacking something. It's the recognition that I'm hard to define. And not just me, but my entire culture. It's not us; we understand us. It's others that don't understand us. Being Latino, we may have certain aspects of our culture that are actually black, and Asian and European and indigenous and native, and all of those things get wrapped up under the title of Latino. Our diversity is in itself the definition. We're a people full of ironies. Many Americans assume that we all speak Spanish. Not necessarily true. So we can't be defined by language, necessarily. And we can't be defined by race because many of us are a hybrid race.

We're so mixed up with other cultures of different conquests and wars that have been part of our Latino culture that sometimes we are "almost white" and sometimes we are "almost black" and sometimes we are "almost indigenous." Many of us, nearly all of us, are mixed in some way or another. So being "almost white" is my ironic way of looking at the world through my eyes. I'm not saying that I'm lacking, or that I'm actually "almost" anything, or that I almost won. No, I am the race and it's not a foot race, it's a steady walk and a long journey. My culture is Latino.

Color is very much a part of the Latino experience. It's important because the Mexican culture, which includes a great number of Latinos in the United States, is part of the *conquista,* the conquest, which came with Hernán Cortéz. He came to Mexico and conquered the land along with other conquistadors linking all the way back to Columbus. The conquerors came to the new world with very few women.

By necessity, life is never defined by borders. Life always wants to get out. Life always wants to re-create itself. So the conquistadors that came to these shores intermingled with the indigenous natives. That's nature. That's life. Different people, running into each other, and color was part of it. Color, in many respects, still hasn't changed; it's still a part of prejudice. It's part of ignorance—the arbitrary decision to make one color stronger than the other, or more favored. Human beings continue this drama even today, long after science has confirmed that we all came out of Africa.

So what was our color back then? It took only a few generations for it to change, and even within our own families we see color degrees and generations changing. My sister is very dark, and I'm very light. We're both brother and sister. That's the reality. But sometimes I would notice people would treat her differently than me, necessarily, because I was light, or *güero.* And that comes with privileges, but also guilt. I think sometimes the guilt I would feel came when I would see people that were my relatives who were dark-skinned being treated differently and I would notice it. So color is a big issue in Latino culture.

There's an old saying in Puerto Rico: *Donde esta tu abuela?* It means

"Where is your grandmother?" Meaning you're hiding your grandmother in the kitchen. So when people would come over, you'd try to shun her from the family because she was dark. So the joke was, where is your grandmother? Why don't you bring her out? Because most likely she's African, whereas the Puerto Rican culture is African-European more than Mestizos and in Cuba and even in places like Veracruz, Mexico, there are over one hundred thousand Africans. Africa is very much part of our culture.

So, culture, race, and color are woven throughout the history of Latinos. And ironically, Latinos that have come to America, in many respects, are continuing the journey.

So, who are we as Latinos? That's a difficult question, because we are complicated and don't fit into simple categories. And that's the answer. When you look for simple answers to a complex culture, then both sides are cheated and shortchanged.

Latino culture is more a choice than destiny. We have to choose to be Latino and enforce that cultural choice, all the while knowing that not even *we* understand what makes us Latinos. Blacks were defined by America's history of slavery and the one-drop rule, which meant that any person who had "one drop of Negro blood" was considered black. Today, a black man may transcend his racial identity with money in some circumstances, but not all. In an elevator late at night, he's a lone black man perceived as a threat by some, but in his office, he's an executive working late.

I'm a light-skinned Latino, so I can pass for white. I have no accent in English. The Mexican janitor who sees me working late in my office may only realize I'm Latino if I speak to him in Spanish. To know what it's like to be Latino, imagine that you're at a convention without a name tag. All the other guests have tags that spell out their name and title. There is no question about who they are. You spend the evening forced to constantly identify yourself.

If you want to understand me, all you have to do is leave your comfort zone and go someplace where you will be the minority, not the majority. Go and be the "other." Latinos are the "other." Not the black other, but the brown other or sometimes the almost white other.

I have a very dark-brown Mexican friend who is not defined by his color. Many people think he's Arabic or East Indian. Until he speaks Spanish. Latinos aren't always easy to define or to recognize.

I could've joined those people who say culture shouldn't define us. The people who say that we're all simply Americans. But even that's misleading, because you can be both Mexican and American, since Mexico is part of the American continent. I chose to be Latino because having two cultures makes my life richer and much more interesting.

The prejudices fair-skinned Latinos face are far subtler than those encountered by brown-skinned Latinos. Subtle institutional racism is the worst. It's the death delivered by a thousand tiny cuts.

Consider recent immigration policies, such as the Arizona law that makes it illegal to transport an undocumented person. If someone gets into my car, I have to police and question his or her immigration status. And according to Arizona Law SB 1070, police officers are now able to detain "when practicable" anyone they suspect of being in this country illegally. It also makes it a misdemeanor not to carry immigration status papers. The problem is laws like these criminalize Latinos based on looks. We are called illegal, not undocumented. You can't be an illegal human being like living is a crime. According to Hill + Knowlton 33 percent of Americans they surveyed believe over 50 percent of the Latinos in their country are illegal. The actual number is 17 percent or 6.8 million.

For example, if I show you a picture of Selena Gomez and Justin Bieber, you may assume Selena is the immigrant based on her dark looks. But you would be mistaken. Canadian-born Justin Bieber is the real immigrant. We must enforce a border sometimes hundreds of miles inland. It seems absurd, right? But, so is that law.

This is how prejudice touches all Latinos. Every time you hear the word Latino, or Mexican, or Hispanic, you begin to unconsciously associate that word or person with illegal immigrants or criminal activity. Suppose I told you the story of a father who loves his family so much that he travels alone thousands of miles and crosses dangerous rivers, borders, and barriers (some man-made, some natural) to get work, get paid, and then send that hard-earned money home to his loved ones. That man would be considered brave and heroic. But if I then told you that same man is an illegal alien, you might now consider him a criminal, not brave and heroic. Illegal equals criminal. And for too many Americans, Latino equals illegal.

Such broad brushstrokes perpetuated in the American media not only shape reality, but also can destroy lives. The FBI reported that in the last five years there has been a 40 percent rise in hate crimes against Latinos. Being *almost white* is like being *almost legal,* as so many Latinos seesawing between the U.S. and Mexico have discovered. When police pull over an African-American because he's driving in Beverly Hills, and he isn't an athlete or an entertainer, that's racial profiling. But according to our American immigration policy, it's not racial profiling when you pull over a Latino in Arizona. It's checking their citizenship status. And enforcing our borders. While some may say it's not racial profiling, I say it is. Many of my darker-skinned Latino brothers and sisters don't get an opportunity to have an opinion.

I'm a Latino who has not forgotten his roots. God chose my color, but I chose my culture. Being in the Latino tribe is a choice because not all of us are as easily defined as African-Americans or Asian-Americans. After a generation or two, Latinos just evolve into me. In all human species, whether we like it or not, evolution is inevitable. And that's a sad fact for some, because eventually the ostrich boots will come off. And the love for *banda* music will end. And the *tapatio* sauce will burn your lips and the corn on the cob won't be smothered in chili and mayonnaise. And you won't speak Spanish. Everyone's ethnic-group identity evolves.

The proudest Indian warrior might evolve into a casino owner after four generations. The thickest-accented Italian grocer might one day evolve into Andrew Cuomo. And the angriest Kenyan radical student's son might be transformed into the President of the United States.

CODE BLUE

"Is that Code Blue for me?"

A Code Blue alarm woke me up. Doctors and nurses rushed to save someone in the intensive care unit. I thought, *Is that Code Blue for me?* I opened my eyes and realized it was not. Drifting in and out of sleep, whenever I heard the words *Code Blue* in my ward, I thought it was me dying. But it was always someone else. I would thank God, and then feel remorse for being so greedy as to stay alive and cheer that it was someone else who was exiting.

A nurse walked in and moved me in my bed for another round of tests. They felt that I was now stable and that I was going to make it, unless of course the unforeseen happened. I was thinking how I lived my life before I arrived in the ICU. So many images and memories flooded my mind as I lay in bed.

Each new visitor brought back a memory. Jacob Vargas (he played Selena's brother) reminded me of my old Hollywood days. He was the best man at my wedding. We had grown apart during my play *Latinologues*. In the pre-Broadway show, the producers didn't choose him, although he was great for the part. That's part of the unfairness of the business. And now he was here for me.

Since the night I'd been admitted to the hospital, my dear friend and producing partner Rafael Agustin was right by my side. After Rafael read my work in college, he decided that he wanted to work with me. But when he saw me at my lowest in an ICU bed, he was shocked. The actor in him didn't miss a beat. "Good to have you back, boss Rick." Rafael always called me "boss." It had become a joke between us.

Others visited. Scott Montoya, a longtime friend and the producer of many Showtime comedy specials, came to visit me one night long past visiting hours. He and I reminisced and talked about comedy. So many people were there for me that I began to ask myself, why was I alive? Why had I returned from my coma? Was there a special message for me? Was there a noble cause for me to join? A job I had to do? My mind was racing.

A nurse came in and rescued me from myself. She explained that in cases like mine, it was normal have mixed emotions. She predicted that I would be experiencing survival guilt and emotional outbursts. "You've had severe head trauma," she said. "You may have lost some memories and you might find it hard to control your emotions." She gave me a blood thinner shot in my stomach. I needed to rest and drugs were the easy answer in the hospital. Oddly, drugs were an easy answer in Hollywood as well. Fade to black . . .

A moment later I woke up, but actually it was a day later. I saw my mother sitting in my room. She had tears in her eyes. She saw I was awake. "You gave us all a scare," she said. "You need a haircut, Rick, but not too short."

I reminded myself of how strong she is. When you are in the hospital, families are all there as witness to the end or the beginning of life. My mother has seen many lives come and go, from her brother being killed in the war to my father's death years later. I wasn't at his side. I was pitching a TV show when I got the word he'd died. I was pitching a comedy, and my own tragedy was unfolding in San Diego. I lost a piece of my history when my father died. He was a great storyteller. With him gone, I find it harder to remember my history. I try very hard to remember all of his stories.

The doctor told me I'd had a seizure, perhaps a stroke. There was a gray spot on my brain. The pneumonia I had was stable, and my brain had stopped swelling. They tested my level of consciousness by asking me the name of the President of the United States. I said, "Saddam Hussein." They didn't hear the sarcasm in my voice. A nurse came in to give me another shot. Tired, I drifted in and out of sleep. Maybe because my mother was there I rested easier. It was like nothing could harm me if she was by my side.

It's strange that no matter how old you are, you never lose the child in you. Like a phantom limb, it's still a part of you. I remember waiting for my mother to come home from work when I was a kid. She was always working. My earliest memory is of her coming home from work in her waitress uniform. I would hug her, my face brushing up against her legs as she stood above me. I remember feeling her nylon stockings against my cheeks. I would hold her tight, not ever wanting her to leave. She was warm and safe. Now, I still remember my beautiful young mother. I felt secure then. With her by my side now, I felt secure again. Then I fell back to sleep.

SAYING YES

"Hello, I'm Rick Najera,
and I'm a writer."

As the '80s progressed, I was a working actor in Hollywood. I was making a living playing a lie—but that is why they call it acting. The problem was that the roles I was playing enforced the stereotypes that I wasn't. My cousins were United Farm Workers (UFW) organizers. Two were married to Cesar Chavez's daughters. I wasn't anything close to the gangbangers and drug lords that I portrayed. Sure, actors exist to play roles, but sometimes I felt that I was lying about my people, playing stereotypical roles written by white male writers who had no idea how their distorted images hurt Latinos.

"You need to work and now is not the time to get political," I chided myself. "First, get your foot in the door." I both hated and loved this time in my life.

I didn't fit the classic Latino stereotype. I was not brown-skinned. The other actors thought life was easy for me because I could pass for white. It was ironic that Latinos felt I could pass for white, but in reality I never could. Because I didn't want to. I wanted to be me. I was a good actor, not a stereotype mascot. And I was doing well. At least financially.

In 1989, I remember a bunch of cholo gangbanger types befriended me on the set of a movie called *Ghetto Blaster.* I went to San Diego State, they went to Penitentiary State. One day after filming, I asked them if they wanted to take a picture with me. They thought it was a big deal to take a picture with a star. And they thought I was a star playing them. It was so far from the truth. To them, my life seemed much more exciting than theirs. They were wrong. I was playing them because Hollywood romanticized gang life.

The more they liked me the worse I felt. I didn't want to be the monkey who dances. I had to play a stereotype of them to get jobs. Sometimes I would darken my skin and dye my hair jet-black to look more Latino. What I really looked like was a punk rocker with a tan. The networks didn't portray the real Latino on TV or on the big screen. The more false I became, the more miserable I was. I was becoming less of me—invisible.

In Hollywood, too often I felt the burden of inauthenticity. I was not telling the truth. I was not being real. I was getting paid and making a living, but I felt I was playing roles not true to myself. Actors are sensitive to false dialogue, and the dialogue and roles were false. Mostly because they were not written by me or Latinos who knew the culture.

Of course actors play stereotypes, but when you're a Latino, you can't unpack it. Why? Because you see the consequences of how we're treated as a people, and you feel you're helping to perpetuate a lie. I played gangbangers in neighborhoods where real gangbangers lived. It felt as if I were mocking the people I portrayed. I would be filming and real thugs would be looking at me shaking their heads. "Hey, homes!" they'd yell. "He's not a gangbanger, I am!" Then they would show off their real tattoos while I got to wash mine off at night and return to white suburbia. I was like a Civil War reenactor in the middle of the real Gettysburg.

I chose to be an actor, and, when you are Latino, sometimes you can choose that, too. But, acting roles are not normally written by a Latino, so the Hollywood lens remains out of focus. All people of color must, as actors, play roles normally not written by people of color. Okay, more specifically, roles normally written by white males. The Hollywood writer's room, even today, is seldom diverse. It's changing, but the change is slow.

Whoopi Goldberg had told me that I should write, and that I should write my experience—write myself, the way she did. Slowly, I began to realize that Whoopi was right. Since I wasn't playing the roles I wanted, maybe I should write them. And that was an epiphany. I was tired of acting in roles that reinforced stereotypes. I decided to write myself free.

As I acted, I realized I wanted to write because I believed I could change my world. I realized that the blank page was my destiny. All I had to do was fill it up and then, instead of waiting for a casting director to give me a job, I could create one. I was in charge of my fate.

I never thought I could write. I was in the shadow of the greats—Shakespeare, Eugene O'Neill, Arthur Miller. However, I'd read an early play by O'Neill and it was God awful. Then I saw comedian Richard Pryor do a bad set, and I realized that geniuses earn it. You have to be bad before you become good; horrible before you become great.

In truth, I had started to write but I hadn't proclaimed it. I didn't own the title. And why not? I didn't say I was a great writer or a famous writer. I wrote, therefore I was a writer. A writer's job is simply to write. The rest is up to God.

I remembered Whoopi telling me that if I called myself something, I would become it. But I also needed to proclaim it. That's what she had done when she said yes to going solo, and her show was born.

Using the affirmative really helps. *No* is a stop sign; it's so definitive and negative. Like the words *cancer, terrorism,* or *victim.* There are very few happy cancers, peaceful terrorists or delighted victims. There are negative words and there are positive words. Each one attracts one or the other. So I reconsidered.

"Yes," I said to myself. "I'm a writer."

So I started to write in earnest at the end of the '80s. I coauthored a play called *Latins Anonymous* with Chris Franco, Luisa Leschin, Armando Molina, and Diane Rodriguez to embrace the brave new Los Angeles. This was ten years after Luis Valdez's play *Zoot Suit* chronicled the world of Chicanos in the '40s whose puffy pants, long coats, hats, and key chains set them apart from mainstream America. I had wanted to tell the story of who I was, and after seeing George C. Wolfe's play *The Colored Museum* in New York, I thought we needed a Latino version. So, the idea for a sketch show for Latinos was born. Writing, acting, and producing *Latins Anonymous* was the fulfillment of that dream. The play premiered at the Los Angeles Theater Center in September 1989 and it was a hit. It was the beginning of my work as a playwright. It was the beginning of me taking control.

One day as I walked up the street to the mailbox on my corner, I saw my neighbor getting his mail. In the stack he held in his hand, I saw a green envelope. "What's the green envelope?" I asked. "It's a residual check," he replied. I get them for my TV shows." His name was John Wells, and he would one day be executive producer of *The West Wing*.

John had noticed I was writing plays. "Why aren't you writing television?" he asked. "John, I'm a playwright," I said. He opened the green envelope and showed me the amount of his check, not to brag, but to emphasize his point. I looked at all the zeros. And then I remembered my mantra: say yes. So I did. "Yes, John. I should write television."

John also encouraged me to do standup comedy, and to try to join the Warner Brothers writing program. It was a very competitive program. Hundreds apply each year. I said yes, and I applied and was accepted to the program in 1990. I was one of a few lucky ones who got in.

Always say yes! Often you are the biggest roadblock to your own success. You can become good at excuses, at coming up with reasons why you can't do something instead of saying, "Why not?" There are always odds against you. So what? There are only three Latinos who have written and starred in their own shows on Broadway—Lin-Manuel Miranda, John Leguizamo, and me. I don't even want to calculate those odds, because if I did, I'd have never tried to do it. But I said yes!

I see this principle at work all the time. When Arizona made it so difficult for undocumented workers to work in that state, many of those same people began to work through a legal loophole. They said yes, started their own companies, and hired themselves. It's not illegal to create a company. You don't need proof of citizenship for that. All these so-called illegal immigrants were not taking jobs, they were making them. Their businesses had to register and be taxed.

Too often, we limit our opportunities and then blame it on the world around us. So stop saying no to yourself, and start saying yes, because "yes" is a choice you have to make every single day.

That was another lesson I learned in Hollywood. Say yes to your life and proclaim it. Tell all your friends what you are committed to doing, because no one wants to end up a liar. Once I told people I was a writer, I had to become one. The power of saying something out loud begins the journey, and the more people you tell the more you have to do. It's an action that starts a journey. I had to stop criticizing myself and move to action. The same was true in writing. I never said I was a good writer or a bad one. That was for critics. But I owned myself. I said I was a writer, and then I became a one. You need to proclaim who and what you are and be about your work.

I write first to be understood and second to understand.

Years later, after refining my craft and paying my dues, I could say with confidence, "I'm a professional writer or a critically acclaimed writer," but those are just descriptive adjectives. Back then, I called myself a writer and I began to write. I refused to allow myself to be a liar, so I worked on owning my title. For me, becoming a writer began with a simple choice. We make choices every day, all day. Who you become is up to you.

"Hello. I'm Rick Najera, and I'm a writer."

MY TRIBE
OR YOURS?

*"A Spaniard is only a Mexican with
five thousand in the bank."*

Most Latinos are racially mixed, but we can go regional and tribal in a flash. No matter how it looks to the outside world, Mexico is tribal. If you're from Guadalajara (a *Tapatio*), you're not really a Mexican according to the Chilangos (Mexico City natives). Then again, most Tapatios don't think Chilangos are really Mexican, either.

There is a saying written on the walls outside of Mexico City: "Be a patriot, kill a Chilango." Like ethnic peoples around the world, Mexicans often don't get along with each other. Why? Because we are a tribal people. It's not who you are but where you're from that's important. Many fights in the ghetto have been started with the line, "Where are you from?" In Mexico, it's more like "Who are you from? Cortéz or Malinche?" People often recoil from this statement, but it's true. What tribe or family do you belong to? That's how Cortéz's Spanish army could defeat a larger army of Aztecs.

Latinos are tribal. We're more than 53 million Latinos in the United States, but we're not united. We are not a homogeneous, united tribe. We are thousands of small tribes and alliances. At times, even we view ourselves through the lens of stereotypes. Just like Cortéz found when he conquered Mexico.

In truth, Latinos have always been a hard people to define. Especially when no one is trying. We cannot be defined racially because we are mixed with so many races that it's confusing even to us. We are a fasci-

69

nating, diverse, modern culture. I once saw a Chinese Cuban speaking Spanish, and a Japanese Peruvian enjoying sushi and speaking Spanish. There are black Cubans and German Mexicans and Italian Argentineans and Mexican Jews and Lebanese Mexicans. Salma Hayek is Lebanese and Mexican. Shakira is Lebanese and Colombian. And yet Latinos remain oddly invisible on television because our images are often not even created by us or by people who understand us first historically, next culturally, and finally personally.

Has there ever been a successful Latino in television? The answer is a resounding yes. Desi Arnaz, that wild cultural propagandist, was our only true sitcom star. He was a Latino singer-comedian who also happened to be a very smart businessman. He wanted a piece of the American dream. Desi created and developed *I Love Lucy,* and sitcoms are a very hard nut to crack. He also invented the three-camera technique, and the rerun, and built an empire—Desilu Studios, which produced such hit shows as *I Love Lucy, Star Trek,* and *The Untouchables.* Eventually it was sold and renamed Paramount Television.

Desi confused many Anglos because he was Cuban-American. America knew Cuba through Teddy Roosevelt and the Spanish-American War, but not much else. Sure it was our entertaining little colony to the south filled with friendly, sexy Caribbean people. Cuba was the playground to America, and it was a great party. Their dances were sexy mambo and salsa. They smoked cigars, dressed elegantly, and drank mojitos and Cuba libres. Every American dreamed of Cuba, the exotic Caribbean island, with warm breezes, beautiful beaches, hot and cold running cabana boys, and sultry Latinas.

Desi reminded America of Cuba. He was fun. He was an escape. He portrayed the Latin lover image so well—the same one later played by other Latinos, such as William Levy, Antonio Banderas, Adam Rodriguez, and before them all, Rudolph Valentino. But Desi was Latino to his very core. He didn't want to be considered the "Latin Lover." He wanted to be seen as a stereotype not yet imagined. He would become the Cuban "Business Mogul."

When I was in the hospital recovering from pneumonia, I had plenty of time for channel surfing. *Where are all the Latinos on American televi-*

sion? I wondered. On channels few and far between. Even if you do manage to find a Latino show, you'll discover that a Latino didn't write the script. Whatever the story, it's marginalized. There is no truth or veracity behind it. Or, if the story does happen to be great, Hollywood changes the ethnicity of the lead. Ben Affleck played a Mexican-American CIA agent in *Argo*. Naomi Watts and Ewan McGregor played a couple that was originally Latino in real life in *The Impossible*. Robert Downey, Jr., played a Latino journalist in *The Soloist*. Al Pacino played a Cuban drug lord in *Scarface* and a Puerto Rican drug lord in *Carlito's Way*. Marlon Brando played a Mexican revolutionary in *Viva Zapata!* Yul Brynner played a Mexican revolutionary in *Villa Rides*. Anthony Hopkins played a Mexican revolutionary in a Zorro movie. So did Douglas Fairbanks, Robert Livingston, Guy Williams, John Carroll, and Frank Langella. The only Latino who played Zorro other than Antonio Banderas was Henry Darrow, a great Puerto Rican actor. Hank Azaria played a Latino butler in *The Birdcage*. Natalie Wood played a Puerto Rican seamstress in *West Side Story*. Madonna played an Argentinean first lady in *Evita*. Hollywood likes to copycat what works. And what works for Hollywood is non-Latinos playing Latinos. Once they find a winning formula, they don't want to deviate from it.

When it comes to Latinos, show business is actually in the business of business more than show. Rarely do they bank on Latinos in leading roles. Why risk it when Latinos themselves, the number one ethnic group that see films, spend their box-office-ticket dollars regardless of whether a Latino is the big-screen draw or not?

Since Hollywood won't look out for Latinos, Latinos need to start looking out for themselves. And that philosophy doesn't end there. Politics should follow suit as well. (But I'll talk about that later.) I'm not paranoid, but let's face it. When the ship is sinking, no one ever bothers to send the lifeboat back for the people who aren't in first class. And Latinos, as valuable as we are, in reality remain in third-class steerage, waiting for our turn to get in line for a life raft. What we don't realize is that everyone who could help us was in first class and already in a life raft, rowing quickly away from the sinking ship.

Old America, meaning my parents' generation, lived for pensions and nice retirements playing golf. My generation is uncertain of our future, and think we may be eating a delicious cat-food meatloaf smothered in tragic sauce for our Thanksgiving dinner. Or end up as one of those old greeters at the front of Walmart. I could end up working at Mickey D's by the time I retire, stealing ketchup packets and adding hot water to make soup. Who knows? But when I read the news lately it seems we're all scared.

Like the great recession, or as I call it, the *great minority depression,* the majority of celebrated gains won by minorities during the civil rights era have been turned back and lost because of the economic downturn. A recent study from the Department of Labor said that Americans lost 40 percent of their net worth. Most minorities invested in homes—not stocks and bonds. When the housing market crashed, subprime mortgages defaulted and jobs were lost. Communities of color were hit the hardest. A study by the National Council of La Raza confirms the data that minorities have been devastated by loss in housing prices, and, that for African-Americans, the unemployment rate is the same as it was during the Great Depression. The difference in our recent economic downturn was that the faces of the poor were more and more dark, and more and more white. President Lyndon Johnson created a war on poverty in the '60s and now, economically, we're back to those same exact poverty levels today.

I remember when I was a child my best friend and I went across the border to Tijuana. He was shocked by the poverty and people begging in the streets. "We're American, Rick," he said. "You'll never see that in America." Well, he was wrong. According to the statistics of the William C. Velasquez Institute, there are 12 million unemployed Americans. In 1933, the height of the Great Depression, there were around 12.8 million unemployed. Currently, there are more than 48 million people on food stamps. That's 15 percent of the population. Add to that more bad news: There are more than 11 million Americans collecting social security checks for disabilities. In 1992, there was one person on disability for every 35 workers. Today, 1 in 16 workers collects disability.

In minority America, 2008 marked the beginning of a genuine economic depression. During an economic crisis, income inequality becomes even more devastating. In an economic meltdown, minorities compete over the few remaining resources. Like a gentleman's agreement, the idea is that if you ignore the minorities (47 percent of America), they will go away. Maybe they will go away. It's a quality of life issue. However, your quality of life in Hollywood will never be equal. After an exhaustive study, the Writers Guild of America found that statistically, Latino writers were better off ten years ago than they are today. If the statistics were horrible for Latinos ten years ago, just imagine how bad 2013 really is.

I'll say it again: Latino writers were better off ten years ago than they are today. Recently, all WGA writers lost 5 percent of their earnings due to the impact of reality TV. In that equation, staff writers are eliminated in favor of producers. Imagine what that means for Latinos. Latinos are essentially the canaries in the coal mine. If we are doing badly, the miners are next. That's why I tell people inequality is a matter of injustice. An injustice for one is an injustice for all. "Woe to him who builds his house by unrighteousness, and his upper rooms by injustice; who makes his neighbors work for nothing, and does not give them their wages." (Jeremiah 22:13).

This is why I support unions and guilds in Hollywood. Collectively, they fight for a living wage, and that little necessity called health care insurance. Without health care insurance, you can lose your life. I was learning that lesson in the ICU. My hospital bill would have been hundreds of thousands of dollars had it not been for health care insurance provided by my union. My grandmother taught me to love unions and not trust upper management. When I was a child, she told me that bosses normally don't care for workers because they don't see themselves as workers, but as a distinct breed.

She used to have a joke when someone who obviously was of Mexican heritage tried to label himself or herself as "Spanish." "*Mijo*," she would say, "a Spaniard is only a Mexican with five thousand in the bank."

Fear has invaded our lives. Fear and need. And now America is closing its borders. Bigger and better walls are under construction in the national psyche. The government tried to build a virtual wall along the Mexican border; it didn't work. They tried to build a bigger *real* wall with millions of taxpayer dollars only to watch a 16-year-old Mexican girl scale it in less than 18 seconds. I saw it on the news late one night and thought to myself, *The people in the red states will have nightmares tonight.* More walls and better security measures to guarantee that we become more separate and less and less equal. Even with our social networking and the Internet, we have become more isolated and far less capable of intimacy. We poke, like, tag, and post our daily updates on Facebook. And we tweet and hashtag and trend on Twitter. However, none of the new social media has brought us closer to one another as human beings.

As I see it, the world has always been ethnic and tribal. Once as a kid I was on an Indian reservation, the Laguna Pueblo reservation. I was in high school, and I stayed there with my friend, who was a Laguna Indian. I remember how much they hated the Apache tribe. I thought, *Wow, the world is divided.*

Then you look at Compton, and you see the Crips hate the Bloods and all that. You look and say, "You're black." "No, I'm Crip." And within the Mexican culture, in East L.A., they say, "I'm with the White Fence Gang or Frog Town or some other block."

In Los Angeles, it's not tribal. It's location. In neighborhoods in East Los Angeles it's "Where you from?" not "What tribe are you from?" Either way, such questions can get you killed. The outcome is the same. It's war. Genocide, hatred, and death, just on a smaller scale.

I once had a cholo tell me proudly, "I'm down for my hood. I'd die for my hood. I'm down for my hood." I asked him, "Do you own your house?" He looked at me with confusion written all over his face. "Do you own your home?" I repeated.

"No," he stuttered, seemingly more like a confused kid in school than a cholo gangbanger I had met on a film set. Hollywood has a bad habit of using real gangbangers as extras. It makes things more authentic. They even have an agency called Suspect Entertainment, known for having former gang members on their talent roster.

"No, fool. I don't own my house. It's an apartment. I rent it."

"Then you're dying for rental property. It's really not your neighborhood if you don't own it," I said.

Some would say I'm wrong. I'm not. Tribalism is one of the easiest ways to see life's glaring differences. It starts with family first, then city, then state, then nation, and finally global corporations. We are defined more by our tribes than our citizenship, especially in America. No one who comes here ever fully gives up their past. We all cling to our tribal identities in unexpected ways. We need identity to feel part of a tribe, to belong to a group. And this is not just defined by heritage, it may be defined by shared goals—there is the Republican tribe, or the liberal Democratic tribe, or the Corporate tribe.

Global corporations are tribes that worry more about their profits than their own nations. That's why they rank over states. They get government tax breaks and move their companies to foreign countries for cheaper labor in order to make a profit for their shareholders. That's corporate tribalism. They might occupy the same lands, but not the same loyalties. Corporate loyalty is to the almighty dollar. Invisible shareholders only care about the bottom line, not for their country or fellow citizens. And no one in the corporate tribe views any of its activities as un-American.

Corporations are inviolable tribes and have initiation rites unto themselves. In the corporate culture, they reward their members with stocks that go up in profit because of their undisputed skill in exporting and eliminating jobs. In corporate culture, if one overworked laborer can do a job instead of two happy union members, the most insecure worker wins every time.

In the ICU, I experienced another corporate culture—the medical culture. I woke up and asked a nurse to help me walk to the bathroom. She looked at me and said, "No." I looked at her and asked, "Please?" She stared at me. "Look, just go in your bed," she said. "We'll clean you afterward." I looked at her, my eyes pleading for a little understanding and dignity. She offered neither. It was the lowest moment of my life.

COMEDY
WRITING HELL

"I was ecstatic. A writing job on In Living Color. *Then, I woke up in comedy hell."*

*L*atins Anonymous was one of my best "yes!" moments. By 1991 I even wrote a TV pilot for a show based on it. Unfortunately, having four Latinos write a show and perform in one together eventually destroyed us.

With internecine warfare squabbles like the Mayans and the Olmecs and Toltecs and every other tribe in ancient Mexico, we eventually became extinct. The group continued, but once I left, it was over. They replaced me when I got my next job—a high-profile TV writing gig—so in reality, it was not my choice. I could have stayed, but I thought the next one was a huge opportunity. Even though it was a shaky job that I could've gotten fired from at any given moment, I thought I had to try to make it work. I was like Cortéz, but it was my *group* who burned my ships. When I left *Latins Anonymous* in 1992, I had no group of friends or anyone to support me and life was hard there. We had all just lived through the Los Angeles riots during this time and I had been targeted during the melee. That's right, me!

I was walking on a side street when I saw three black and four Mexican teenage gang types walking toward me and I thought, *Isn't it great to see Latinos and African-American youth united?* Apparently, they were united in trying to kick my ass, so as they got closer, I got enraged. They didn't see *me*. They couldn't see my ethnicity. They ran up to attack me. One yelled, "Let's fuck up this white boy!"

I screamed at them, "White boy? Muthafuckers! You wanna piece of me? Well, bring it on, *putos!*" They were shocked and walked away. I imagined their conversation—"Man, did you see that shit? That mother-fucking white boy got possessed by a Mexican. That shit was crazy." There were the riots, earthquakes, and a fire in Los Angeles all at the same time. I just needed Godzilla walking down Hollywood Boulevard to cement the disaster I was living.

It was one of the worst times of my life. I was at an identity crossroads. I was an actor who was becoming a writer. In Hollywood, what you do is who you are. My Hollywood agents were very stereotypical. They wore suits and all had a fast-talking banter like carnival hucksters. They all seemed to survive the '70s and looked like if you brought out lines of cocaine, they'd join you. For example, when I brought a girl, who was just a friend, to watch a big Evander Holyfield versus Mike Tyson fight in Vegas, my agent asked me, "Why would you bring a girl who is just a friend to a fight? Women get hot at fights. You want a girl you can have sex with. Listen, I can get you a girl and she'll be clean." This was my agent speaking, but he sounded more like a pimp.

And he was the one who got me an interview with Keenen Ivory Way-ans. "Hey, Rick, I got a call from *In Living Color.* Go in and make Keenen laugh."

I had just completed the Warner Brothers writing program, and now I was in line for my first writing job. You never feel like a writer until you get paid, and this was a job that would pay me. I was ecstatic to get the interview. *In Living Color* was a Fox TV show that started the careers of Keenen, Shawn, and Marlon Wayans, Jamie Foxx, Jim Carrey, and Jennifer Lopez. It was the biggest show of its time in sketch comedy.

The next day, I went in and made Keenen Ivory Wayans laugh. It was not an easy task. I remember meeting him. He had a shaved head, wore dark sunglasses, and was flanked by two other black guys. He was eating lunch. He looked me up and down and said, "Okay, make me laugh." Just like that. My agent was right.

So, I looked at Keenen and did a character Jamie Foxx had done on the show, named Wanda, the Ugly Woman. I acted out Wanda meeting Stevie Wonder. I did a few "I-got-yous" and other expressions, and Keenen laughed. That laugh saved me.

He asked me to tell him why I thought I could write for *In Living Color*. I said, "Funny is funny, in any color. And I just did a play that toured around the country called *Latins Anonymous*." And he said, "How did it do in ticket sales?" I said, "It made a million dollars in ticket sales."

I think the *million dollars* in that sentence made him hire me. I was ecstatic. A writing job on *In Living Color*. Then, I woke up in comedy hell.

I wrote on that staff with Keenen until he left the show, nearly a year later, and I learned a lot from him. The biggest lesson was this: tell your story, because it's unique. Keenen looked for original stories and with him, I was a certified original. I did 37 episodes of *In Living Color*. It seemed like ten years.

In Living Color was my comedy boot camp. That was my first paid writing job. People called me a writer and paid me for it after that. When you're a writer, it's the check that validates your profession. You're not a hooker until you get paid. It's the same with writing. I began to feel the creative power surge of the keyboard. I could write, "A waiter walks in," and *bam!*, a waiter would be cast and walk into the world I created. I would write down a location and *bam!*, someone would build a set.

At the same time, *In Living Color* was ground zero for comedy and race in America. I was excited to get the job, but when I did, I entered comedy-writing crusades. That's the meaning of the old saying, "Sometimes the best thing and the worst thing in life is getting what you want." There are TV shows that help define you either by how hard they are or how hard they should never have been. *In Living Color* wasn't just my boot camp, it was my comedy hell. It never had to be this hard, but funny is only funny if it's tragic. My big television-writing break came this way.

It was an amazing and excruciating experience all at the same time. It always amazes me when people tell me stories of waiting for *In Living Color* to air on their TV sets. But to write on that show? It was one of the toughest experiences of my life. It was *Survivor* without the prize money. It was *Big Brother* without the ending.

It was the race-card rally on steroids. I had a black writer telling me, "Hey, we don't need a Mexican writer. We need a brother on this show."

It was a full-blown racial WWE smackdown. I fired back, "Wait, look at the Jews here. And the white guys. Why don't I belong and they do?" The black writer looked me straight in the eye. "They don't count," he said.

The race firing range was even worse in the writers' room. In retrospect, the issue really wasn't race per se—it was economics. Jobs on a hit show are rare, and for writers of color, it's *Survivor*. I once found "Taco Boy" written on a piece of paper taped to my office door, along with a cartoon drawing of a Mexican smoking marijuana. The truth is, I wasn't smoking marijuana; if I had been, my experience would've been much nicer. I was working all night long, sometimes sleeping on a couch in my office that was three inches too short for my body. I felt like a pledge slated for a washout in a bad fraternity.

At least there was a production assistant who would come to my office and take my food order. They fed us well, but I felt like pampered veal in a cage being prepared for slaughter. They'd suck every good idea from us, and on Monday, we would pitch.

Pitching is when you tell your idea about a sketch and hope someone will say, "Great job." That's when you sell your idea. Then they'd ask you to work on it. In this sink-or-swim Hollywood boot camp, there were never any words of encouragement. I heard one of the producers yell when a writer was in mid-pitch, "Goddamn, somebody bring me some funny! Rick, pitch something funny!" And that intensity was re-created every Monday. So, you'd write Tuesday through Thursday, film Friday, sleep in Saturday, get up and think Sunday, and pitch Monday.

What the hell am I going to pitch on Monday? You felt the constant pressure to be funny. It was like a test every Monday at 10 a.m. I saw grown men crumble under the weight of the pitch. Then you had to add the African-American and the urban side to your sketch, and you had to be both street and hip. Street and hip did not describe many of the writers I knew. If you were white and had to do the pitch, it was like doing one round in a gladiator fight without a weapon. And if you weren't white, if you were a minority writer, it was even harder, because if you lost a comedy job on *In Living Color,* you would never get another one.

There are many success stories from *In Living Color,* but the cost was enormous. Shortly after the show ended, one of my writer friends died of a massive heart attack. Was it the show? Well, we were all overworked back then. The Monday pitch was my fiery crucible, yet somehow I pitched every week and managed to survive.

One thing I learned was to be fearless. I was a Mexican-American writer surrounded by African-American writers, and I wasn't afraid to be politically incorrect. I would do stereotypical black and white characters and act them out. Keenen was definitely an equal opportunity offender. He even made me write a sketch about Edward James Olmos, played by Jim Carrey, just to make sure I was loyal to comedy. Jim Carrey played Edward James Olmos cleaning up the neighborhood after the LA riot. Years later I would have dinner with Eddie. I was worried that the sketch might have offended him, but he wasn't upset. "It was a funny sketch," he told me. Whenever I pitched an idea, I tried to make it as unique as possible. Keenen said to me once, "I hired you to be you, so write like you." I would tell my story and how I saw it.

One time, a Fly Girl (dancer) came to my office. She was Puerto Rican, cute, and fun, and I could see ambition in her eyes. "Rick," she said, "I want to act." I wrote her a monologue about a beauty queen who refused to give up her crown. It was funny and perfect for her. Keenen said, "She dances and you write. She doesn't do both." That girl was Jennifer Lopez, and she would go on to prove Keenen wrong. That monologue later became part of my play *Latinologues* and it ended up on Broadway played by a Puerto Rican actress. I believe there are opportunities all around us. We just have to recognize them.

A writer's life is hard. It's long hours. Sometimes you sleep at the office. You constantly deal with deadlines and huge egos. How can anyone take the scorn and humiliation of being a writer? I don't know. But I knew if I could survive *In Living Color*'s countless demands, I could never be broken.

BACK IN THE
ICU

*"Some of your memory might be lost, but you are a lucky guy.
Yes, I thought, if they were bad memories."*

I'm awakened at night in the ICU for a trip to the MRI machine. Getting an MRI is like being in a washing machine where you can't move. This is my second week in the hospital after my fall, and the doctors want to see why I have high blood pressure. I could tell them why. PRESSURE!

They wake me up and wheel me and my ICU bed everywhere, like I'm a human petri dish they can do experiments on any time during the night. They don't like me to sleep. They give me shots in the stomach. They like to wake me for shots to ensure that I experience the full effect of the pain.

The MRI clangs and shudders as it rotates around my body like I'm on a rotisserie. The doctors think that my condition might have something to do with my kidneys; they might be shutting down.

My wife visited me in the ICU. I was there joking and keeping the nurses laughing. Everyone was surprised by my recovery. Fern Orenstein, vice president of casting at CBS, came to visit me. Nina Tassler, the president of CBS, sent me a gift card. I got so many gift cards for coffee, I could have opened a coffee shop, which is ironic since coffee and high blood pressure don't mix. Cheech Marin sent a note.

But the best acknowledgment was a note from a writer who had worked for me years ago. It read, "I used to not like you, until I realized you wanted the best from me. I had to go through the Rick Najera boot camp." It touched me deeply.

Lots of people came to visit me in the ICU. It was then that my wife reminded me that I used to say I never felt like I had a Hollywood community.

After I had been in bed for two weeks, I vowed to walk for the first time. I felt like an astronaut coming back to earth. A nurse came into my room to help me. They call it "physical therapy." I got the bill to prove it.

Another woman came by with a dog. They felt the dog *was* physical therapy and would cheer me up. Then the doctor visited me after breakfast. He said my MRI showed that I had damaged my prefrontal lobe. "Some of your memory might be lost," he said, "but you are a lucky guy." . . . *Yes,* I thought, *if they were bad memories.*

How did memory loss equal lucky? *Some* memory loss? What memories? I wasn't feeling lucky or even looking lucky. I was hooked up to IVs and a catheter. No, I wasn't feeling lucky at all.

I was in so much pain that I had fits of anger and emotion. One physical therapist asked me to smile for him. I did. He didn't smile back. "Your smile is slightly crooked. There may be some paralysis," he said. "No, that's called a 'red carpet smile,'" I explained. I never liked posing, so I had in my muscle memory a Hollywood smile from red carpets and photo ops. "It's not crooked on camera." Image is everything in Hollywood, but not in the ICU.

Looking around from my hospital bed, I felt things like career and Hollywood were trifling. Then I got my phone back and somehow I began to feel whole again. It's funny how a phone can do that. Many of my friends in Hollywood had left me messages. They had all heard the rumors. Being a minority in Hollywood was rough enough, but being a wounded one was even worse.

I remembered my early years in Hollywood and how I struggled. I was in for an even bigger test now. Physically, I was a wreck, and somehow after waking up, my confidence in myself failed me. I was shaken to the core. I couldn't trust in my future. Not sure what I remembered or what memories I had lost, I suddenly realized I was mortal. I wondered if I would ever again be ready for any job. I was at a point where I could've stayed in bed, given up, and died, but my spirit wouldn't allow it. I had to get better. There was more to my life. I survived *In Living Color.* And *Townsend Television.* And *Culture Clash.* I could survive this. I had to.

HOLLYWOOD

REDUX

"People look at you like you're a success when
you know you're one step ahead of the repo man."

After *In Living Color* I started to go back to theater. It was 1993. I was part of a solo artist series at the Goodman Theater. The Goodman Theater had Spalding Gray (*Swimming to Cambodia*), John Leguizamo (*Spic-O-Rama*), and myself with my new play, *The Pain of the Macho*. My show was directed by John Bowman. Unfortunately when I arrived in Chicago, I learned he had hurt his back and couldn't travel. I remembered how I felt back then in a new city at a prestigious theater in a solo series with the greatest monologists in theater at that time. I was scared.

There is a very odd thing about being a performer. An audience almost inherently knows what's in your heart. If you come out there and you have hate in your heart, they will pick up on it. Mean-spiritedness can set an audience against you. I always approach the audience as if I'm joining a wolf pack. A wolf exposes his neck, submits—this is who I am, you can chomp down on my neck and kill me; but he knows that the other wolf won't. This is my posture when I stand in front of an audience—I open up and surrender. So as I approach an audience, and open myself up, I find they're very comfortable laughing. Because the audience becomes, at the end, a part of a community. I become a part of their community, they become a part of mine.

Good satire is very healing, because the laughter itself always comes as such a surprise. There's nothing controlled about laughter. It's free. It's natural. Laughter is the closest thing someone can have to an orgasm with his or her pants on.

The night before my show opened, I had a dream where I woke up onstage naked with all my costumes scattered about. I was embarrassed, scared, and ashamed. Not because I was naked, but because I couldn't find my costumes. I woke up and changed the beginning of my show. I'd lived through the L.A. riots. So, I decide that's how I wanted to start my show. With a riot. I started like this:

> ### ANNOUNCER
>
> Ladies and gentlemen, the role of the macho performed by Rick Najera will not be performed by Rick Najera tonight. I repeat, the role of the macho will not be performed by Rick Najera tonight.
>
> ### VOICE #1
>
> *(A Latino-accented voice offstage)*
>
> Oh, man, I really wanted to see him.
>
> ### VOICE #2
>
> Oh, man, I bought season tickets here. This is some bullshit.
>
> ### ANNOUNCER
>
> I repeat, the role of the macho will not be performed by Rick Najera tonight.
>
> ### VOICE #2
>
> I'M RIOTING!
>
> *(SFX—rioting sound) The stage is full of rioting. Rick Najera appears trying to calm the crowd.*

RICK

Please, Mexicans, stop inciting the Puerto Ricans. Puerto Ricans, stop inciting the Mexicans. Cubans, stop inciting everyone. In the name of Edward James Olmos, I order you to stop rioting.

(SFX—the riot sound effect stops suddenly.)

Thank you. (sheepishly) I'm sorry. I just don't feel all that macho. I know the show is called *The Pain of the Macho,* but I don't feel all that macho. I've been in therapy. I don't argue so much. I learned not to use aggressive speech. I don't use words that hurt or judge. I say things like, "You make me sad when you act so stupid," instead of "You're an idiot." I'm Latino and I don't feel like living up to a stereotype tonight. But I must say this. There are Anglo machos, too. The only difference between Anglo machos and Latino machos is this that Anglo machos attack in large groups, but only after UN approval. Latino machos attack whenever the beer runs out.

And that's how I started the show, vulnerable and alone onstage. The audiences loved it, and more importantly they loved the honesty of it. *The Pain of the Macho* was a hit. I used a tactic that I've always believed in. It's in every artist's toolbox: tell your truth onstage and audiences will admire your bravery. I wanted to tour my new one-man show, but my agents did not want me touring. They wanted me in Hollywood, pursuing television. So they called me to tell me I just got an offer to write *Townsend Television,* a sketch comedy show. I told my agents no, I wanted to tour in my one-man show. They called again and offered me even more money. But I knew there was talk to go to New York with *The Pain of the Macho;* maybe Broadway. Then my agents were offered even more money for me to write and star in *Townsend Television.* The offer was too tempting; against my own better judgment, I took the job. Then disaster struck—after a four-month run on the Fox Network in

1993, *Townsend Television* was canceled. My shot at New York was gone. That was a hard time for me. No New York and a failed show all in four months. Things began to go more wrong.

Often a victory is followed by defeat. That's why you need to make peace with defeat. Because there are more losses than wins in Hollywood. I remember the time, between *In Living Color* and marriage, as an ADHD-filled Hollywood daze. I began to get seriously depressed. I was fighting an unknown and invisible enemy. I would hear, "We love your writing, but not what you write about." My agent even said, "Why don't you go to Mexico? They would love you."

They probably said the same thing to the thousands of Mexican residents rounded up in boxcars during the Great Depression. "Why don't you go to Mexico? They would love you there." I hadn't been Mexican in a hundred years. It would be a like telling Jamie Foxx, "Hey, Jamie, how about playing the Congo? They would love you there. Man, you would be so great in Tanzania."

I began to get bitter. Jobs were scarce, and the one thing that derails a Latino is unemployment. It's a shameful thing for us. Hollywood life is hard, and for those not welcomed, it's even harder. I wrote TV pilots with Latino themes for almost every network, and time and time again I'd hear, "It's not time for Latinos! Not yet."

My year after I left *In Living Color* in 1993 was an odd time in Hollywood. I'd done various other TV pilots, but everything seemed to be slowing down for me. Work was hard to come by. Be a humble laborer or a king, but whoever you are, you better work. I began to slip and slide. I stopped calling my folks and my friends. I cut myself off from everyone.

I was becoming a character from *Sunset Boulevard*. People look at you as if you're a success when you know you're one step ahead of the repo man. I was like a gambler. Everyone convinced me it was only one second more and I would get my big break. So, instead of living in the "Now," I was living in the "After I Make It" world. The whole truth: never hold off living in the "Now."

Then I finally got a deal to write and star in my own sitcom called *An American Family* for Paramount Studios. It was about a Latino veterinarian. They pitched the idea to me like this: "It's called *An American Family* because they are one. Even though they're really Mexican-American. You get it?" You can add the fake humility of a TV writer to the pitch. I was in the room when the very white executive pitched the idea. I almost threw up in my mouth. Then they gave me a Paramount jacket with a star on it. "Look, Rick, there's a star on the jacket because you are one!" Add my cringing face to that scene.

So, they cast me in a sitcom about my life, and then they said I wasn't good-looking enough to play me. I always felt Tim Allen and Jerry Seinfeld weren't good-looking enough to play themselves, either. Apparently, I was too ugly to be convincing as me.

Now you might begin to understand Charlie Sheen. They fired Charlie Sheen for being too Charlie Sheen. They fired me from playing me because I wasn't good-looking enough to be the TV me. Luckily they kept me on as the cowriter. Nothing was more humiliating to me than watching the "better-looking me" act badly. Then, they rewrote the script and made it so bad that I wanted to take my name off of it.

Even "better-looking me" hated the script. He had a six-pack, but after reading the script, he summoned a twelve-pack and a gallon of tequila to get the story out of his mind. Of course, the studio didn't pick it up. One producer told me, "Rick, hey, no big deal. I'm like a Jewish deli. I just say 'Next!'" I looked at him and said, "I'm not. I can't say 'Next!' I just let down millions of people and lost countless jobs for Latinos. We won't get a 'next' for years." And it was true.

The next Latino show was ten years later—*The George Lopez Show*. And after six seasons, George's show was replaced by a caveman pilot. When they didn't pick up my show I felt that I had proven, once again, that "Latino" does not work. Of course, Latino shows are seldom run by or written by Latinos. Then another producer on the same show said, "Rick, don't take this so seriously. I'll get another job. But for you, it's gonna be tougher." With that, he left.

I knew it would be some time before I'd get a job, and I sunk into despair. Hollywood has built-in failure, and if you can survive failure, you might just make it. And I had failed. *I failed.* My agent and everyone else told me I had. They also told me not to worry. In a year or two, I'd be able to come back to Hollywood and give it another shot. I thought about cryogenically freezing myself and putting myself in my mother's freezer next to the Christmas tamales. I went from Pacific Standard Time to depressing time. And I stayed there for several years.

Only Russians can get as depressed as Mexican-Americans can. At least the Russians kept their land. We Mexicans, especially Mexican-Americans, can wallow in depression and mariachi music for days. We get depressed like no one else. Our depression goes back thousands of years.

Life was not easy in the new millennium. The terrorist attacks, oil spills, terrorists, new diseases, and worse yet, reality TV. It was 2001. I was single in Hollywood, and I was miserable. I had a failed TV pilot from ten years earlier that I was still mourning. I was wondering if I'd ever get another shot when my phone rang.

I'd been up all night, as usual, switching channels and brooding, watching too much television, searching for my entertainment fix, craving it like a junkie. Anyway, I had dozed off . . .

All of a sudden, my fishing lines start peeling off my reel. The line zings and hisses off the spool, being ripped from its coil. I have a fish on the line. My reel screams as the line tears off my spool. The fish is diving. I'm nearly diving with it. I'm pumping the rod up and down. The fish is pulling me over the stern. I can see its skin now, a flash of blue. It's translucent, colors changing to every shade of blue. Deep in the dark ocean, I see my opponent. The fish looks like a creature not from our world, but from some aquatic alien planet. It was left here on Earth centuries earlier from a doomed starship. The fish is beautiful. It can't even be described as a fish. It's more than a fish; it's joy itself. I almost have my fish to the boat. It pulls away again. It's translucent colors explode in the blackness of the ocean. It looks like it's suspended in deep, black space. The fish begins to rise. It rises toward me. I'm going to land this giant. I'm going to land this prize. The fish is nearly mine.

The blast of the phone startles me. My fish! I look around. Where's my fish? My fish is gone. Grogginess keeps me from realizing where I am. Then the weight of daylight lands square on my forehead. The phone. I'm hearing a phone ring. Then I'm awake. I'm awake. I pick up the phone.

"Hello?"

"Hello, Mr. Najera?" It was an accented voice that could be a Latino credit detective calling me. My mind raced with different possible scenarios. Did I owe money to some guy in Mexico? I was panicking. My mind raced some more. It always does. "Mr. Najera, could you come to Mexico?"

"Who is this?" I asked.

"Excuse me, we are from a production company in Mexico and we understand you are a writer."

Well, I thought, *a writer?* Some might argue with that. Mostly me. I never wanted to be writer, and writers always have voices of doubt that whisper, that threaten—*How can you call yourself a writer?* I liked people too much to be a writer. It's lonely, hard work.

"Mr. Najera, we understand that you are a good writer, and we have a project that might be great for you. Could you come to Mexico so we could speak about it in person? There is a ticket waiting for you at Aeromexico."

"Which city?" I asked, like I was really going to go.

"The capital, Mexico City. The only city in Mexico."

I instantly recognized that Mexico City attitude. The call was real. "Can I get your number in Mexico?"

Here's a rule: Never sound like you want to go anywhere. You may be willing to crawl naked on your knees over broken glass to get a job, but never act like you would.

All great endeavors start with the tiniest, most insignificant gestures. An insignificant thing can lead to a great thing. The ordinary leads to the extraordinary. We are the accumulation of a million happenstances, but I think there is a divine plan. There must be. I've seen it my own lifetime, time and time again.

There are no coincidences. If you look closely, you'll notice patterns in your life that are orchestrated by a divine hand. Faith is the engine that gives you courage and moves you forward toward your destiny. My father met my mother at a bus stop. They went on their first date at Horton Plaza in San Diego, then love, romance, a margarita, and me. A seemingly random event. But things that appear to be trivial never are. A phone call opens another door—another chapter of your life.

I got a call. I got on a plane. I flew to Mexico.

CORTÉZ AND MALINCHE: A DYSFUNCTIONAL LOVE STORY

"How do they keep citizens from asking tough questions in Mexico? Entertainment."

I'm on a plane to Mexico, secure in the knowledge that I have a meeting in Mexico City. I have a destination. The Capital, De-EFEH, the *Distrito Federal.* The center of the Mexican in me. This is a kind of pilgrimage for me, being Mexican and all. Knowledge of my culture has never changed me. The way I see it, with too much knowledge, you're miserable. With too little, you're miserable. Perhaps if I'd been born with a little less intelligence, I'd be the happiest man on Earth. We just discuss and overanalyze how our history has served us up with the same old problems.

People a hundred years ago definitely had less knowledge, but I guarantee you our ancestors were happier. What we are is simply more entertained. I work in entertainment. It's my job. And I'm a Latino. Latinos are very entertaining. We are a salsa-dancing, Babalu-yelling, baby-making, switchblade-toting, Medellin-cartel-dealing, and entertaining people. Oh, and all with a big side of diabetes and high blood pressure on the side. I'm Mexican-American on my way to the land of my forefathers.

Every time I go back to Mexico, I realize how my people are still paying for Cortéz's invasion. I see the sad results. I see the prejudice and destruction left behind every time some dark little "Aztec," or "Mixtec," or "Zapotec" indigenous child with dusty bare feet tries to sell me Chiclets on a street.

As legend would have it, the Aztecs moved from place to place until they saw an eagle eating a serpent on a cactus. That was where they should have built their city of Tenochtitlán. I could imagine the Aztecs seeing the same thing in California. Maybe they could have wandered like the Jews wandered, but to La Jolla, or Napa Valley, or Eureka. I always wondered why the Jews didn't wander to Saudi Arabia instead of Israel, to a promised land with oil under it. With a slight course correction the Jews would have been oil magnates.

The Aztec tribe had been so beaten down that they had to serve as weary mercenaries for other tribes. The Spaniards who would conquer the Aztecs a thousand years later were actually similar to the Moors who had conquered them. The conquering conquistadors were mostly from Andalusia in southern Spain, having fought perpetual wars with the Moors, until they finally kicked the more educated Moors out because they were better in medicine and science. Those Spaniards were mercenaries, too.

The Aztecs founded their empire in a swamp on an island they could defend. They were a bloody people. They felt their gods needed blood to survive; at least the sun god who gave them maize did. They had conquered hundreds of other tribes in the Mexican basin, and now they were going to meet another would-be conqueror, Cortéz.

They believed the Spaniards were gods, and that was the beginning of the Mexican insecurity complex. The Aztecs had a bigger army, and could have easily destroyed the Spanish army, but they let the Spaniards into their city. There was a legend that Cortéz was the great god Quetzalcoatl, returning to claim his crown. If Montezuma would have looked and listened more closely at this odd-sounding, paella-eating Spaniard, he would have seen that the man on horseback was no god. Everyone else who met conquistadors knew they weren't gods; they were just humans with a need for world domination.

In 1519, Cortéz was not even a conquistador, he was only a tourist looking for gold and adventure. He and his men stunk of sweat, leather, and horse. The Native indigenous tribes were disgusted by their appearance. Their skin was white, like the smoke that came from the urns filled with copal.

Cortéz was amazed by the height of the buildings. No buildings in all of Spain were as tall. The villas and temple were so high that even Cortéz was tempted to believe the gods really did live in them. After all, most of his men were from the region of Andalusia, the poorest parts of Spain. They were a rough lot—a legion of skinheads, bikers, gangbangers, and thieves. They barely scraped a living in the harshest part of Spain, a region scarred by years of oppression by the Moors who had conquered them, following Islam's path out of Africa.

Cortéz understood conquering a people for religious reasons. The only way you could tell when God was on your side was by who won the war, and the Spaniards had defeated the Moors. In celebration, they could eat ham. That's one of the reasons Spaniards love ham.

Cortéz migrated from Spain to Cuba, then from Cuba to Veracruz, Mexico. Once in Mexico, he burned all of his ships in the harbor so that his men could not retreat. He rolled the dice. Then, with Malinche, he created the mestizo. Their son, Martin, was the first.

I'm of 100 percent Mexican descent, but I can choose a side in a race riot. There are many light-skinned Mexicans and Latinos; it's the Spanish blood coursing through our veins that makes us light. It's the African or indigenous blood that makes us dark. We are a calico people. Mexico and all of Latin America is mixed between blacks and native-born indigenous. The United States has a much more mixed past than it acknowledges. Look at Civil War pictures. Not everyone is Nordic looking. People were mixed with African and native blood. You tell me if you look at Abraham Lincoln, you don't see some Cherokee in those dark eyes and cheekbones? My children are mixed. We are all mixed.

We are Aztec and Spanish. We are mestizo. And that is why we carry the conqueror and the conquered inside of us. We are living with a race war inside of us every single day. Because when you are Latino, it's like waking up half North Korean and half South Korean in the middle of the DMZ (demilitarized zone), a gun in each hand pointed at your head, threatening both sides inside yourself to pull the trigger. That's me.

Before I left for Mexico, I had picked up a few essentials. When going to Mexico, always bring money. With enough money, you can buy your way out of anything. Even if you don't have a lot and you're in Mexico, always bluff like you do. Bribery is a particular Mexican problem. Then again, after watching high-priced lawyers in Hollywood get enough people off, I realized that money doesn't care if you're Mexican or American. It respects no one, but demands respect from everyone. Money can be evil everywhere, but in Mexico, it's even more so.

As I prepared to fly to Mexico, my depression hit me hard. I visualized myself driving myself into my garage, sealing the door, turning on the car, and sucking on that sweet carbon monoxide air freshener called death. So, I read a lot in an attempt to keep my mind from overloading. I found histories and biographies fascinating; what I liked about them was that they were true. I needed to know the truth, since in Hollywood, everyone had a publicist, so what people saw by design and necessity might have nothing to do with the truth.

I learned about the problems of Mexico on the History Channel, but that's nothing compared to the indigenous child whose painful reality requires that he or she sell me some Chiclets or he or she goes hungry. The complexities and troubles of modern Mexico make me shudder. All I need to do is watch a blonde Mexican television anchorwoman speaking Spanish way too quickly for me to understand to really see what a horrible situation we've inherited.

I have worked in Mexico, and guess how they keep the people from asking those tough questions like, "Why am I always poor, hungry, and exploited? Especially if I'm dark and indigenous?" "Why are the rebels in Chiapas fighting the government? Why do the rebels look like me, but the people who are supposed to lead me don't look anything like me?" and "Why does the government look like Cortéz's children, and I look like one of his defeated bastards?"

How do they keep citizens from asking tough questions in Mexico? Entertainment. The people are too busy being entertained. I worked for one of the largest entertainment companies in the world. This company rules Mexico, and it does so via entertainment. Through telenovelas, to be exact. It's the same strategic plan that the Roman emperors had for their "Bread and Circuses," but their entertainment wasn't Barnum & Bailey clowns; it was gladiators and death. Telenovelas entertain all of Latin America. They were modeled after decades of daytime soap operas in America. Same plot lines, just more priests. These telenovelas, however, are exported all over the world. Romance is romance, anywhere you go.

A telenovela actress was sitting across from me on the plane. I knew she was a telenovela actress because back in the airport terminal people were asking for her autograph. Separated by a few seats, a language, and a culture, we were both professionally polite. Maybe it was my imagination, but she stared at me for a moment and puzzled like she knew me. I looked at her and I knew her. She was like every other actress on a quest for fame and everything that came with it. Say what you want about this actress, just don't spell her name wrong when you smear it in the paper.

Since I was transitioning from a Latino actor to a Latino writer, I looked at actors differently. Once you are the other side of management, you always do. An actor becomes a tool. It was hard for me to look at actors that way, because I knew the work and the skill you needed to be one; I had trained for years.

In the early days of my acting career, I put on brown makeup so I would look more like a stereotypical Mexican. I had once guest starred on Columbo with George Hamilton. When they put me next to him, I looked even whiter than I was. They had to put so much dark makeup on me that I ended up looking more like Othello. I looked like a dark-skinned Mitt Romney on his famous Univision interview.

Playing stereotypes always bothered me. Stereotypes exist, but when there is no other image to balance the image of a people, eventually a stereotype becomes a reality. The Latino stereotype is a skewed image of Latinos. Ironically, I was on my way to Televisa, a studio in Mexico City, the heart of Latino images and stereotypes. However, these class stereotypes involved fair-skinned, blond, blue-eyed Europeans, the sons and daughters of Cortéz. The dark-skinned indigenous Mexicans played out the lower-class roles.

Someone gave me a book about Mexican history for my trip, so, I pulled it out and began reading about Emiliano Zapata, a great revolutionary general of Mexico who fought for the peasants and was loved by the working class from which he came. He said, "Better to die on your feet than live on your knees."

I stopped the flight attendant and ordered another drink, my favorite— Bombay Sapphire and tonic. I looked at that telenovela actress again. She seemed confident about who and what she was. I settled back in my seat and dreamed of Mexico. I wanted to sleep, and hoped I could dream of fishing again, but I couldn't. So, I thought about Zapata. Zapata had a mission in his life. What was mine? What was I doing traveling to the soul of Mexico?

Then, quite magically, I discovered a magazine on the plane. There was a picture of Emiliano Zapata, my greatest hero, with a poem written about him.

> *Little star in the night that rides the sky like a witch.*
> *Where is our chief Zapata?*
> *Who was the scourge of the rich?*
> *Little brook, what did the flower say to you?*
> *It says our chief didn't die, that Zapata's on his way to you.*
> *Beware of those that steal from the poor.*
> *Zapata still lives, and he's looking for you.*
> —Old Mexican *corrido*

There was another picture of Zapata, dead in Morelos. He had died on his feet in an ambush. Strangely, though, the picture of the dead Zapata didn't quite look like him. His face was puffy. Maybe it was death. No one ever believes anything that happens in Mexico just happens, like the assassination of Luis Donaldo Colosio, the Mexican presidential nominee in the '90s who was gunned down in Tijuana. No one believes one assassin killed him. No one will ever believe the authorities caught the man behind his murder. Just like not many people believe that a lone gunman killed John F. Kennedy. Bobby Kennedy, who was loved by the Mexican-Americans in Los Angeles, had a Mexican busboy hold his head while he was dying on the floor. He prayed over him. A busboy and a great man, holding hands in death, the great equalizer for us all.

Assassinations are the thieves of destiny, because one man ends up deciding the fate of many. One lone assassin has the ability to change history. Jefferson Davis, the president of the Confederacy, said the worst thing that happened to the South was the Civil War and the assassination of Lincoln. What would've happened if Lincoln had survived? This is just one of history's great unanswered questions.

I continued to read. There was a picture of Cortéz and his Malinche, who helped him defeat the Native indigenous empires of Mexico. Cortéz christened Malinche and their son. That christening was the act that legitimized and created the first Mexican. Their child was now a citizen of Spain. Born of a European father and a Native indigenous mother, the child was a mixture of defeat and victory.

The Mexico I knew, filled with thousands of years of history, and its capital, Mexico City, never existed in San Diego where I grew up. We were taught that there was no Mexico; there was only Tijuana, where you could buy cheap tequila and cheap lobster dinners. If you were underage, you could drink in bars. If you were older, you could visit whorehouses. But that was not the Mexico I was reading about.

In my mind, I'm cuing swelling music and sweeping panoramic views of Mexico and America during a sunrise as the sun gently kisses the soil one last time. Slowly and deliberately, it moves into the cosmos, like an Aztec god ascending into the heavens. Maybe that's too dramatic. Mexican-Americans are much more casual because we are constantly being asked to look at both sides of every issue. We need to translate to each of our sides.

Our Mexican side explains to our American side why watermelon tastes better with chili and salt on it. Our American side explains to our Mexican side why we want to hire Mexicans for their cheap labor without wanting them to live here. Or, in the case of California, not pay for their education. We have cut over $20 billion from education in the last three years, and laid off more than 40,000 teachers. This has affected nearly 3 million Latino schoolchildren.

"Señor, would you care for another drink?" The Puerto Rican flight attendant interrupted my thought. The Puerto Rican flag on her lapel pin was a dead giveaway. She normally flew in from New York to California and back to New York, but she took the Mexico City flight for extra money. Puerto Rican women are irrepressibly exuberant and make delicious, strange foods, from fried plantains to pork that melts off your fork, and I kid you not, it is good. Their diet is rich in fried food and malted drink calories; they need the extra calories to fuel them so they can argue with you longer. It takes a lot of calories to burn so brightly. "We're not crazy, we're just Caribbean!" a Puerto Rican woman once told me proudly. "Yeah, sure," I replied.

A Puerto Rican actress once reminded me that they are born with American citizenship. She loved holding that over me. "Puerto Ricans are born with American citizenship," she boasted. "Your people have to cross rivers to come to America. We take planes." It's strange how Latinos can be victims of prejudice even from their own people. Ignorance comes in every shade and color.

The flight attendant brought me another gin and tonic. I tried not to think, but the drink fueled my thoughts. I reclined my chair back and imagined this scene in my head:

EXT-AIRPLANE RUNWAY-DAY
The FBI SNIPER holds the TERRORIST and HOSTAGES in his sight. The blazing-hot roof is like a frying pan. The hot tar melts under his weight, nearly burning through his clothing, but he doesn't move. He won't take the shot until given the order. His radio crackles with excitement.

RADIO V.O.
Can you see the hostages? Can you see the hostages?

FBI SNIPER
Yes, I have them in my sights.

The NEGOTIATOR is on the phone with the terrorist.

TERRORIST

I want three million in bills. A helicopter now. Where is my money?

The lead negotiator steadies himself. ANGLE on the MONEY in a suitcase near his side.

TERRORIST

I want the money! Where is it? Where is it? I will kill these hostages.

The negotiator wipes sweat from his brow. He was trained to be cool, but somehow this terrorist was winning this round.

NEGOTIATOR

Alright, you will have your money. Just let the people go.

TERRORIST

I will kill this black man and this Asian man and this Mexican man if I don't get my three million.

The negotiator turns to an FBI AGENT by his side.

NEGOTIATOR

Hold on. Did he say he has a Mexican, a black guy, and an Asian guy?

The sniper looks through his glasses.

FBI AGENT

Yes, sir. He's right. I see a black guy, a Mexican, and a Chinese guy.

The negotiator smiles as he speaks into his phone.

NEGOTIATOR

Look, Habib, three million in bills and a helicopter for a Mexican and a black guy and some Chinese guy is really steep, don't you think? We'll get back to you.

The negotiator laughs.

FADE OUT.

I awoke as another flight attendant came by to check my seat belt. The Puerto Rican flight attendant returned and offered me a local Mexico City paper. I looked at the headline: "Narco kills three Americans in Acapulco." This was so early in the current drug war that I barely noticed.

I always wonder, if a terrorist ever captured me, would I be considered an American hostage? I can only hope to God.

I looked out the plane window at the smoking volcano in the distance and thought about the day before I ended up on the plane. I had gotten another phone call from my commercial agent. I was acting and doing commercials. "Have you ever been in a gang?" she asked. "What?" I couldn't believe the question. "We have an audition for some tough guys in a beer commercial at a biker bar and the casting director wanted gang members," she said. "So, I told her you were in a gang. So, if they call you and she asks, tell her you were in a gang."

Who was she talking about? I didn't grow up in the barrio. I didn't belong to a street gang. I wish. I would have loved it. Gangbangers were always having so much fun running around, learning hand-eye coordination, marksmanship, salesmanship, and having great parties to boot. Every street gang member I know has plenty of money and they never pay taxes. But there was no street gang where I grew up. I was the only gang member in my neighborhood. I used to have gang meetings by myself. I'm the only gang that used Robert's Rules of Order.

"All those in favor of disbanding this gang, say aye! Aye! Opposed? Nay. The ayes have it. All those in favor of wearing baggy pants and shaving our heads, say aye. I move for discussion. I second the discussion. I don't like baggy clothes because they make me look fat. I say no to baggy clothing. Let's put it to a vote. I second. All those in favor of baggy clothing, say aye. Aye! Opposed? The ayes have it. Next on our agenda, bald heads versus full heads of hair . . ." That was a typical gang meeting from my hood.

I grew up in a nice neighborhood. On weekends, I would spend time with my grandparents in their so-called bad neighborhood. Everyone was afraid of my grandparents. They were a gang unto themselves. They were always drinking, smoking Pall Malls, and arguing about something. They always had a house full of family and extended family. I never knew if someone was my cousin by blood or by beer.

Mexico was 30,000 feet below me and coming up fast. We had begun our descent. I leaned back in my leather seat and read some more about Mexican history, which was flying past my window as we descended into modern-day Mexico City.

THE DEAL

"They eat whatever we feed them."

Mexico City seemed to reach up with an invisible hand and pull the plane from the sky. Once you're on the ground, you immediately notice the swell of humanity. Old ladies that looked like they might have personally met Zapata would talk about him like he was their first crush. "Zapata, yeah I knew him," one said. "We went out one time when he invaded Mexico City. I remember his moustache. It used to make me giggle when he kissed me. Ay, he was hung like a stallion."

As I passed a luggage counter, an old indigenous Mexican woman was crying hysterically. It seemed her luggage was lost. A haughty, light-skinned woman obviously of Spanish descent cut in front of her as if she were a piece of furniture. I looked at her standing there, scolding the old woman: "*Ya,*" she told her, "Enough." I was reminded of Cortéz.

A purposeful, professional-looking man walked up to me. "Mr. Najera?"

"Yes," I replied, my attention pulled from the ancient drama unfolding before me.

"I'm here to take you to your meetings," he replied. Dressed in a perfectly creased clean suit, my escort definitely looked like much more than a driver. Together, we moved past customs. I thought that was strange.

"No customs check?" I asked.

"No, that's not necessary with you."

Not necessary? I thought. Since when was customs not necessary? Apparently in Mexico, it wasn't necessary. We were outside the airport in no time. A car quickly sped us through the city.

"First time in Mexico?"

"No," I answered. "I've been to Guadalajara and Puerto Vallarta."

"This city is the real Mexico. Those cities are not the capital. If you haven't been to the capital, you have not been to Mexico."

The capital stretched for miles. It was late, but it didn't seem to matter. The city was full of people. In the middle of traffic stood a teenager. His eyes red and blurry, he wore a red clown nose and was juggling dirty balls in the air. He was obviously drugged out. He wasn't a first-world clown. He was a poor third-world Mexican clown. A true clown, pitiful and sad.

The driver dismissed the teenager from his window. We pulled away from the light. A town car with bulletproof windows followed by, and another car with six armed men inside passed us. "I have been instructed to take you to your hotel so you may rest," my escort said. "Is this alright with you, Mr. Najera?"

A smile slowly lit up my face. I was a gringo; an American writer from Hollywood. In the United States, I was a hyphenated name, but in Mexico City, I was bringing a different kind of ethnic flavor—the American flavor. Here I was a Hollywood writer, with no hyphen in my history. Not a Latino writer or Mexican-American writer. Just a writer. The irony engulfed me like the thick Mexico City smog outside my town car.

Later, the driver brought me to the studio. The car pulled up to San Angel, Mexico City, and the huge gates opened and there it was—the City of Gold. It was like no studio I'd ever seen before. Grupo Televisa is Mexico's largest and oldest studio. *How many starlets had been treated as badly as Malinche here?* I wondered. We continued to drive into the abyss of the lot and finally ended up in an executive courtyard. A little security guard opened a small gate. "Why don't they have an automatic gate?" I asked my driver. He laughed. "Well, they could, but then *he'd* be out of a job."

I took in the essence of my driver for the first time. His name was Javier. A heavyset man; part driver, part bodyguard. He quickly faded back under his dark sunglasses. He had an uncanny ability to hide in plain sight, no doubt perfected over years of being discreet and invisible. As we pulled up to a building, a few guards watched our every move.

They were not like American studio guards who would give friendly tours to tourists. These guys were trained to be attack dogs, not lap dogs. They would bite without ever bothering to bark.

"Should I bring my luggage?" I asked Javier.

"The bags are secure in the car," he replied instantly. Then just as quickly, he disappeared behind his sunglasses.

As I walked into Televisa, a new Mexican empire with ambitions in America, I was filled with my own ambition to work here. I wanted to be part of the good alternative to bad programming. I would later work for a different network that was the bad alternative to good programming, but that's another story.

The office seemed nice enough. I noticed a model Gulfstream jet and a model Ferrari on a shelf behind the desk. In fact, the room was filled with small models of luxury items—planes, exclusive cars, custom yachts. Whomever this office belonged to, if he couldn't afford to buy the *real* thing, at least he owned the *miniatures*. I sat down on a leather couch until my host finally arrived.

"Hello, I'm Manuel Garcia." (This name has been changed to protect the less-than-innocent.) "Thank you for coming. If there is anything you need, don't hesitate to ask. I need you to start writing the script. Let me take your passport to change your ticket."

He took my passport and left. It was the quickest, most succinct meeting I have ever had. Here I was stranded in the middle of Mexico with no passport or return plane ticket. I felt like Cortéz, only I hadn't burned my own ships. Someone else had just done it for me.

Manuel Garcia's wake rippled in the room. He was a Mexican producer. A Mexican producer is like an American producer, only crueler, possessing even fewer morals, with fewer unions to deal with, and who pays whatever his cold, cheap heart deems as a fair wage. There's white-guy entitlement and Spanish-language-producer entitlement. They're both the same. Either way, someone's going to walk away unhappy. He had no real recognized opponents or agents to argue with him. If you were not at Televisa, you were not in entertainment. Televisa's only rival was TV Azteca, and they didn't really measure up. Suddenly, I began to understand Mexico.

A week later, after having gotten paid, I was walking around one night with a Cohiba cigar in my hand when I called my father. "Dad, I'm back in Mexico." He hesitated. "Where are you?" I took a puff of my Cohiba. "In Mexico," I said. "I'm in the Zocalo, next to the Templo Mayor, the Aztec temple. I'm in the same place Cortéz, Montezuma, and Malinche walked. I'm in the same spot Villa and Zapata came to after they entered Mexico when they had won the war. I got paid, and I'm smoking a Cuban cigar and taking a walk." He hesitated again. "Okay, watch your wallet, Son. You will look like a tourist walking around there." I loved my dad.

I worked at Televisa on and off for about a year, and what happened during that time in Mexico changed me. In Mexico, I wasn't Mexican. I wasn't Mexican-American, either. To them, I was a Hollywood writer. That's all. This new identity began to free me. I started to see myself with more possibilities and fewer excuses. I slowly begin to grow hopeful and confident.

I remember being in meeting with Televisa executives, and I advised them to develop shows with a Latino point of view, the way BET does with a black point of view. Black Entertainment Television doesn't air programming brought to them from Africa. They air programming from America *for* American African-Americans. And the millions of Latinos in America should do the same. We shouldn't have to go to Mexico to get Mexican programming to air in America. I advised Televisa to go after the huge American Latino market. In *English* . . .

After a few tequilas, one of the executives let me in on a secret. "Rick," he said, "we don't want Latinos to assimilate or join the United States; we want them to remain separate. We don't want them to improve. All we want is their money. Our second-largest source of earned income is American dollars sent back to Mexico from Mexicans living and working in the United States. They're our market, and we don't need them living here. They are not us. We don't want them. We don't even like them. They are the people that could cause us problems if they stayed here.

"In the United States, we give them *patria*. We tell them to love Mexico and be proud of their roots. And we tell them they are not gringos. They are Mexicans. And we give them telenovelas and gossip shows and bad programming that is cheap and costs us nearly nothing.

"The right wing prays they return to Mexico, but they won't return. And we don't want them to. We only want their money, so we give them bad programs and hope no one encourages them to learn English or become what we don't want them to be—good American citizens. Because if they do, they will question us here. They will begin to ask why? Why do we have such corruption in Mexico? Why is there no opportunity for the poor? Why do gringos own beachfront property and we don't? The only way for them to be on a beach in Cancun is if they're bringing a cold margarita to a tourist."

"But they're your people," I said.

He laughed. "They are not my people. They belong to no one and no country. They are abandoned and lost. We don't want them to ask why. Because if they do, they will get angry at that injustice and plot a revolution just like Zapata did. Only this time Mexico's brand name political parties like the PRI or PAN won't be able to steal it. Those abandoned people that live in the United States, those Mexicans, are not my people. We can't have them stay here in Mexico and change Mexico. I think it's best for them to go away and belong to no one. Don't you, my friend? Better they go to the United States than stay here and ask for justice. The United States is a release valve for the pressure cooker that would explode in Mexico if they knew how this county cared so little about them and how much the wealthy have stolen from them."

Cortéz never left Mexico, I thought to myself. *He stayed, like an old Aztec curse. In Mexico, his conquistador children rule.*

"There is no home for the poor here," he continued. "So, they go to the United States, become successful, and send money back. We make fun of them and say with disdain that they are *pochos*. We tell them that no matter how successful they become, they will never truly be American. They will be almost white, but not white enough. We say they are not real Mexicans, and shame grows deep in their souls because they are stuck between two worlds and are wanted by neither."

I was stunned by his brutal honesty. I think there was some cocaine involved, too, because I couldn't believe what he told me. Obviously he didn't view me as a threat. In his eyes, I was just a Hollywood writer.

Then, looking at me like he was about to lecture a schoolboy, he said loudly, "We don't care about the Latinos in the United States, but Spanish television keeps them in our grip. Spanish television is the illusion of a place that does not exist for them. We sell them Mexico on their TVs. Whoever controls the media controls their minds. On English television, they are not seen or welcome. But on Spanish television, they are blond news anchors, blond European telenovela stars, and everything else they can't be. We show them that they are nowhere to be found in any language on the air. So, they remain in purgatory, not wanted by gringos or by Mexicans. They eat whatever we feed them."

My host drank another glass of tequila, not sipping it this time, and just as quickly stopped talking. It was a moment I'll never forget. The media is the subconscious of our souls. If you put in good images, expect good things. If you put in bad images, expect bad things.

I drank my tequila, and knew it was time for me to go back to Hollywood and write my story. My story was not in Mexico, it was in the United States. The only way you win is when you decide to win. I got on a plane, returned to the United States, and began to write again.

In Hollywood, the phone is a revered instrument. It's a direct line to your fate. A phone call is a command performance from God. Normally, some predestined event or divine intervention is involved. In Hollywood, everyone also shares the gambler's mentality: Every phone call is a roll of the dice. With every call, the numbers might come up in my favor. Not long after I came back from Mexico, the phone rang and I picked it up.

"Rick?" The voice waited. "Rick?"

"Yes," was my casual reply.

"I have Art on the line for you."

They always have someone on the line. No agent would ever call you himself because in that millisecond, he might make a call or miss receiving one that could change your fate, and more importantly, his. Fates are decided, fortunes lost, and egos boosted as we all hang on the telephone line. Agents don't make direct calls. Their time is too valuable.

Would you expect Michelangelo to make his own calls as he wrestled with the unforgiving marble that held the *Pietà* in its grasp? No. Would you expect God to make his own coffee during creation? Hell no! So don't expect an agent to make his own calls.

"Rick, Art here."

"Yes," I said, on pins and needles with anticipation.

"I got some interest on you for this show. It's real edgy."

Edgy? Has anyone ever admitted to creating a non-edgy show? *"This is our new show, the most amazingly bland idea that our overpaid minds could ever come up with."*

"They want to meet you."

"Great," I said. One always had to be positive.

On meeting day, I was ushered into a room. Three people stood before me. An older black man, distinguished and somber; a young, beautiful black woman; and a nebbish kind of Jewish guy. I'm hopefully the Andy Garcia–type Latin guy, not the Paul Rodriguez kind of Latin guy. The head writer was introduced to me. He gave me the once-over. I almost opened my mouth so he could count my teeth to see how old I really was.

"Rick, we really like your work," he said. "Did you see the tape we sent you?" I had. It was a horrible show, the kind of show that makes you realize that you somehow died and you've been sentenced to purgatory. It was so bad that someone had to have been fired over it. These people were smiling, so I knew I was dead and we *were* all in purgatory.

"What do you think?" he asked.

"It was edgy!" I replied cleverly. They smiled. They knew I was lying, but the fact that I would collude meant I'd be a team player and join the spinning-plates game with the rest of them. I knew I had the job. The head writer and executive producer looked at me. He stopped me at the door just to prove he was the alpha dog and said, "Hey, look, I might send your scripts back to you stapled to your head, but I think you've got an ear for dialogue. I think you'll do." I'd have preferred that he ask me to lie down on my stomach and expose my neck. That would've been less humiliating. But I needed the job, and they knew it.

"We need you to bring the ethnic flavor," said the black female producer. I felt I was being asked to a picnic. *"Could you bring the ethnic fla-*

vor? I'm bringing coleslaw. He's bringing drinks. And she's bringing hot dogs."
I knew I was in trouble, but it's the money that moves you. Actually, no, it's really about the chance to work. Work is what most people try to get out of. In Hollywood work is what defines you. The question is never *Who are you?* It's always *What do you do?* With work, you're valued. You belong to something bigger than just you. They hired me. I was back to writing in America.

I did a comedy sketch show for those producers called *Off Limits,* with Jacob Vargas and Aisha Tyler, for the United Paramount Network, now gone the way of the dinosaurs. They had promised me "edgy." It was not. UPN is gone, but I'm still here.

That meeting was more than 13 years ago, and it seems like it was yesterday. Since then, I've written for *Madtv* (2003–2005); seen my play go to Broadway (2005); begun writing and directing the *CBS Diversity Showcase* (2006–2013); been vice president of LATV (2007); released the film I wrote, *Nothing Like the Holidays* (2008), a Christmas classic that received an ALMA award in 2009; toured and starred in my Showtime special, *Diary of a Dad Man* (2010); survived the recession (2011); gotten a book deal (2012); and—right now, today—am beginning to see hope in the United States for a Latino story. It's not easy, and every time it gets hard, I remember my father's mantra: "Rick, you have to hear a lot of 'nos' before you hear that one 'yes.'"

MI AMOR

*"Latinos tend to create family and friends
not by blood, but by loyalty."*

One of the biggest blessings in life is family. You only realize that when you don't have one. I thought I would be fine without one. My career was the love of my life. I was obsessed with my art. They say a life in art is never wasted, but a life alone is never easy. I was alone and lonely and unhappy but I did not know it. I needed a woman to explain to me how miserable I was.

My family life began at a New Year's Eve party. I was living in Chicago doing my show *Latinologues* before Broadway. It was late in 2001 around Christmas. Life was moving fast. It was the height of my bachelorhood; "-hood" meaning I hung out with a lot of minorities, including myself. I'd left Hollywood because I simply got sick of it. I began to live my life in that purgatory between "Do I want a family?" or "Do I want a career?"

I was going to spend New Year's Eve alone. It was post 9/11 and everyone was trying to act like the world would return to normal. The United States was in a collective numbness. I was even more numb because it was damn cold in Chicago—too cold and way too much snow. I had an "escape clause" in my contract that said I could travel to California any time I wanted to. I wanted to. I wanted to badly. I don't know why, but I simply had to go home to San Diego. I had a "feeling."

I remember the night I left because it seemed unreal. A limo picked me up. It was snowing as I left my place in Wicker Park. I got in the limo. An Andrea Bocelli song was playing. The limo, the snow, the song—I thought I might actually be living a movie. I took a flight back to where my life had started—San Diego. Things had changed back home. My father had died. My mother seemed older. Somehow, Christmas seemed shallow. "Why don't you go out?" my mother asked. "It's New Year's Eve." Normally I would have said no, but I had a feeling I should go.

"Won't you be lonely?" I asked.

"Won't I be lonely?" My mother smiled. "It's New Year's Eve, Rick. I'm going to bed at nine."

After she kissed me I headed to a friend's party. At that time, I knew very few people back in San Diego. I'd grown up and changed. San Diego had, too.

So, I'm now at a very Latino party with lots of politicos, community leaders, and sharply dressed Latinos with their dates. It was the first New Year's Eve I could remember being without a date. I kept noticing this beautiful woman across the room. I was a Hollywood guy. *Hey,* I thought. *Be confident. You're a writer. You've written popular TV shows like* In Living Color *and* MADtv. I'd hung out with Tupac Shakur. I'd given advice to Fly Girl Jennifer Lopez, and told her she could be an actress. I had costarred with George Clooney in a really bad movie.

I was a Hollywood player, dating models. I dated a Corona girl, which was more classy than those cheap 40-ounce Schlitz Malt Liquor girls. I partied with the biggest Hollywood guys. I did tequila shots with Quentin Tarantino. He called me a genius. Or maybe his tequila did. I'd hung out with Mexican telenovela stars in Mexico City.

Here at a New Year's Eve party in San Diego, I saw this beautiful, petite, blue-eyed blonde across the room. I was slightly drunk. All night long people were buying me tequila shots. I was a mini-celebrity. I walked over to the beauty and introduced myself. I told her I was the "celebrity guest."

We talked for a bit, and then she looked at me and said, "You know, Rick, you're not really happy." I laughed. Her name was Susie. She spoke Spanish and was involved with Mexico. She loved Mexico like only a Mexican can. She helped set up water stations in the desert. Her last name was Albin. For a second, I thought she was Latina. I pronounced Albin with a Spanish lilt, al-BEEN. But she wasn't Latina. She was Irish and Scottish and very Anglo.

We talked for a while. Her date was engrossed in business talk with a group of guys and barely paid any attention to her. Later I found out he wasn't her date; he was just her neighbor. I told her about my so-called Hollywood life and Chicago where I was living and doing my show. She wasn't impressed. "I have to tell you," she began, "I think you're living an aimless, unhappy life. And you're really depressed. The only thing that'll cure you is changing your carefree bachelor lifestyle, getting married, and having a family. Right now you're a man with no direction. You may think you're having what seems like fun, but you're really depressed and don't know it."

Wow! She was right. I had no idea. I didn't know it. How could I? I FELT GREAT! I had no responsibilities. I didn't have a care in the world. In fact, the world took care of me. I was like Cheech Marin in a 24/7 medicinal marijuana shop. "Wow, she's good," I thought.

Now I was confused. So, I did what any confused man would—I started dating her. *I'll show her how happy I am,* I defended. It was about a month later when she asked me, "Hey, you wanna go on a trip to Spain with me to meet my family? They're on a vacation in Spain visiting my sister on her honeymoon. She just got married and everyone is going to Spain to have some good family fun."

I'm thinking, *Spain? Well, I haven't been there in like five hundred years, why not?*

It was about six months after 9/11, and the horrible tragedy was still a fresh wound around the world. Spain was tense. A side trip to Morocco was even tenser. Being there reminded me how American I was. We were in the middle of a bazaar in Morocco, and a man came up to us, screaming in Arabic. "He is only reciting poetry," our translator said. I was skeptical. How do you rhyme *kill* and *infidel?* No, my Spidey senses were telling me I was being yelled at, or cursed, or threatened in some way. It was a fear-ridden time, and Americans abroad were vulnerable. And I was with the whitest people in the world, riding camels. I was happy to leave Morocco.

I'd made a promise to try my best to make Susie happy, and going to Spain was my way of doing just that. And Spain is a very romantic country. I think she knew that. A week into the trip, we got engaged. I asked her if she would marry me in the little coastal town of Salou. I was on bended knee in front of an *El Rey de Burger*—Burger King. They served beer there, which was more surprising to me than the fact that I was engaged to Susie. I looked in her eyes and thought, *Wow. They've got Burger King in Spain? And they serve beer and wine? Europeans really know how to live. Why did we ever leave? Oh, yeah, the Inquisition and a chance to steal gold from the Aztecs.*

Susie said yes. I wanted her more than I can describe. I knew it was the best thing I would ever do. Then I had to go home.

En route back to Los Angeles, I had a stopover in Switzerland. I was tired, and they lost my luggage in Spain. I was waiting for my Swiss plane to taxi off the runway. I needed to start writing *Going Green,* a pilot about a Latino man marrying an Anglo girl and the two families they bring together, for famed producer Ben Silverman. I was up for an ALMA Award, an accolade given by the National Council of La Raza, a civil rights organization for Latinos equivalent to the NAACP, so I felt good.

It was one of those "everything is right in the world" moments. I had an economy ticket and I was in Zurich where everything is on time, except my Spanish luggage handlers. So, there I sat, newly engaged, tanned, tired, and happy to be heading home to the United States.

First, I hear an announcement over the intercom—"Messieurs et Mesdames . . ." It's in French and I can't understand it. All of a sudden, a few French people sitting next to me leave, without even a goodbye. They were French, so I assumed they simply didn't like Americans. Then came another announcement in German. More people around me leave. Blond, blue eyed, punctual, intense. Then there's yet another announcement, this time in Italian. The dark-haired, fashionable people leave. I'm beginning to catch a word or two. Finally Spanish! More people exit the plane. I'm seeing a pattern here. Then, finally in English—"Ladies and gentlemen. There is an emergency. We need you to evacuate the plane immediately."

The only two people left are me and a big American tourist. He's fat and he blocks an aisle when he tries to get his luggage. I'm thinking, *"Damn American, move it!"*

Since it wasn't long after 9/11, people were easily panicked. I thought, *He would be a good hostage, better than me, so he needs to stay.* Finally he moves, and we scurry off the plane. Outside, there are police dogs and a bomb disposal unit. They have us take off our shoes for no apparent reason. They're going through our luggage. Everyone's luggage is outside on the tarmac and I'm thinking, *What if there had been a hostage situation with some guy yelling in an untranslatable language out a window and me with a gun to my head?*

Of course, he'd be screaming, "We will kill this American if our demands are not met!" And I'm thinking, "Finally, I'm just an American." But I'm also thinking that if they kill me, then the headlines will read, "A Mexican-American was killed today when a gunman's hostage demands were not met." Identity is everything.

The Swiss police interrogated me because in Spain they had lost my luggage, and there was an unclaimed bag on the tarmac. Someone told them it was mine. I think it was the American couple that said they didn't think I was really an American. I looked a little dark, although my ancestors had fought the Moors six hundred years earlier. Now I was barefoot on the tarmac and accused of being the same people my forefathers had died to oppose.

Meanwhile in the identity war on an airline runway, the Swiss police are trying to get me to claim some luggage on the tarmac next to a bomb squad. They attempt a "good cop versus bad cop" thing. But it's more of a "polite cop versus more polite cop." They cannot identify two pieces of luggage and, since I have no luggage, they think it's mine and that I'm lying to cover up a hidden bomb threat.

After several hours, they finally let me go. I wasn't a terrorist, just a barefoot American. Once they released me, they tried to act as if nothing out of the ordinary happened. They re-booked me on a flight back to America. I demanded an upgrade. I got it. Sitting in first class, I recognized the American woman who had regarded me with such disdain when I was a suspected terrorist. I now sat across from her.

As the flight attendant was taking her meal order, she explained that I had just taken the last order of lobster medallions. "Oh, no," she exclaimed. "I really wanted the lobster." The flight attendant looked at me.

"Would you be so kind to give her your order?" she asked. "No," I said. "I'm not *that* kind. I'll keep my order." And I enjoyed my lobster medallions all the way to New York. Then, after wonderful homemade cookies and a mousse parfait dessert, I felt bad—further proof that I wasn't a terrorist. A true terrorist would have eaten the lobster medallions with hatred in his heart.

A few days later, I attended the ALMA Awards. Susie joined me. We walked down the red carpet next to Antonio Banderas and Melanie Griffith. Melanie was his blonde. I walked down the red carpet with mine. We were living the Hollywood Latino life, and on that red carpet with the cameras flashing, Susie finally began to believe I worked in Hollywood. She had fallen in love with me knowing very little about me. I think that's why I loved her. She accepted me on faith, not because I worked in Hollywood. Susie had no idea what I did, she just cared about who I was. That's what impressed me most about her.

When we got engaged, I thought her folks would be happy, but after we announced it, her parents were like, "Ohhh, really? Maybe you should go to counseling."

I don't think they were prejudiced because I was Mexican; I think they were prejudiced because they thought I was a *broke* Mexican. If I had been a rich Mexican, I'd have been an Italian. They didn't trust this Hollywood guy who'd just asked their daughter to marry him. But I was in love. And for whatever reason, I wanted to change for this woman.

"Look, now that we're engaged," Susie said, "I'm going off the pill, but don't worry, because it'll take me years to get pregnant."

Now, there's a voice in your head that occasionally tries to warn us of danger. Your mind screams "NO!" but your mouth says, "Yes." Just like the executive who thought *Waterworld* was going to be a good film. Or, the guy who said, "Invade Iraq. We'll be out of that country in no time. And while we're in Iraq let's invade Afghanistan, too, because that fun country will be even easier to exit than Iraq." I call this voice in my head the "inner dad" voice. My inner dad voice has given me advice throughout my life.

Imagine a thick Latino-accented voice speaking in your head. *What's wrong with you, Rick? Come on, son, it's a trap. You know how fertile we are. We had a cousin who was a lifeguard. He got a girl pregnant just by resuscitating her. She won't let you be Mexican. She won't let you walk down the beach in your cowboy boots and jeans listening to Los Tigres Del Norte. She's going to make you be everywhere on time. It's a trap!*

Even white guys have an inner dad voice. It sounds like this—(imagine a hillbilly accent) *Run, you dumb son of a bitch! Pack up the crystal meth, hook up the trailer, and run! Don't forget the banjo. That's right. Let's go, Cletus!*

Susie told me it would take years before she got pregnant. Years! But she was Irish. I was Mexican. We were the perfect storm of fertility. Irish and Mexicans are unnaturally fertile baby makers.

Fertility and children are big in the Latino culture. Back in ancient Mexico, we created sacrifices to get rid of any excess virgins. You can either be a virgin sacrifice or you can be a party girl on spring break. Only virgins die.

I imagine an ancient Aztec priest saying, "Okay, girls, welcome to the virgin sacrifice. We've got a line backed up here. Now, all you virgins can get your hearts ripped out or you can have sex with me. Because if you screw me, ironically, I can't touch you. Okay, what's it going to be? Your heart ripped out? Or sex with me? Heart ripped out or sex? What's it going to be? Why don't you all have a margarita and think about it."

So now my inner Mexican dad voice was yelling, *Are you crazy? She's Irish and you're Mexican. That'll make your kids double alcoholics! You're going to have to check their sippy cups for tequila and whiskey every night!*

Susie was calm. "Look, Rick, relax. It might take a long time for us to get pregnant. I might not even be able to get pregnant at all. All of my friends are doing in vitro." My inner dad voice was screaming in my ears. *"In vitro" is nothing compared to your magic "chor-IZO!" You are going to get her pregnant!*

Susie smiled at me. "Is it true that Latino men can make love all night?" she asked. "Uhmm, yeah, sure, but those guys are unemployed," I replied. "I've got a job, so try to get some sleep because you have to get up before me and make me breakfast, just like my mother did!"

Julian was conceived that night, and Susie walked down the aisle six months pregnant. It was like graduation day at an inner-city high school. I went from hard partying Hollywood guy, to dating guy, to engaged guy, to parents-not-liking-me guy, to the-guy-who-got-our-daughter-pregnant guy, to married guy, to dad all in a matter of months. And I broke five hundred years of pure Mexican lineage in my family by marrying a white woman. However, there are advantages to marrying a white girl versus a Latina, I would joke. With a white girl, during a domestic disturbance, I'm going to jail. With a Latina, I'm going to a hospital.

Okay, so I'm not all that brown to begin with. I'm Latino light. (Pause) A *güero*. (For you non–Spanish speakers, remember *güero* simply means "tall, sexy, good-looking Mexican-American man.")

I imagined getting a phone call. "Mr. Najera, your FICA score is 750." And I thought, *Oh my God, I'm going to die!* Then they explained that it was not a medical thing and that after marrying Susie, my credit had improved. Sure, I married my wife for love. And her good credit. I jokingly tell people I did not marry Susie because she was white, I married her because I thought she was rich.

January 11, 2003. Goodbye Hollywood guy. Hello married guy. It's a date I'll never forget, because now I have someone in my life to remind me why it's important. But Hollywood isn't a great place for a marriage. Marriage needs stability and unifying moments. Christmas, Thanksgiving, family meals, family vacations—a life that is shared. By contrast, Hollywood is completely unstable. It consumes your life 24/7. Hollywood is where you work, and if you're lucky it's where you build a career. It's not where you find love. Hollywood doesn't visit you when you're sick or text you an "I love you" whenever you get on a plane.

Marriage is a life-altering thing for any man. It certainly was for me. Most of my life had been defined by my occupation or my culture. I was a Latino actor and writer. I was a cultural warrior in Hollywood. But now my identity had been completely redefined; I was a married guy.

Cultures share different defining ceremonies, but marriage is a universal ceremony. It keeps traditions alive and unites us with our ancestors. Sometimes when I indulge thoughts about how hard my life is, I remember my ancestors. My father had five children that he raised with only a high school education. My grandfather had seven children he raised with even less schooling and opportunity. How can I complain?

My marriage makes me feel closer to my father and mother because the challenges of raising children helps me to understand them more. Little things I do remind me of my father. When I try to set up a meeting to get a job I think of my father going house to house, selling his wares. Then I think of my great-grandfather leaving Chihuahua, Mexico, to avoid a revolution that would kill over a million Mexicans, and the bravery that it took to do so. I imagine him with all his family and children crossing over to New Mexico to build a new life.

I could relate to my great-grandfather when I bundled my family up and took them to Broadway with me. Marriage is a union of love between two people bound together for each other's betterment against the harshness of the world. That's my definition of a partnership.

Through our union, Susie and I are building the new America. Our children are the new reality. We're a mixed family—Latino/Anglo. Our kids are *Mix-icans.* Mexico has a long tradition of cultural mix-it-ups. The Spaniards and Aztecs got together to create the Spaztecs, more commonly known as the mestizo race. The Mexicans and Irish mixed and created twice the poverty. The Mexicans and Jews mixed and became Mexi-cohens. The Mexicans and Africans mixed and they created the Dominicans.

Latinos were put into a cosmic blender and pureed to be us. The only real Mexican was the Aztec emperor, Montezuma. He was stoned by his people in his feathered robes. He was the true Mexican or Aztec or Mexhica. But of course, all the other tribes thought they were the real Mexicans, too.

I used to get the "I'm a real Mexican" minority game at college. There was a Chicano group that decided I was not Mexican enough. I thought, *Please, oh please, let me join your oppressed minority group.* But, surprise!— sometimes minorities aren't even accepted among their own. It's true. We have problems with self-loathing and jealousy among ourselves.

I once lost a writing job with a Latino comic. A producer had asked me to join his writing staff. Then I got a call from my agent. "Rick, it looks like the job isn't happening. The comic doesn't want you on his show. He wants a white, Jay Leno–type writer."

I didn't know what to say. "Really?" I asked. "Why not me?"

My agent paused. "He said you're too Latino."

I was shocked. I couldn't believe the Latino comic wanted the white writer and not the cheaper Latino writer. The show was on Comedy Central, and his funniest material was Latino. (And just to be clear, it was not George Lopez, Gabriel Iglesias, or Paul Rodriguez.) The truth is he hired the white writer and the show was cancelled.

Years later when I confronted him, he said, "Oh, yeah, I was getting pressure from the network to make my show more white. Sorry, bro, they wanted me to get a white writer." I couldn't believe my ears. "Okay. Jesus, now I feel so much better." I don't know if he was telling me the truth, but at that point, I didn't care. In the end, we both lost a job.

Years earlier, I had learned an important lesson from Keenen Ivory Wayans. "Keep your family close," he said. He was more my family than my so-called fellow Latino. What I know is this—Latinos tend to create family and friends not by blood, but by loyalty. If you're friendly with a Latino or welcoming to a Latino, then you're in the family. Blood has very little to do with it.

The Great
White Way

"Thank you for giving me, someone with no voice, a voice."

My journey to Broadway started in 2005 and began with a promise. I'd been a writer on *MADtv* and received two Writers Guild of America nominations during my tenure. I was also still performing my play *Latinologues*. Just like a shark that always has to be swimming or else it dies, in Hollywood, you always have to be working, because you never know what project might get the green light next. It's like fishing with multiple poles; with more than one pole in the water, something is sure to bite.

Latinologues had started out in 1994 as a protest against California Proposition 187, the bill that denied illegal aliens basic services and health care rights. Instead of anger, I wanted to protest with laughter, so I wrote a series of monologues about the Latino experience and all our colors and diversity. That boy Bradley, who called me "wetback," even found his way in.

Latinologues was born during the time that I was creating pilots for the TV networks. I'd write a pilot, or a show, and producers would tell me, "Oh, we love this script but we don't have any Latino stars to be in it." Star wattage is a very big thing. In film, they'll say, "How many Latino stars do we have that can sell the movie?" In other words, "If I give you $3 million to film, which star is bankable? Can I have a good feeling that I'll get my money back, either internationally or on DVD/pay-per-view?" There aren't many Latinos who have this kind of draw. That's one of the reasons we're not seen. It's the same thing working in TV or in theater as well, that's why we don't have the opportunity to advance in that direction.

We didn't have the time or connections to chase theatrical producers or filmmakers. We didn't have enough people around us who could actually see us, so after too many rides on the merry-go-round, I said, "Hey, you keep telling me we don't have any Latino stars, so I'll start making them."

Part of my plan was developing a showcase; that's how it works with comics. Comics will use seven minutes on stage and then get development deals. The producers are like, "Wow, he's so funny! But he can't act."

So I said, "Let me change comics into actors. I'll put them in this showcase, and then help build their careers. And in the end, it will give me an opportunity to write and discover great talent, and then the next time someone says, 'We want a pilot but we have no Latinos,' I can say, 'Look. Come here to this place. You'll see Latinos on stage. They all deserve a TV show. They're great!'"

That was my capitalistic strategy to build the market. That's why I did it. It wasn't to showcase me; it was to showcase other people. In the end, it showcased me in a lot of ways, but most importantly it showcased hundreds of other actors. Just think of all the actors that have been in *Latinologues* over its lifetime and how they have all impacted entertainment. It's been amazing.

The play was first performed at the Odyssey Theatre in L.A., with comedians including Debi Gutierrez, Rudy Moreno, and Gene Pompa, as a showcase for Latinos written by and produced by Latinos. Over the years, I wrote new monologues—over a hundred—that I'd change every year to keep it fresh and relevant to the whole Latin experience, from busboys to border crossers to the producers of shows like this. Since it began, more than two hundred Latino actors have performed in the show—everyone you can imagine, from Cheech Marin, to Edward James Olmos, to Geraldo Rivera, to Eugenio Derbez (Mexico's modern Cantinflas). And it's been performed in theaters around the country, from the San Diego Rep to the Victory Gardens Theater in Chicago to, finally, Broadway itself.

One night on tour in Portland, Oregon, a Mexican man with a dark moustache, jet-black hair, and dark brown skin came up to me. He was wearing a red velour jacket and wore a gold pinky ring on his finger. Smiling, with silver-capped front teeth and an accent so thick that he needed subtitles when he spoke he said:

MEXICAN STEREOTYPE

Chewwww . . . should write better Mexicans. Why do you do chewwwwwse people that talk wheet de accents? I no like that. I like to see gooood Mexicans. Show me nice Mexicans. I no like stereotypes.

RICK

But you're a stereotype. Look at you! Central Casting would love you. I think I saw you in a John Huston movie talking about badges. But, okay, it's folkloric dancing and noble Mexicans in all of my shows from now on.

MEXICAN STEREOTYPE

Good. Why don't you write in da Spanish?

RICK

Because I speak horrible Spanish. Why doesn't Woody Allen write in da Yiddish? But I'll try. I'm trying to avoid insulting Woody Allen.

MEXICAN STEREOTYPE

Okay. Can you write on the program something poor my keeds?

RICK

Sure, what are their names?

MEXICAN STEREOTYPE

Stephanie and William.

RICK
Your kids are Stephanie and William? Not Cuauhtémoc or Maria or Guadalupe or Malinche?

MEXICAN STEREOTYPE
Hey, we live in Portland and I work for Nike. Okay, just signs the program. *Pinche coconut!* I should have bought tickets to *Disney On Ice.*

I prayed this man would never have to go to Arizona.

In 2004, I was on the road with *Latinologues* and touring in Miami with René *"People en Español* Magazine's 25 Most Beautiful People" Lavan, and Carlos Gomez (of Broadway's *In The Heights*). I was in Miami in the thick of my Caribbean Latinos. Miami's a great international city. It's the only American city where it feels like you need a passport to visit. I'd been there before, working on a show with Cuban rapper Pitbull, one of the nicest people I've ever worked with. However, we Mexican-Americans tend to be deep thinking and depressing; Cubans tend to be happy and inviting. Of course, unless you've ever had your picture taken with Fidel Castro and you're hugging him.

In *Latinologues* at one point, I did a sketch about Elián González with Eugenio Derbez. In 1993 Elián became a symbol for thousands of Cubans who longed to go back to Cuba. He was their baby found in a raft floating in the water; like Moses, but in the Caribbean instead of the Nile. He was forced to return to Cuba by Democratic President Bill Clinton. This decision echoed an earlier loss felt by many Cubans who had been stranded without the promised air support during the Bay of Pigs. The Cubans felt they were lied to by then Democratic President John F. Kennedy, and with the fresh memory of the returning of Elián back to Cuba, the Democratic Party lost the Cubans for good. The Democrats would, years later, lose the White House because some Republican-leaning Cubans were enraged over losing Elián and the Bay of Pigs. The Cubans in Miami and Florida voted for Bush and the Democrats lost the White House. Modern history today is affected by the past.

Wearing an inner tube and flippers, I was Elián in *Latinologues,* walking behind Eugenio as he was talking on the phone, cursing out Castro for not fulfilling his promises to Elián's father after he returned his son to Cuba. I was cursing Castro, too, yelling, "I want to go back to America! Cuba sucks!" Needless to say, Miami loved it. One of our actresses performed a monologue about a Cuban prostitute who dreams of old Havana. It was tragic and poignant. People in the audience cried.

While in Miami, I was cast in a National Lampoon co-ed spectacular called *Pledge This,* starring Paris Hilton and a slew of other B-list stars. I won't turn this into a "tell-all," but it was filled with drinking clubs and a lot of debauchery. One night, the producers of *Pledge This* came to see me perform as Buford Gomez in *Latinologues.* Buford is a redneck border patrol officer. The character has always resonated with audiences because he's based on truth. I've seen border patrol officers that are zealous in their desire to enforce that line between two countries. Buford introduces himself by walking on stage in his full green border patrol outfit, wearing aviator glasses and holding a stop sign.

"Hi. Allow me to introduce myself," he says with a thick, Texas drawl. "My name is Buford Gomez. I put the panic to the Hispanic. The pepper spray to Jose. The baton to Juan. Deportation is my business. And business is good." Imagine playing Buford Gomez to Latino audiences across the country. Surprisingly, people understood the joke.

Driving a Rolls-Royce, the producers of *Pledge This* take me out one night for an incredible dinner. I end up telling them about my biggest dream—going to Broadway. "Rick, my boy," one of them says, "I'm producing you on Broadway. I think you're a comic genius. You make me laugh, so the hell with it—I'm paying for Broadway." So, I tell the cast of *Latinologues* and everyone's excited.

Cut to a few months later. That same producer has been indicted by the SEC in a $300 million Ponzi scheme. His last known whereabouts— Brazil. He's at Carnival somewhere in Brazil and I'm in trouble. I've already told the cast we're going to Broadway. I promised them! I gave my word based on an SEC-indicted man on the lam. So, I come up with a plan. I'll rent the Town Hall in New York. Located just off of Times Square, it's a 1,500-seat Broadway-type house. Actually, it's more of a concert hall, but it's the next best thing to a real Broadway theater.

I'll fly the cast to New York. I'll use my savings and produce the show myself. It's exciting and it's all my money. I feel like a gambler, betting everything on *Latinologues* to win. So, I do it. For one night only. A week before the show, and I've sold only fifty tickets. FIFTY TICKETS! At this rate, I'm going to lose about $30,000.

I panic and call a New York radio station that just happens to have the biggest Latino morning show in the city. I'm desperate to get on that show. I have Eugenio Derbez go to the station. His mission—to get into the control room. I call the station and ask if Eugenio can be on their morning show. "No," they say. I'm shocked. "No? You can't say no," I tell them. "He's outside your door now. You have to let him on."

And they did. Eugenio went on the show and begged people to come to Town Hall. And they did. Opening night—February 19, 2005. We sold out. The show was a hit. Then I get a call from producer Robin Tate. He wanted to produce *Latinologues.* Robin Tate produced John Leguizamo's one-man show on Broadway, and now he wanted to produce me.

I think I wanted to be on Broadway for one reason: the slogan. "The Great White Way." I had to cross that border at that time. Luis Valdez was the only Mexican-American who had attempted it, and he failed. His play *Zoot Suit* was never extended. Now, ironically, New York's immigrant world was not embracing the Latinos. Most Latino-themed plays on Broadway had failed. *The Capeman,* the Paul Simon musical, died a horrible death. And *The Mambo Kings* closed in San Francisco before it ever opened in New York. That was a preemptive death. Still, I wanted Broadway.

Latinologues opened on the *real* Broadway at the legendary Helen Hayes Theatre on October 14, 2005, to critical acclaim. And since many of the readers of this book may never have the chance to see the show, I believe that this brilliantly written review sums it up far better than I could. It re-creates the Latinologues experience.

San Diego, San Antonio, Los Angeles, Houston, Miami . . . Is there a port city, border town or other immigrant mecca that this brash Latino revue (shrewdly cast and improbably directed by legendary stoner Cheech Marin) has not played over the past eight years? Oh, right—New York. Well, "Latino-logues" finally came to town, and if word of mouth gets out to the boroughs that the cast is hot, the humor is spicy and the Latino sensibility is authentic, it should have a healthy run.

What we've got here is a modest (Did I say "cheap"? I did not actually say "cheap") production performed on a bare stage with canned music, cheesy graphics, retina-damaging lighting and spotty sound effects. None of that seems to matter, though, once this high-energy show launches its first mono-logue—a nose-thumbing view of illegal immigration from the perspective of a Mexican border-skipper named Erazmo, currently employed as a dishwasher at a New York restaurant.

Having found an ingenious way of getting a free vacation to Puerto Val-larta, Erazmo is on his way back to New York when he stops to explain to the audience the "natural migration pattern" of illegal workers. Eugenio Derbez, a comedian with timing you could set the sun to, keeps the savvy audience in stitches, even as he squeezes every drop of irony from Erazmo's performance in the "Third World Olympics" of border jumping.

"Erazmo trains by working 80 hours a week with no overtime, picking to-matoes, picking peaches, picking lettuce," Derbez tells us, putting a sharp edge on his comic delivery. "He's running and crossing 5,000 miles just to pass out flyers for strip joints in Times Square." The rest of the monologues in the show are constructed in the same vein, with layers of pain, anger and bitterness cushioned by comedy.

With directorial assists from Marin, scribe Rick Najera engineers a bit of interactive byplay for these janitors, busboys, dishwashers, drug dealers, in-dulgent mothers, pregnant teenagers and veteran sex workers. But even when that loose (very loose) narrative thread breaks—as it does, for instance, for a hilarious Cuban visit with Elián Gonzales and his father, or the rebellious last hurrah of the Miss Puerto Rican Day Parade—the energy keeps flowing from scene to scene.

With only four thesps in the cast, that energy is the premium fuel that keeps the show pumped up. Although the comedy sketches are nominally per-formed in English ("because we don't want the Anglos confused—they paid full price"), the Latin rhythms, Spanish curses and breakneck speed of deliv-ery give the monologues the hard-to-catch quality of street-corner outbursts.

There's enough good material to go around so that this sturdy cast of pros can play to their distinctive comedic strengths.

Shirley A. Rumierk takes on distaff roles that, in Najera's table-turning writing style, present themselves as stereotypes but go on to reveal surprising depth of character. Thesp clicks on the clueless rap of a visibly pregnant teenager ("I'm a virgin, and don't you fucking doubt me"), and puts terrific comic snap into a hard-bitten hooker trying to peddle her hard-luck story on the streets of Havana ("Oh, my God, you're unmoved—you must be an American"). All the while, however, she's setting us up for the pathos she finds in their lives.

The versatile Derbez plays the diva roles, delivering his tour de farce as a Latina mother, the driving force of the Daughters of the Inquisition and a real ball-buster, who is volubly grateful because her son is a vampire, not gay. (Although almost buried by such flashy roles, his cool and creepy turn as the bodyguard to a drug lord is a special treat.)

René Lavan has the satirical hook on Latin loverboys like Alejandro, who racks up extra macho points by bedding blonds. But after holding this Colombian busboy up for ridicule, thesp takes him down gently when his ego is bruised.

"Hey, don't feel sorry for me," says Alejandro, who, like all the resilient characters in Najera's gallery, has more self-knowledge than most people give him credit for. "I'm a macho, and as long as I'm a macho, I'll never be just a busboy."

Najera is himself a hoot in multiple roles—from a chubby, bratty Elián Gonzalez ("I want to go back to Miami, Cuba sucks") to Felix "Veterano" Nogalez, a powerful drug lord aghast at the inefficiency of professional hitmen who can't shoot straight. "They kill the old woman, the baby, the guy with the full scholarship to Princeton," he says in disgust.

In the best application of his performance chops (picked up in regional theater, TV and films like "National Lampoon's Pledge This"), the switch-hitting scribe scores big as Buford Gomez, a Tex-Mex officer with the U.S. Border Patrol who makes the generous gesture of educating the audience about border jumpers. Having established that "not every single Latino is Mexican," he goes on to define the ethnic differences in pointed barbs aimed at every Latin American cultural group (presumably) sitting in the audience.

"Puerto Ricans are legal Mexicans . . . Cubans are Mexicans with rafts . . .

Dominicans are Mexicans who play baseball really well . . . Venezuelans are Mexicans with oil." Although Buford chickens out on Colombians ("Colombians are real nice"), he even has a cutting word for any Argentineans in the house: "Argentineans, you are not European. I repeat, you are not European."

This is funny stuff; and no, you don't have to be Mexican to get the jokes— or the message.

—Daily Variety

I loved that review because they understood the show. What I wrote was understood and accepted, and that is a basic human desire shared by all. I was in the greatest city in the world on Broadway and it only took ten years and 25 cities to do it. I was proud of the reviews and to be on Broadway. Being one of only three Latinos to write and star in a Broadway show was a huge accomplishment for me.

Latinologues lasted 127 performances on Broadway and has toured the nation for over 15 years. I had accomplished everything I wanted to up to that point. Life was good.

One night, the ex-president of Mexico, Ernesto Zedillo, came to the show. He was a professor at Yale and his daughter was friends with Eugenio Derbez's daughter. He came backstage and said, "I want you to know, Rick, that not all Mexicans are busboys and illegal aliens." I smiled. "Yes," I replied, "but those are the people I like to write about." What I really wanted to say was, *Those are the people I like to write about; not the privileged, like you.*

That same night I went to Sardi's. I noticed a busboy had been staring at me. I actually thought, *I hope I tipped him enough.* Then he came up to me and said apologetically with a *Poblano* accent, "I'm sorry to disturb your dinner, but you gave me free tickets to your show." I'd done that because many of my people (Latinos) could not afford to buy them. He looked at me. "I wanted to thank you for giving me, someone with no voice, a voice." I was stunned by his eloquence and the beauty of his words.

Broadway was for me a moment of triumph and a revelation, because I never wanted to be the only Latino in anything. A lot of times in Latino culture there has been a feeling of "me only" or "I made it!" I never thought of it that way. I always said, "A true measure of success is to have people around you that are enjoying your success because they're part of it."

You know, my attitude was born at an Indian reservation when I was a kid. The Indians had a ceremony at Laguna Pueblo where they would get on top of the roofs and they'd throw their belongings to people down below and people would take them. They'd go from one roof to the other and do that. I remember the concept was, in their tribe, there's very much a commitment to sharing, and so you might have some-body's belongings that come off the roof during this giveaway sort of thing, but it's redistributed throughout the entire tribe. That feeling of sharing and helping one another was a big part of why I thought, *I never want to be the only Latino at an event.*

I was not the only one on that stage. My work represented the hopes and dreams of many Latinos. That busboy gave me the greatest compliment I've ever received.

On December 31, 2005, *Latinologues* made its final performance on Broadway. Immediately after the show, I wheeled my suitcase through Times Square to catch a cab and to take my last memories of Broadway through pouring rain and a crowded New Year's Eve celebration beginning. A cab stopped for me, I jumped in, and off we went. I celebrated New Year's Eve in-flight. I had to get back home to California; I had two jobs waiting for me. One, directing the Diversity Showcase at CBS, and the other, director of programming at LATV, a new bilingual network in Los Angeles that had a digital signal in 27 other cities. In programming, I would create new shows for LATV.

I had decided to take both jobs, mainly for my wife and kids. I became a corporate executive to provide for my family. I wanted stability and financial security, so I put acting and writing on hold and joined corporate America. I wore a suit. I drove a nice car. I took people out for power lunches.

Within months, I was promoted to vice president of development. That sounds fabulous, but I had two presidents over me. LATV was run by two white presidents—two very white Anglo types who were presidents of a Latino network. Not that an Anglo can't run a Latin network, but it was like having a blind person as your cameraman—confusing, unsteady, and out of focus. And if that wasn't enough, neither of them understood any of my programming, or even liked it. I helped to develop, write, and voice a cartoon called *Ceasar and Chuy,* and I created a stop-motion animation called *The Homies Hip Hop Show,* and *LATN* (*Latino Ahora Today Now*), a Colbert-type fake news show.

My audience consisted of Latinos and anyone hip enough to relate to Latinos. And I got some great ratings for the network. But I was locked into the eternal battle between advertisers and the network. The network promoted the fact that they spoke in English for a bilingual audience. The advertisers loved this, but in truth, internally, there were a lot of people at the network who had a Spanish-language agenda. They were used to programming in Spanish and Spanish only, and they didn't want to transition to English. The constant tug-of-war between the two camps affected everyone. Once again, I found myself involved in a cultural war. The belief that the only way to reach a Latino audience was in Spanish was called "Univisionitis," referring to people who wanted Latinos to remain in a Spanish-language world and never evolve to a bilingual capability.

Univision was getting huge ratings producing Spanish-language-only programming. I'm not against the Spanish-language networks, but I think it's a double-edged sword that further alienates Latinos from our fellow Americans. A foreign language makes Latinos foreigners, instead of equal participants in English-speaking America.

You *can* reach Latinos in English, and when you do it's ratings gold. However, there was a steady propaganda campaign to turn the network into a Spanish-language-only network. How could the executives resist getting programming from Mexico in Spanish for practically nothing? All networks cater to their audience. And so did I. I've always known my audience, and was looking forward to creating programming for this network.

After spending years traveling across America speaking to audiences and selling tickets to predominantly Latinos, I knew the programming they wanted. Over the years, I had learned how to speak to that audience, and looked forward to doing it on television. Unfortunately, these two very white Anglo presidents over me who were running the bilingual channel considered me a threat. I quickly learned about corporate politics. They would "hate" a good idea because it was not their idea.

An executive came up to me one day and announced, "My daughter said she doesn't get your programming." I laughed. "Really? The one who attends the very white private school called the Academy of Entitlement?" He glared at me. "Yes" he replied, tight-lipped. "She doesn't like your *Homies Hip Hop Show.*" I held his angry gaze. "She's not our target audience. She's your daughter."

Life as an executive in corporate America in these new trenches was depressing. The reality was that the network was going Spanish even though the ratings were slipping as a result. Whoever gets to tell their story is the winner of the culture war. I wanted to tell my story. That has never changed. But at LATV, I ended up developing shows for Anglo executives, not Latinos.

In Hollywood and Mexico, there is only one color: green. To me, the two presidents at LATV were the cultural enemy. I always love white people who are born with an incredible ability to understand "my culture." Some even speak Spanish better than I do. It's the relative cultural superiority theory based on such indisputable examples as the man who tells the feminist, "Hey, I feel cramps, too." Or the hip young thing who says to the blind man, "I can absolutely relate. I need glasses to read." Or a white man telling an American Indian, "I'm part Cherokee."

I was born in the market, but the Anglos were the gatekeeping interpreters. They were never going to approve programming they didn't understand. *Ellos no comprenden Los Latinos.* (They did not understand Latinos.)

Once, these executives decided to fire an on-air personality. Then they changed their minds. The on-air personality was so happy to get her job back, she kissed one old president's cheek. The other remarked, "That's one thing about Latinos. They're so affectionate." The comment felt like praise for a unique characteristic of a particular breed of dog—"Golden retrievers are so affectionate." Either way, when these two unassailably distant gentlemen shared their views of Latinos and what they were like with me, I knew my days with the gringos supreme would be numbered.

ME AND GOD
IN THE ICU

"I think God has a great sense of humor."

When I was in the ICU I felt out of control and weak. I stopped watching TV news. Was it just me or did the "news" seem skewed? Consider the news slogan, "If it bleeds, it leads." Lately, it seemed like there was a lot of blood in the news. It's as if the world were bleeding out. From oil spills to tsunamis, to war and rumors of war. There is definitely blood in the streets. In Afghanistan. In Iraq, in Mexico, in the United States. The drug war in Mexico has claimed over 50,000 lives. That's more than all the Americans lost in Iraq and Afghanistan combined.

America has changed since I was a child. I see time differently. Now is now. The past remembered in the now is always present. As for the future? Who knows? I feel like my entire life has raced by in a millisecond. Until my close call, I'd never really stopped to think about my life. The ICU strengthened my faith. My life has been marked by many close calls—from auditions to screen tests. Many times I almost "made it."

My recent scene at death's door was a serious reminder. Every day is a new day and a gift. In the hospital trauma unit, I sipped my drink and ate my Jell-O; I thought about the new people who had entered my life and those who had left. I had traveled and seen much. My father loved *Man of La Mancha* and the song "The Impossible Dream," with the lyrics, "to fight the unbeatable foe." That play inspired me deeply. I had been given a second chance at life. When you wake up in an ICU ward, something in your life definitely needs changing. I was going to do exactly that. Change.

As I lay in the ICU, my wife, Susie, came into my room, looked me in the eyes earnestly, and said, "Rick, you have to change for your family." How could I change? She wanted me to work less. I thought I needed to work more. I had worked myself nearly to death, but that was the Mexican way. I'd seen it all my life. It's all I knew. I'd watched my family nearly work themselves to death. Now, as an adult, I had so, so many responsibilities—I wondered what my father would do. He was gone, so I couldn't ask him.

Months later, I would receive a call telling me that Lupe Ontiveros was in the hospital dying. She had cancer and never told a soul. It was her private suffering. She was a classic Latina mother. She would suffer alone and bear all the agony, shielding her family from her pain as long as she could. When I saw her in the hospital just before she passed, she was in a bed, pumped full of morphine. Her loving family was by her side. She was no longer full of life as I remembered her. This is what Susie desperately wanted to avoid—a husband on life support after a heart attack or stroke. I put my hand on Lupe's, said a silent prayer for her, and left.

I called Edward James Olmos. "Rick, this will hurt bad," he said simply. And he was right. On our way into the hospital, we ran into Esai Morales (*La Bamba*) as well as a group of other close friends and actors in the industry. Esai was visibly shaken. I felt for his loss and mine.

Edward James Olmos gave a great eulogy at Lupe's funeral. She had touched so many lives.

Jimmy Smits was there, as well as Eva Longoria, Los Angeles mayor Antonio Villaraigosa, and countless others. And I saw how someone so full of life could go so quickly. And, remembering my time in the ICU, I realized one thing: Life is now. The dress rehearsal is over. Curtain up. That's why when the doctors had advised me to stay in the hospital for a month, I knew I had to leave. People have often asked me, "If you were that close to death, did you have one of those white light moments?" The answer is no. There were no white lights, just red lights from the ambulance taking me to the emergency room. I did not come back with a message from God. God has already given us all of his messages. He's just waiting for us to act on them.

My near-death experience? No white light. No voice of God. Just peace. I felt like I was deep within a cave in a tomb like Lazarus. I wasn't dead, I was in a cocoon, separated from friends and family, yet never alone. I was still alive and loved. I did have a few moments where I saw people in the hall or outside, like I was above their heads. Was it my spirit traveling outside of my body, or just my imagination? It didn't matter. God was there with me.

I could've lied and said I actually met God or Jesus. Or that an angel told me great secrets that I needed to share at seminars around the world. Or I could tell stadium crowds about the people I met in heaven who gave me great understanding and wisdom, and advised me to return to the living and release all that I'd learned on an audio book for the low price of $19.99. And that's not all, folks. If you act now, I'll throw in a set of Ginsu knives. If I did, I'd be making millions. But I didn't and I'm not. Because after a near-death experience, you want to be your best. Not out of the fear of God, but rather, out of love and respect and faith.

You see, I think God has a great sense of humor. My God laughs. My idea about God is best told this way: There is an old story about a man walking on a beach. There are two sets of footprints behind him in the sand as he walks. He has faith. He knows the other set is God's footprints as he walks alongside him. At one point, the man's journey gets rough and he sees only one set of footprints in the sand. *God has deserted me,* he thinks. He passes through a storm and finally meets God. He tells God, "Look, Almighty, why did you desert me during that hard time in my life?" And God said, "I didn't desert you. The single set of footprints you saw were mine, not yours. You only saw one set because I was carrying you on my shoulders during your hard times."

Then the man said, "You really carried me?" There was a pause. "Well, no," God admitted. "You were complaining and whining. Geez. It was really annoying. Have you ever listened to yourself? Well, I have. So, I bailed on you."

That's my God story. After my accident and time in the ICU, I had deeper understanding of the plan. God was at my side. But my God expects me to meet him halfway and to trust him on my journey and have faith in him. He expects me to keep on walking in any storm. He will walk with me, but he wants me to walk and to pick myself up, because sometimes just trying to walk is an act of faith. I have faith because I could've easily died yet, by some miracle, I didn't. I could've had brain damage. I didn't. I could've been paralyzed. I wasn't. My experience was no accident; it was definitely God's doing.

When I look back on my life, I realize there was a divine hand protecting me as a child. That same hand protects me now as an adult. When I was in the coma I know I was protected. I felt it. Yes, I know you supposedly can't feel anything when you're in a coma. But I did. You won't find that on the Glasgow Coma Scale. I was not in my body, which at that time was good, because the pain would have been excruciating. I was on the other side of a wall. I knew there was life on the other side, I just wasn't part of it. I was in a cocoon waiting to emerge from a deep sleep. There were people waiting for me on the other side and I had to get back to them.

I remember the time my son Julian and I were fly-fishing in the High Sierras. We were crossing a stream when he fell on a rock and almost slipped into the rushing river below. I quickly grabbed his hand. "Don't worry. I've got you. I'll never let you go." He looked at me. "I know," he said simply. He wasn't afraid. At that moment, I saw faith in my son's eyes. Faith in my love and presence.

I felt the same way in my coma. I knew God wasn't going to let me go, either. He had my hand. Once you have a brush with death, if you survive it, that's when you really begin to live. That's what I got out of my time in the ICU. That, a few scars, and lots and lots of bills. March 3, the day I landed in the hospital, would become a bigger birthday for me than my entry into the world.

When I was just starting to walk again in the hospital, Jeremy, my lecture agent, called and asked how I was doing. I had morphine in me and was feeling no pain. "Great," I said. "It was just a little fall." He was quiet for a moment on the other end of the line. "I may have a job for you," he tested cautiously. "Do you think you can do it?" I never turned down a job. Luckily, Jeremy couldn't see me. Flat on my back, IVs sticking all over me and unable to walk, I said, *"Yes!"*

As I recovered, the doctors advised me to stay in the hospital for a month. But I knew I had to leave. Then my phone rang. It was Jeremy, my lecture agent, again. "Rick, you got the job," he said. "You're going to speak about diversity at the World Bank in Washington, DC. Last year they had Dr. Henry Louis Gates." He's the black Harvard professor who was arrested for breaking into his own home in Cambridge. (I'm sure it had nothing to do with racial profiling . . .) "This year they want you."

God speaking through my agent via Hollywood's preferred divine instrument—the telephone. The one thing that I truly needed to motivate me to get up out of my hospital bed was a job.

"Can you make it?" my agent asked.

"When do they want me there?" He paused. "In a week." I was in the ICU, my eyes were swollen, and I looked like a pincushion with IVs still stuck in my arms. "Sure," I said. "I'll be there."

I had now lost my mind.

WALKING
MIRACLE

"Don't tell dirty jokes."

O n the plane to Washington, DC, Jeremy was sitting next to me. He looked at me with a controlled calm, no doubt wondering whether or not I'd make it. I was wondering the same thing. My doctors had warned me not to fly. And yet there I was. I had a headache and thought if I die, Jeremy will have to sit next to a dead guy for six hours.

I'd texted my casting director, Fern, and told her I was on a plane to DC to speak at the World Bank. It was March, and the World Bank was doing a month on diversity. There's a month for everything.

"We're flying first class," Jeremy said, "because you've only been out of the ICU for a week. I didn't want to put any extra strain on you." He makes me laugh.

"Thanks," I said, "but I've just survived a severe head injury and air pressure changes could kill me. First class or economy, either way, I could die. But at least you'll be sitting next to me in first class." Jeremy doesn't think I'm funny.

The only reason I'm even able to fly is because I spent a week at the very Hollywood-type health spa called the Optimum Health Institute. The Institute is a strange little place. It's a vegan raw food boot camp. After a week of wheatgrass, organic food (uncooked), and slow yoga-type moves, I was able to walk haltingly. I brought my friend Rafael Agustin with me. He understood my condition, and in the event I had a relapse, he could at least detail my recent history for the medics.

Jeremy looked at me again. "You look great, Rick!" Of course, he was lying. Fern texted people confirming that I had lost my mind. "Poor Rick," she shared. "He's texting me from his hospital bed thinking he's going to speak at the World Bank."

Curtain up! I now stood in front of a huge crowd at the World Bank. A vice president sidled up to me and whispered in my ear, "Don't tell dirty jokes and keep it clean," she said, with a smile. *Lady,* I thought to myself, *I'll be lucky to just finish my speech. The only dirty thing would be me soiling myself after I die onstage.*

My speech began like this:

Thank you so much. I'm honored to be here at the World Bank. I see over 170 nations are here today. You represent millions of people, and here you are in the United States, changing the world. All I ask is for you to stop and see a miracle. Look to your right. The person on your right is a miracle. Imagine their hopes and journey from thousands of miles away to be here today. Look to your left. Another miracle. A person from the farthest part of the world who has come here to work and make a difference and perhaps change the world for the better. Now look in front of you. I'm a miracle. A week ago, I was in a coma. Today, I'm here. There are no coincidences. I'm here for a reason that I can't yet fathom. Look at me and know I'm a miracle.

There was instant applause. I definitely had gotten my audience's attention. I went on to speak about such topics as diversity, Hollywood, and my life. In front of that audience, for the first time since leaving the hospital, I felt certain that I was coming back to life. What were the odds of speaking at the World Bank in Washington, DC? What were the odds I'd be on Broadway with a play I wrote and costarred in that was directed by Cheech Marin? I listened to his *Up in Smoke* record album for hours as a kid. What were the odds? Receiving these gifts in life suggests that there's some sort of plan. And if there is a plan—a script, if you will—there has to be a head writer.

After my appearance, I returned home to a steady diet of Xanax, Vicodin, and other meds. I was weak and in pain. The scar on my forehead was still a prominent reminder of my injury. It had barely faded. I'd used makeup to cover it for my speech.

Once home, I saw my blood-soaked mattress in the alley, waiting to be taken away. I also witnessed the incredible strain my entire ordeal had put on my family.

I was done with Hollywood. I had collaborated with Hollywood to put me in the ICU. The adrenaline of a never-ending obstacle course had taken a toll on me. My new plan? To keep myself out of the ICU and focus my attention and energy on my family. The Vicodin helped, but I began to need it too much. When my doctor wanted to refill my script, I said, "No." It was the hardest no I remember saying in a long time.

When I went in for a checkup my doctor told me I should have stayed in the ICU longer. He had forbidden me to fly. I didn't tell him about the World Bank trip. My experience in the ICU had shattered my self-confidence. There could only be one cure—giving the speech at the World Bank. I needed it and it came at the perfect time. It was a recovery triumph for me. It was no coincidence. And I needed to do even more to prove to myself that I was regaining my health.

Until my wake-up coma, my career had always been the top priority in my life. Now, I only wanted to hold on to one thing: my family. Being in a coma had changed me in a very profound way, and I needed my family more than ever. But I held off embracing them. I held off seeing my kids. I was ashamed of being weak, and I refused to let them see that. It was an illogical thought, but I recognized it. My collapse was a result of overwork. I was ashamed that I hadn't made more money, worked less, and spent more time with them.

I wanted to protect my family from seeing me in the hospital. I remember as a child when I saw sick relatives in hospitals, like my grandfather or grandmother. When they were sick, I felt helpless. If someone in the family ended up in the hospital, it was as a last resort. It meant the end. My grandfather. My grandmother. My father. They all died after stays in the hospital. I didn't want my family to see how fragile I was. I didn't want to remind my family that someday I would die.

Once I was home from the ICU, my biggest goal was to make sure I never returned. I began to walk religiously every day. I increased my distance until I was doing five miles a day. It became my meditation. I listened to songs on my iPhone. One in particular moved me—"100 Years," by Five for Fighting. It's about a man who recalls his life from the age of 10 to 99. The irony of the song is that life is short. You don't have a lot of time. I wanted to do more with mine because I didn't have "a hundred years to live." I walked and walked and walked. A month out of the ICU and I was a walking miracle.

THE GOOD DAD

*"How I treat myself
is how I was treated by my father."*

Looking back on my life, I've been many things—writer, actor, director, husband. But now I realize my biggest job would be my father years. I have three kids. I'M A DAD!

You can't really prepare for fatherhood. Becoming a father happens way too fast. One moment you're in a club with bottle service and the next you're in a delivery room asking about diaper service.

I remember our first pregnancy and birth; it was Julian. DOB: May 18, 2003. (I texted my wife for that date while writing this.) Our first birth was painful and messy. Not for me, luckily. Susie did all the work; I just supervised the horror.

I was Susie's birth coach. I wasn't a good birth coach. I got all NFL on her: (football coach voice) "Come on! You can beat this, baby! He's got a big head, but you've got a big heart. Come on, don't cry! Remember when it seemed like a good idea nine months ago after that piña colada in Puerto Vallarta? You wanted a baby then, remember? That's it! Use that anger at me to help forget the pain! Come on, push, push, PUSH!"

Now, ignorant anti-immigration-reform types might think a Latino birth sounds like this: (Mexican accent) "PUSH, PUSH, PUSH, Maria! Over the fence so we can have an American baby!" But in reality, the birth of my next child will sound like this: "PUSH, PUSH, PUSH, Susie! Over the fence to Canada so we can have a Canadian baby and get free government health care!" Birth is not cheap.

My wife wanted to do "natural" childbirth. However, there is nothing natural about childbirth. Women don't give birth in the forest anymore, biting down on a twig and hiding from the wolf. We have hospitals. If I was the one giving birth, I wouldn't do it naturally. I hate pain. Guys, the best way to explain natural childbirth is this. Imagine going to your dentist and he says, "Would you like natural root canal? A natural root canal is so much better than a drug-filled root canal. I think the natural experience is the way to go. You'll bond with your molar. There'll be candles and incense. We'll play some Enya and natural whale-song music. There'll be no anesthesia or negative words near the root canal area." Right. I don't want natural anything! Men want to tame nature; to put buildings and landfills and gas stations on it. We see the Alaskan wilderness and think it would be so much prettier with an oil rig.

We rationalize our treatment of this planet by saying things like "Global warming doesn't exist." However, in my own lifetime, I've seen the abalone, edible sea snails, disappear in California. Growing up in San Diego, I remember neighbors who ate abalone steaks and had abalone shells in their yards. Try to find one abalone around San Diego now. The sea otter, our California grizzly bear, and the giant black sea bass are as rare as fair-and-balanced media. The weather is also strange, with hurricanes Katrina and Sandy. Tornadoes have devastated the Midwest and blizzards have buried the East Coast. When you have children you think of the world you'll leave them.

I was involved in the birth of all three of my children, but women don't really need men to assist them with childbirth. I was more involved with the conceptions. I was very involved with the conceptions. I was a better conception coach than birth coach.

Men are great conception coaches: (football coach voice) "Oh yeah, that's the right lingerie. Keep going with that uniform. That makes me want to score. You're ready to hit the field. Oh, you're doing fine. Oh yeah, don't stop, baby. Okay, I'm done. I'll see you at practice tomorrow night. Come on, don't say no to your coach! You've got to keep practicing conception. Now, hit the showers with me."

I was a birth coach more than once, so that proves I'm Mexican. I've had three children and don't plan on having any more.

At the hospital when Julian was born, I had to fill out a questionnaire. Name: Rick Najera. That's with an 'h' sound, not a 'j' sound. Occupation: writer, actor, producer, director. Race: . . . Race? My dad's voice was screaming in my ear, MEXICAN! *QUE VIVA LA RAZA!* (Long live the people!) Then I looked at my son. Was he white? I was expecting him to be just a shade darker. I looked at my son again and wondered how anyone was going to know he was Latino.

I suddenly remembered something I heard Edward James Olmos say: "There is only one race. The human race."

It shouldn't matter whether or not anyone knew that my son was Latino, but it mattered to me. My newborn son looked really white. My Mexican gene seemed to have been completely washed out of him.

Once, when he was a baby, I put a taste of tequila on his tongue as a baptism of sorts to keep him in touch with his Mexican roots. Now looking back, that was crazy, but I was so desperate to have him keep a part of his culture, to keep a part of me, to keep a part of my father and grandfather as well. I wanted a Mexican *Lion King* moment where I held my little cub Julian up for all the animals to salute him.

There is only one race. The human race. QUE VIVA LA RAZA!

Now Julian is ten. He loves music and dance and boxing and fishing. He's that odd mix of little boy and little man. Whenever he cries I'm reminded that he's still just a little boy. Sonora, my second born and my oldest daughter, is eight. Gentle and kind, she loves cooking and all of the domestic arts. My youngest, Kennedy, is five. She is a total terror. She wants to be a pro wrestler and drive a "monster truck." However, she also has a feminine side. She'll give you fashion advice whether you want to hear it or not. Then she'll put you in a headlock.

When you become a dad, you create life, and you're responsible for that life for the rest of yours. But I don't look at my children as extensions of me or my wife. They are unique individuals. Each one surprises me. I don't own them. I only have the privilege of guiding them and teaching them for a short time. Then they're grown and gone. I can keep them young only in home movies, not in real life.

I'm not an Anglo dad with 2.5 kids. I'm a Latino dad with 3.0. And,

I'm a great Latino dad, because I had a great dad myself. He taught me everything I needed to know about being a dad. Many Latino comics joke about their families, but my father truly was a good man. He never hit me or spanked me; he'd just look disappointed in me. That look of his was all it took to get me in line. As an adult, I understand him more because I'm a father now. I have three kids. I'm only five away from having my own reality show. You need a minimum of eight.

I wrote about my children in a Showtime special, *Diary of a Dad Man*. I began to talk about my life and children in my work. At first I wondered who would want to hear about my children, but I noticed people wanted to know about my life as a father. The fundamental rule of comedy is to talk about your truth. Fatherhood is my new truth; it's who and what I am. If you're a dad, you'll appreciate what I'm saying, and if you're not, then this is your only warning because hormones will do you in. It did me in. My wife wanted children. I wanted Susie. So, I had beautiful children with Susie.

Most single men don't want to be fathers, but testosterone talks them into it. I did not run to fatherhood myself, but being a dad has changed my life. I went from ME to WE in an instant. And when I say WE, I don't mean WHEEEE like a fun carnival ride. I mean WEEEE like we need health care, diapers, babysitters, and college education. WEEEE need things now! One year I paid $1,500 a month for health insurance. I was praying I got sick just so I could justify all the money I spent.

A woman sees a child and says, "How fun." A guy sees a child and says, "How much?" When you have kids, you have more maxed-out credit cards than not. I have credit cards, mortgages, and bills for things I thought we didn't need. Like zoo passes. I took my kids to Petco and I swear they were just as happy there as when I took them to the zoo. They saw a snake eat a few rats and they were in animal kingdom heaven. And it was FREE.

Today I'm broke, because I'm a "daddy" and no longer a *"papi."* A "papi" is a Puerto Rican or Cuban daddy. I'm just a daddy.

I once dated a Puerto Rican girl. They're very different from Mexican girls. They're like, (in a Puerto Rican accent) "Ay Papi, ay Papi."

It totally shocked me. I was like, "Hold on!" Then she explained,

(Puerto Rican accent) "Look, Rick, you call me *Mami* and I call you Papi when we make love."

I was like, "Is there someone you need to talk to, because to me, sex is not ever mentioning your parents in bed." But then, I really got into it. She's saying "Ay Papi!" and I'm saying "Ay Mami!" and I'm like, "Who's your daddy? Who's your daddy?" And she yells, (crying in a Puerto Rican accent) "I don't know! I don't know who my daddy is! He left my family at Christmas when I was three!" Whoa . . . whoa . . . this dysfunctional sex is turning me on. "Who's your daddy? Who's your daddy! Daddy's home!"

And, now we have a recession. Thank God it's not a depression. There's a difference, you know. A recession is when your neighbor loses his job. A depression is when YOU lose your job.

It's tough out there. I remember the beginning of the recession. I saw banks closing. I saw a bunch of Anglos waiting outside a bank, and they looked desperate. They had the same look that white people have when there's a GOING OUT OF BUSINESS sale at an Ikea store and they can't get in. It's scary to Latinos when we see white people lined up outside a bank, withdrawing their money.

The only good thing I can say about this current recession is, welcome to being Latino in America. You, too, can adjust to being non-white. Come on, Anglo America. Sit down on that plastic-covered sofa over there—the plastic-covered sofa we got on layaway—and let me help you cope. We Latinos have been in a recession a lot longer than all of you. You will adjust, America. It's not the end of the world. We have survived. So will you.

I work and write late at night because being a professional writer is mostly a game of writing then sifting through the junk you wrote down during the day just to find a nugget or two of something worth keeping. A writer becomes sort of a gold miner. And there's no guarantee you'll even find any.

Recently, I wrote a treatment for a film I think is great. It's a true story about a man who started a mariachi program at his school. Mayhem Pictures loved it. They had a deal at Disney Studios. Disney Studios had another Latino movie in development and decided to go with that one. So, Mayhem Pictures had to pass on mine. That's the life of a Hollywood writer. Most of the time you are writing scripts that may never be seen or read. And when you add how long it takes for films to be made, script writing is a long trek through the jungle that could lead to oblivion.

But I work hard in Hollywood for my children and my people. That's what keeps my artistic engine running. Even writing this book—it's my last will and testament for my children. When I'm gone they might read and understand me and my love for them better.

For everyone else, it's my way to shine the spotlight on a people, at least in the media, who are seldom seen. I want people to understand me by understanding my children. My children are the new America.

I love my family and I work really hard for them. I work 14 hours a day; 8 hours at the office and a few more driving around in circles to avoid my kids. I need sleep. When I come home I'm on their time.

At first, I was not a good dad. I had to learn the ropes. My wife came home one time and saw me in the backyard with a garden hose on Julian, washing him down. "What are you doing?" my wife yelled. "Changing his diaper," I said. "I'm wiping him. It's a green thing. He's clean and my lawn's getting fertilized. It's never looked so green!"

There are definite cultural differences between my Anglo wife and Mexican me. My wife's idea of a fun afternoon is going to a you-pick-em farm. Who takes a Mexican to a farm where he picks the fruit? And then pays for it?

My wife thinks it's fun going to the Alamo; I see a dark stain on Mexican-American relations. Susie also believes in health care; I think doctors are scary people who live off your medical problems. Susie worries constantly about the kids' health; I don't like taking my kids to a doctor. Doctors always, always find something wrong. They even invent problems that I can't understand.

I don't know what it is with white women and doctors, but my wife feels we need doctors for everything. If a child coughs, we need a battery of tests. One day my wife took my son to the ER because he had a fever of 103. "A hundred and three?" I asked. "Honey, that's like a cool day in

Cancun." She didn't laugh.

I remember a phone call I once got:

SUSIE

Rick, Julian's head is tilting to the side.

RICK

Maybe he slept on it wrong.

SUSIE

No, I'm taking him to emergency.

RICK

No, don't do that. Calm down. What do you mean, his head is tilted? Like a Pez candy dispenser?

SUSIE

It's not funny! Meet me at the emergency room.

So, we go to the emergency room. It's a Friday night in Los Angeles. There are gangbangers waiting for "La Sad Girl" to get out of surgery, and we're sitting next to a guy with a hatchet in his head. His name is "Little Puppet." He's over six feet tall. And to top things off, there's a man who has some sort of Asiatic flu. We wait for hours. Luckily for us, everyone dies. The doctor finally sees us.

DOCTOR

I ran a battery of tests and I think his neck is a little sore because he slept on it wrong.

RICK

He "slept wrong"?

I was stunned by the ER carnage, fear, and worry for a diagnosis of "He slept wrong." Two thousand and fifty dollars later, and I've got an irregular heartbeat after seeing the bill. Then I had to get THAT checked out! Twelve hundred dollars more!

Mexicans don't go to hospitals unless they work there. They won't go there unless they are wheeled in on a gurney. My wife, like most white people, takes our kids to the doctor whenever they're sick. I, like most Mexicans, take my kids to doctor if I can afford it.

I need to provide. That's my responsibility. Kids cost money and we live in an uncertain world. We can't just hunt to provide. I watch the Hunting Channel. I see guys do it all the time. I watch them hunt deer. It's strange, but the thought of going out into nature and returning with a meal is so primordial and simple. Providing a meal for the family is everything and it's no different in Hollywood or anywhere else.

Dad is a title, not a location. How I treat myself is how I was treated by my father. My father gave me love and respect, so, I love and respect myself. I teach my son about being a man just like my dad taught me.

My daughters are different. I need to give them love and affection. Studies show that a girl's relationship with her father determines how she will get along with men. I'm the first man in my daughters' lives, and they will judge men through me. That's a lot of pressure.

My Alamo

"My children give me a reason to be exactly right where I am."

With three kids, life is moving so fast. My comedy career became serious at breakneck speed. I took jobs for my family that I would have never taken before. I became a television executive, otherwise known as "a suit."

I worked at that network job for nearly two years, and I wasn't happy. I'll do anything for my family. Case in point: I went to the beach with my family and we were walking along the boardwalk. I pushed a stroller with my daughter in it. Suddenly, my wife says:

> SUSIE
> Honey, you know what would be fun? Taking our kids out in the stroller and walking on the beach.

> RICK
> Honey, this is a stroller, not an all-terrain vehicle.

> SUSIE
> Honey, do it for the kids.

So, I started to push the stroller. A baby stroller on the sand rolls an inch and then becomes the Great Pyramid of Giza. Now I'm knee-deep in the hot sand. Everyone on the beach is in real bathing suits and they're

155

looking at me saying with their very white voices, "Look, Shannon. They're so cruel to their gardener. They're making him push a stroller in that hot sand." Old men are looking at me on the beach saying, "Poor son of a bitch, that was me 30 years ago." I'm loaded with baby toys, pushing a stroller in hot sand. I'm waiting for Roman soldiers to come up to me, whip me, and yell "Look at him! KING OF THE MEXICANS!" I'm screaming and cussing, "Why, Lord, why hast thou forsaken me?" That's me at the beach.

I try to be a good example to my kids because the world can be a criminal and cruel place. I want my kids to have values. I even started taking my kids to church. The Church has these great ideas such as, one day, they ask us all to fast so we understand and think about the poor. Okay, so I fast. And now I'm thinking how mad I am at poor people for making me fast. I'm thinking that we've got to kick these poor people out of here. They have only brought me hunger and pain. Then I ask them to pray for a job for me, so they pray and I get 20 jobs, but none of them pay, so I've got to be more specific. Pray for a job that pays money.

My mother was a proper Mexican woman with Midwestern values. So I want my kids to have religion. I want them to be "good." My mother's a sweet woman who always said (old mother voice) "Never cuss, Rick!" I try not to cuss, but when you have kids, that is a promise you can't always keep. Julian asks me to help him put together a Transformer toy. An hour later I'm screaming "Damn Optimus Prime!" The transformer has transformed me into a screaming maniac. I go off! "You can't fix it?" my son asks. I'm cussing. "How does Optimus Prime turn into a damn truck? This shit is hard!"

MOM

Rick, never cuss unless it's appropriate. In the old days, no one cussed unless it was appropriate.

RICK

So, let me get this straight. In the old days people never cussed unless it was appropriate? Like in Custer's last stand, did he say, (Southern accent) "Holy shit, look at all the Indians"? Or, did the captain of the *Titanic* say, (old man voice) "That's a big fucking iceberg"? Or, did Davy Crockett in the Alamo yell, (frontiersman voice) "Well, I'll be a goddamn son of a bitch, that's a lot of Mexicans"?

(Beat)

                    MOM
Yes, that would be appropriate.

Sometimes you come to realize that what we learn as history is actually a myth. That's part of the reason I love history; it helps me decode certain truths that you just cannot gloss over or hide. For example, in 1848, President Ulysses S. Grant said the Mexican-American War was unjust.

"Generally the officers of the army were indifferent whether the annexation [of Texas] was consummated or not; but not so all of them. For myself, I was bitterly opposed to the measure, and to this day regard the war [with Mexico] which resulted as one of the most unjust ever waged by a stronger against a weaker nation. It was an instance of a republic following the bad example of European monarchies, in not considering justice in their desire to acquire additional territory." (U. S. Grant, *Personal Memoirs of Ulysses S. Grant* [New York, 1885])

The unjust Mexican war occurred because we invaded the Mexican territory without sufficient provocation. The invasion was advanced by Southerners who wanted to introduce slavery to Texas. Slavery had been abolished by the Mexican constitution, so they couldn't allow slavery there. The Southerners wanted Texas to be a slave state. The Civil War was brewing within the country. And even Lincoln himself said it was wrong for us to take Mexico. Renowned poet and activist Walt Whitman and other respected thought leaders were opposed, too. Not all of America was into grabbing Mexico.

The funny thing was, an American statesman reportedly said if we should take Mexico, it will be "like a poison pill to America." Stealing Mexico is a poison pill to America? Really? So a lot of people were against the war, and after generations, you start to forget that. You start to think, *Oh, no, this war was just and right.* Instead of looking at the facts.

I took my son to the Alamo on a family vacation, and it was a strange experience. Speaking of lost history, did you know there were Mexicans inside the Alamo? They were Texicans, loyal to their fellow Texans. They died fighting with the white man, Davy Crockett. I tried to explain to my son that you can be an American and a Mexican; you can be a Texan and an American. That you can be two things at once. I told him, "Son, imagine how it was hundreds of years ago at the Alamo . . ."

Julian loves it when I act out stories. I imagine the scene like this:

Paco, a Mexican, is standing on the fort walls looking out to thousands of Mexican troops.

PACO
(in a Mexican accent)

Hey, you Mexicans! You are going to lose big time! You're going down!

DAVY CROCKETT
Look at you, Paco, a Mexican, standing and fighting next to me.

PACO
We are going to win, Davy Crockett. The Mexicans outside are going to lose.

DAVY CROCKETT
You are brave to taunt a 5,000-man army, Paco.

PACO
I'm not worried. You white guys always win. I chose the right side.

PACO *(cont.)*

He yells out to the enemy troops below.

You Mexicans are going down!

DAVY CROCKETT

That's the spirit, little Paco. Even with no ammunition left and no more troops coming, you still taunt them.

PACO

Don't fuck with me. I'm under a lot of pressure. Where's your army, Davy Crockett?

DAVY CROCKETT

They're not coming.

PACO

Help! I've been kidnapped by the gringos! Help! Somebody rescue me!

And that man, Paco, was shot in the back, retreating or charging, depending how you look at history.

One of the biggest events my family survived was the day Sonora went into surgery. It was in 2006. I was waiting in the hallway at Children's Hospital, holding my wife's hand. My daughter, Sonora, was in surgery. One of the best doctors in Los Angeles was removing a congenital nevus from her back. It was right on her spine. The doctors were worried that the strange red birthmark on her back could become cancerous. As a precaution, they wanted to remove it.

All the doctor saw was a congenital nevus. What I saw was the image of the Virgin of Guadalupe, halo and all. "I think it's a sign," I told the doctors, "and it can't be removed. I think my baby is a miracle and the Virgin is watching her back."

The doctors thought I was just being a superstitious Mexican, the type that sees Jesus on a tortilla. The type that wears his underwear as swim trunks at the beach. The type that is able to buy a green card at a swap meet. The doctors thought I was being too Mexican; I thought the doctors were being too white. I was so worried about my daughter.

Any time your child goes under the knife, you feel fear. I had no control over anything. And anything could've gone wrong. This was my child, and I didn't care about comforting statistics about surgery. Even if it's a-million-to-one odds, it doesn't matter because that "one" could be my child.

Talk about two different views of something. I was seeing a miracle and they were seeing the possibility of cancer. The doctors won the cultural tug-of-war. Medical precaution beat my Mexican faith. The doctors insisted that Sonora not keep the birthmark, and they took my little baby into surgery. They put her under and operated. My wife and I waited. Then after about three hours that seemed like three days, we went into her recovery room. She was crying like I had never heard her cry before. It broke my heart. Nothing makes a parent feel worse than seeing his or her child in pain. The Virgin Mary birthmark was gone, and the only thing left was a huge scar, but Sonora was alive.

What I learned that day was that my children were my Achilles' heel. I've had a great life and lived it well. But my children are pure potential. I want their future bright. They're my encore. They're my curtain call. They're my last bow. The world could only hurt me by hurting them.

Sonora is fine now; she's healthy and beautiful. All of my children are. I look at them and I think they get that beauty from their mother. I want to hold them, protect them, and keep them young forever, but I know I can't. Someday I won't be there to protect them. They will only have the memory of my love and wisdom to help them when I'm gone. My father once said, "Rick, you won't truly understand me until you have children of your own." He must be smiling in heaven now because he was right.

Before my father passed away, he gave me a coat. It was a long coat. I'd been working in Hollywood, so I couldn't visit home as much as I wanted to. I was busy with my career, pitching TV shows and acting. I had worked on a Pax TV show called *Ponderosa*. It was shot in Australia, which was surreal—an American classic Western shot in Australia.

I came back to see my father, who was ill. I didn't know how ill. I went to the hospital to visit him. I didn't know it at the time, but he was dying. He wasn't as strong as I remembered. He'd lost weight. I remembered him as a strong man full of confidence and laughter. He had movie-star good looks, but now age and sickness had changed him.

I still saw a shadow of him in his eyes. His eyes were always warm and loving. He'd smile at my antics and laugh and tell stories about me. I was his *mijo* (son), whom he loved and accepted. I was his artist son. I'd done what he dreamed of doing. I was able to do it because he because he sacrificed at a job for 30 years to give me that chance:

RICK

Hey, Dad. How you doing?

DAD

Oh, great, Son. I just slipped in the shower. That's all.

RICK

You have to take better care of yourself, Dad.

With a smile, he looked at me.

DAD

Remember when you were a kid and I bought you that coat? It was a long coat.

RICK

Oh yeah. You said I looked like a little Humphrey Bogart in *The Maltese Falcon*.

DAD

You were eight years old. You went to school, so proud of your long coat. Then I saw you that afternoon, dragging that coat behind you. "Hey, what happened?" I asked. And you told me, "Nicky said, 'Hey, where did you get that dress?'"

RICK

Yeah, I remember. I was so mad when he said that.

DAD

I told you that you never had to wear that coat again.

RICK

I remember.

DAD

Does it get cold in L.A.?

RICK

Does it get cold in L.A.?

DAD

Yeah, I have an old coat just like the one I gave you as a kid. I won't wear it, so why don't you take it? Does it get cold in L.A.?

RICK

Yeah, Dad. It gets cold in L.A.

I was amazed at the love my father had for me. Even dying, I was more important than anything. I was the future, and he wanted me warm and secure. He wasn't going to be there to protect and shield me from the world. That's the Latino I know and see—a man who worked all his life to provide and protect his family. My father was my hero.

Now I'm a dad and I see the world and I worry. There's swine flu, the recession, SARS, the Ebola virus, sexual predators, global warming, oil rig pipelines spewing black gold into our oceans, the Arab Spring, tsunamis, financial collapse. And then I look at my kids and I see hope. I asked my dad once if he would ever change anything about his life and he said, "No, Son. I'd do everything the same. I'd just do it a lot slower." I have to teach my kids that.

My dad died. I miss him. More for my children and wife than for me. He was a patient, funny, and wise man. I think my father knew what I would see, feel, and become. He taught me one great lesson: to be optimistic. Optimism is in short supply, but my dad always wanted me to be optimistic—to believe in the future is always better than dwelling on the past. Somehow we're all better off looking forward rather than looking backward.

Optimism fuels every journey, and every child is another hope for that better future. When I had my first child I thought, *How will I ever be able to afford kids working in this business?* Ten years later, I thought, *How could I ever afford* not *having kids in this business?* More than ever, my children give me a reason to be exactly right where I am.

HELP WANTED:
NETWORKS THAT
SPEAK LATINO

"Not all Latinos speak Spanish . . .
We can speak English and live Latino."

The only thing I'm really ashamed of as the head of my tribe is my poor command of the Spanish language. Not all Latinos speak great Spanish. I'm one of them. In Miami, I even went on *Despierta America,* Spanish television's number one–rated national news show, and did an interview in Spanish. It was so bad. After every sentence, I thought I saw the host actually get teary eyed and silently curse America.

People think Latinos are taking over with their foreign language. Not true. Trust me, I went to Cabo San Lucas, Mexico, I ate a Costco pizza, bought an apple pie, had Kentucky Fried Chicken, went to Starbucks, watched HBO in English in my hotel room, and the only words I said in Spanish were "Margarita, por favor."

While Latinos may or may not speak Spanish, we still retain our culture. I went to the courthouse and I saw a Mexican guy talking to the judge. There was no question or issue over his culture or race. He was not hyphenated. He was Mexican, not Mexican-American, and he spoke to the judge like this:

MEXICAN GUY
(in a thick Mexican accent)

No, Señor. I no guilty, Señor Judge. I no guilty.

JUDGE
Well, Mr. Rodriguez, you missed your court date.

MEXICAN GUY
I no guilty.

JUDGE
Okay, the fine is $2,000.

MEXICAN GUY
What? That's too much!

JUDGE
Okay, $50.

MEXICAN GUY
Oh no, judge! Too much! Es too much! *Mucho dinero!*

JUDGE
How much can you pay?

MEXICAN GUY
Fifteen dollars.

JUDGE
Okay, $15.

I imagined what I would do. I was like, *Man, I'm turning Mexican! Screw Mexican-American.* I wanted to pull my shirt out, borrow a cowboy hat and some mariachi pants, pour some Tapatio sauce on myself, and speak to the judge:

JUDGE

The fine is $2,000, Mr. Najera.

RICK

(in the same thick Mexican accent)

Oh no, Mr. Judge. Too much! Es too much! Es too much!

JUDGE

Let me get a translator for you, Mr. Najera.

RICK

(same thick Mexican accent)

Oh no, Mr. Judge. I no speak Spanish good, but I have thick accent. Mucho strange, no?

JUDGE

Two thousand dollars or 30 days in jail.

RICK

(in a regular voice)

Jail? Do you accept American Express? I'm not going to jail. I'm too pretty.

That's how I saw that bad Spanish scenario. But I was worried I'd end up in jail for impersonating a Mexican. Or that I'd be charged under the Lou Diamond Phillips Mexican Impersonation Act. The law was passed by both houses after the movie *La Bamba* came out, because Lou Diamond Phillips wasn't Mexican. But he has been loyal to our culture so I say he is. "Welcome aboard, Lou!"

My kids are fluent in Spanish and help me understand computers and technology. I give bad history lessons. My kids asked me why we celebrate Cinco de Mayo. I said it was to celebrate the Mexican victory over the French. Then they asked why we fought the French. I told them be-cause the French wear little beret hats. We Mexicans wear big hats; that's why we fought the French. Then they waited for a smile on my face to see if I was joking. I smiled. My kids think I'm funny and goofy, which makes me very happy. My kids laugh at my bad Spanish and correct me. All three speak Spanish better than me. My Mix-icans have arrived.

Many Latinos define themselves through language. It's also the rea-son they're excluded from American television. Univision and Spanish-language networks are selling to those who control the American mar-keting and advertising dollars. It's a lie that the only way to reach Latinos is in Spanish. Univision gets huge ratings; there's absolutely no doubt about that. Recently they beat NBC. And I'm happy for my Spanish-speaking brothers and sisters. However, I'm concerned that there's a per-ception that Latinos don't speak English. Not true. The fact that Latinos don't speak English separates them even further from the mainstream.

You don't do a Tyler Perry film in Swahili, so why is it they cut our numbers by saying the only way to reach Latinos is in Spanish? There's a finite amount of money set aside for the Latino market, and the fight is to see which network convinces people to buy advertising with them. Univision or CBS? Telemundo or ABC? It's a battle, and Latinos are caught in the middle.

Growing up in San Diego, I remember that many of the local English radio stations would sign off with the Mexican National Anthem. Every night a very white San Diego, a military town populated with U.S. pa-triots (and retirees looking for good weather), would be lulled to sleep by the sounds of Mexican national patriotism. Growing up Mexican-American, on the border, I lived in a constant state of irony.

I was a border child with one foot in English-language television and the other in Spanish-language television. The Pedro Infante films that I watched with my *abuela* (grandmother) went hand in hand with the images of *Gilligan's Island, Star Trek,* and *Bonanza.* My abuela would cry watching wrestling with me because she thought the fights between the muscular Anglo brutes were real.

My favorite image on television was always Desi Arnaz, who loved

Lucy and the America that she represented. Americans loved Desi, regardless of the "Babalu" songs he belted out each week, songs that called for the worship of African gods and *"negra bembonas."* That was TV then. Ironically, Desi remains on the air to this day with his decidedly bicultural love affair with America.

The television programming of today has changed radically for Latinos. The biggest change is programming in English. Comcast, with its purchase of NBC Universal, has become the biggest media giant in the United States. Comcast is reaching out to Latinos in an attempt to ease the fears of the FCC that the mega-giant will hurt diversity.

That's good news for U.S.-born Latinos. According to the 2011 U.S. Census 52.9 percent of the 50.5 million Latinos in the United States were born here and 82 percent of those born in the U.S. are bilingual. The U.S. Census Bureau estimates the biggest growth for Latinos is a result of birth in the U.S., not immigration.

A new 24-hour news channel, Fusion, is the new name of the ABC-, Univision-, and Walt Disney–distributed channel in 20 million homes. Fusion will be launched to see if second-generation Latinos want English programming. I'm a second-generation Latino, and I say "Yes!"

To keep competitive in the market, networks will need a new way to reach those U.S.-born bilingual Latinos. And the way to reach them is through programming in English. Comcast plans to add new networks aimed at Latinos. It recently renewed its distribution pact with nuvoTV (formerly Si TV), expanding its reach to 17 million homes. Founded by Latinos, nuvoTV offers a mix of typical low-budget English-language programming aimed at Latinos. In addition, Comcast plans to add two more English-language Latino channels owned and operated by U.S. Latinos. This programming has yet to be seen, so the verdict is still out.

Other networks like mun2 and MTV Tr3s are targeting a younger audience with their mix of reality shows and music. Comcast and these other networks are trying to reach the acculturated Latinos with programming in English. And that, if done right, could spawn many future Desis.

This was why I left LATV; I wanted to work in programming in English. When programming is done in Spanish, it only reaches part of the market. So I called my boss—not the president but the CEO—and told him I felt I wasn't working hard enough and couldn't justify my salary. He was stunned. I told him that a lot of my shows weren't going forward, and LATV appeared to be turning their English-dominant channel to Spanish.

I noticed the president brought in another vice president as a political checkmate. He was an older, failed actor who wanted to turn the network to Spanish and for a lot less money, but in doing so, he'd go against Univision and the huge Spanish giants to compete for their advertising dollars.

I knew his plan was flawed, but he sold fear to the president and my boss. It was the fear of "falling ratings." "I think the world of you and your family," I told my boss, which was true. "But I want to stay in the English market, so I have to resign."

And that was that. I resigned with no job and no prospects in sight. It was the most freeing thing I'd ever done. To this day, I know I did the right thing. To me, being paid for a job I wasn't doing was unethical. "Why don't you stay, Rick?" my boss asked. I couldn't. I was never in it for the money or the power. I wanted to tell my decidedly Latino story at LATV, and if I couldn't, I needed to try somewhere else.

Let's look at what's happening in the Latino market in film. According to *The Hollywood Reporter*, Hispanics make up only 16 percent of the U.S. population yet represent 25 percent or more of those buying tickets to the cinema. Hispanics also go to the movies more often than any other ethnic group—5.3 times a year on average, compared to 3.5 times for whites and 3.7 times for African-Americans.

In 2012 when *End of Watch* opened over the September 21–23 weekend, 32 percent of the audience was Hispanic. Both Spanish-dominant and English-dominant Latinos went to see this film. It grossed $13.2 million that weekend, a solid number for an indie feature.

Years ago, another movie called *A Day Without a Mexican* drew an incredible Latino audience. (I was a comedy consultant on that movie, which meant I was a secret joke advisor.) With a limited release, the film earned over $10 million in box office receipts. It was a film in English that was supported by a Latino audience. If Latinos are flocking to films in English, they'll flock to television in English as well.

According to the new U.S. census, last year, for the first time in a long while, net migration from Mexico dropped below zero; more Mexicans left the United States than arrived. The so-called exponential growth in the U.S. Latino popluation will be largely driven by Latinos born here. The Pew Hispanic Center found that 70 percent describe themselves as Latinos who can neither speak nor read Spanish well. About 70 percent describe themselves as English-dominant. What once was a combined front from Spanish-language media and Latino advertising agencies to reach Latinos in Spanish may be over. What does this mean to Latinos and all other audiences? Networks are recognizing that there's a new way to reach Latinos: English.

That's good news for Latinos like me. I can hold on to my unique Latino identity and enjoy my story in English because, like I said, I speak horrible Spanish. Better yet, all the members of my Anglo in-law family can enjoy my Latino-themed programs in English as well.

Network programming must be specific to its audience and must understand that audience's identity. BET does it with programming for and by African-Americans. LOGO does it with programming for the LGBT community. And now more and more Latinos can chose programming in English or Spanish. The Fusion channel would plunge Disney's ABC News more directly into the cable news wars, forcing them to compete alongside Time Warner's CNN, News Corp.'s Fox News, and Comcast's MSNBC. Moreover, Spanish television is adding English. Univision and Telemundo are adding English subtitles to their telenovelas. That practice was absolutely unheard of in the past.

All of these efforts are designed to start bringing the 82 percent of Latinos who are bilingual to traditional networks. It's a huge change. All because Latino buying power, according to the Nielsen data, will reach $1.5 trillion by 2015.

Latino programming, at least in Spanish, is usually produced out of the country or in Miami, leaving those who don't speak Spanish or who may not relate to the Cuban experience out of the equation. In addition, in the past, advertisers made the mistake of thinking that in order to reach U.S. Latinos, they'd have to do it in Spanish. Univision continues to do so with a long-standing supply of international telenovelas.

Now Colombian broadcaster RCN and News Corp.'s Fox International channels are launching a new network in the United States: MundoFOX. It will go head-to-head against Univision, Telemundo, TV Azteca, Tele-futura, and other Spanish-language broadcasters that are watched from coast to coast. But to me, like many younger, second-generation Latinos born here, nostalgic programming from Latin America is about as relevant as watching their abuela's travel slideshow.

I'm not saying there's no need for Spanish-language programming. The numbers prove there is. And MundoFOX believes there is as well. But programming for Latinos in English is showing that networks and advertisers recognize that Latinos and their TV-viewing habits are changing. We're living in an English-speaking country; we're not just a Spanish-speaking colony in the middle of an English-speaking world. Why should we not reflect that on television?

Recently I turned on LATV and everything I'd feared would happen did. The network was just bad, rehashed Spanish-language programming: guys dressed as clowns with girls dressed like schoolgirls. Sexy girls and older men hawking bad programming pulling in bad ratings. It was the skewed view of Latinos held by advertisers. If you want to reach Latinos, do it in Spanish, even though the statistics indicate Latinos are watching English programming in English.

The media keeps Latinos in the Spanish-language programming world in order to keep us from joining the media mainstream. I think putting Latinos in a Spanish world is a form of apartheid and ghettoization. Many of the 53 million Latinos in the U.S. recognize that you can watch in English and keep your Latino culture alive. Desi knew that. *I Love Lucy* was coproduced and cocreated by a Latino from Cuba living in America. He told his quintessential American story in English. *I Love Lucy* is the longest-running sitcom on the air today in any language. It wouldn't still be running on TV if it were in Spanish.

Profound changes are coming to our Latino landscape, and they will include more programming for Latinos by Latinos. In English. And it's just beginning; networks on both sides of the language border are recognizing that we can speak English and live Latino.

EL LOCO:
THE POLITICAL
LATINO

"The Latino giant is waking up and he's hungry."

I'm political. I have to be now more than ever, because I want every opportunity for every child. I worry about America and the people who seem to find it easier to spread hate rather than find solutions. I was watching Lou Dobbs on the air a few years back and was shocked at how he could get away with immigrant bashing on CNN, but let Rick Sanchez say something against anyone else, and he's out.

I couldn't believe Lou Dobbs could talk like that, so I started to watch the show. After seeing it, I wanted to turn myself in. I wanted to deport myself, and I'm legal. I was scared. Anti-immigration reformers join Lou in fanning the flame that the Latino giant is waking up, and he's hungry and he wants your job. Law-abiding Americans are next on the menu. Dobbs and his so-called patriots believe that we're losing America; he's scared our borders are being overrun with illegals. He said we have to enforce our borders at all costs. It was amazing.

I got invited to Atlanta to speak at LISTA (Latinos in Information Sciences and Technology Association). After looking around a room full of Latino professionals, I thought Lou Dobbs might be right. I told the audience that night:

Ladies and gentleman, Lou Dobbs has got me scared. He's showing us that Latinos are the problem, not the solution. He's showing us Latinos who are

173

undocumented, invading our borders. Lou Dobbs has images of illegals cross-ing the border recklessly, with a baby in one hand and swine flu in the other, and a big load of drugs on their sweaty backs.

After watching his show and seeing that, I'm scared like most Americans. And isn't that exactly what Lou Dobbs wants? Because he's not in the news business, he's in the fear business. Because fear gets you paid in ratings gold. Lou Dobbs is showing us Latinos that will keep America in fear. The problem is, he's showing us the Latinos he sees, but not the Latinos that I see and know.

You never see Latinos like me or like the Latinos here tonight on TV. This is LISTA. There's a Latino here that worked on the Hubble Telescope. That Latino not only fixed it, he got NASA images from space, HBO, and ten other channels for free. That's a Latino scientist.

My father is a Latino we never see or hear about on TV. My father fought in World War II, landing Marines on a beach in Tarawa. More than once, he was ordered to keep doing that job. Keep doing that job, son. He'd keep doing it until he was killed. And the odds were that he would be killed—at 17. That was his job, but he didn't die. He lived and came home to the United States. He fought and raised a family of five. He worked at North Island Naval Air Station for 30 years.

He even went to Vietnam as a civil servant for overtime during the Tet Offen-sive. That's like being a Jewish pizza delivery man in Baghdad during Desert Storm. That's the Mexican-American work ethic. My father's a Latino we never see or hear about on TV.

My mother was a Mexican-American woman raised in Boone, Iowa. Her brother fought in World War II and was killed in a Japanese concentration camp. He was another Latino that we never see.

I've had a cousin, brother, or father in every one of this country's wars. La-tinos are the most decorated, because the first wave of soldiers sent out in any battle are the Latinos. We never see working Latinos buying homes, paying taxes, or raising families. Where are those images?

Where are the Latinos that never got a corporate bailout and gave more to this country than they took because they chose to be here? In fact, being Ameri-can is a choice. We cherish that choice. Every immigrant chose to be here. Even the slaves forced from Africa made a choice to survive and flourish against all odds. We all chose to be here.

Immigrants are among the bravest and the hardest-working citizens of any culture. And we have a country that does what no other country in the world does. It turns people into Americans.

America has always created Americans. It takes a generation or two to create a President Obama and a generation or two to create a Latina woman on the Supreme Court like Sonia Sotomayor or an astronaut like Ellen Ochoa. Because ladies and gentlemen, America creates Americans.

In America, we make Americans, and we're civil and good. At least this is my wish. I covet traditional American values like civility. We are not the country that tolerates an angry old white senator that says to our President, "You lie." You lie?

I understand his misguided anger because sometimes when I see the media I want to yell, "YOU LIE!" At least when it comes to Latinos. Because only showing the worst of us on TV is the lie. Scaring and polarizing a nation for ratings is a lie. You won't see a newly arrived immigrant with a sign that reads "Will work for food." They're too busy working.

Almost all my relatives are Latinos we don't see on TV. Nobody writes about them because they're hardworking, tax-paying, contributing Latinos that the media ignores. I remember being at a breakfast for the National Council of La Raza once with Ellen Ochoa, the first Latina astronaut. I'd just finished speaking and she leaned over to me and said, "Rick it's me, Ellen." I said, "Yes, Ellen, glad to meet you."

Then she said it again, "Rick, it's me, Ellen. Elena Ochoa." I didn't get it. Then she said, "Rick, don't you remember me? I'm Ty Ochoa's big sister. Ty, your buddy from Junior Theater, remember?" I knew her in my little town of La Mesa, California. I realized then how small our worlds are, but not our spirits. We came here to work and live and thrive.

We're the American Dream and, ironically, Lou Dobbs is married to a Latina, so I can't get too angry with him because he's now in our extended Latino family. He's one of us, at least by marriage. We're in your own home, Lou, and you're in ours. At least on my TV. That's what's amazing about this great country. I'm not against Lou Dobbs. I'm against a media that never seems to show the other Latinos, the Latinos you never see. And if we don't change our attitudes, America, we'll all lose and we'll all lose together. We need each other. I even need Lou Dobbs to remind me to remember and to see the Latinos we never see.

I gave that speech and CNN taped it and planned to air it, but Lou Dobbs quit. I wish they would've aired it. I really wanted Lou Dobbs to hear that piece, because I'd heard his take on immigration for too long. I wanted him to hear mine.

I'm sitting at my computer writing. It's my daily ritual. I think it's more like a ritual that monks do. I hear our nanny Carmen in the next room. She's really more of our friend, an extended family member. I'm just the crazy "American" she works for. Even though I'm Mexican-American, to her I'm just an American.

The house phone rings. A heavily accented voice asks to speak to Carmen. He sounds serious. I call Carmen and she takes the phone. She takes it as far away as the cord can reach, five feet to be exact. For privacy, I try not to listen. Then she hears some news. I hear her say simply and tragically, "No, no, no, *mi primo* no, no *mi primo*." Over and over again. Then she begins to cry a soft whimper of hurt and pain. It is a cry of loss deeper than I can imagine. Tears flow down her cheeks. I assume someone close to her is dead.

I look at her and ask the question that I know the answer to: "Are you okay?" She tries not to cry. "My cousin and his whole family have been arrested. The immigration came this morning. I don't mean to bother you."

I assure her that it's okay, but I know it's not. She tells me her cousin's family has been in this country for 28 years, paid taxes, and bought a home. They were all just out the night before, celebrating Father's Day. Only their daughter wasn't arrested. She was in Europe working for an American corporation. Disney, no less. She had just got her papers, and she was in Europe with Disney, the company that proclaimed, "It's a small world after all." A world of laughter. A world of joy. The paradox hits me square in the face. They're now gone and she doesn't know where they are.

In front of their neighbors, they were arrested like a mob family. In reality, they're just a simple Peruvian family that slipped through the cracks. I'm feeling angrier and angrier and more ashamed of the country

I love; the country my uncle died for and my father fought in two wars for. A country where countless cousins have fought. And this morning, I was ashamed. I know Obama wants immigration reform even after the Republican defeat. After Obama's first three years in office, it's estimated that around 1.2 million Latinos were deported. That's after Obama promised he would make immigration reform a priority.

Everyone wants to look at someone as either the villain or a hero. And the truth is, human nature is complex; sometimes we're heroes and sometimes we're villains. But that reality doesn't play well on the newsstand, and that's the whole point. If you're going to work in stereotypes, you must define a person very quickly.

The problem with stereotypes and distorted images is that they become a prison with no escape. No judge. No jury. No parole. You're thought of in one fixed way, and it doesn't allow people to ever look at you in a neutral fashion. The beauty of being born is that you're a unique, individual, perfect being. And then you enter life and things happen.

So when you say "Latino," who do you see? That's always the question. You know, I see my family. I see good people. I see a wonderful, vibrant culture. I see all those things that are not shown on the news. And not because I'm Latino; it's because I really observe life.

Georgia, with its harsh immigration laws, lost millions in crops because of our failure to address immigration reform. The face of the immigrant or the undocumented worker is not always what the media portrays. I've seen this in my own life among my friends. My own friend and producing partner, Rafael Agustin, was undocumented and only found out when he applied to college. His parents came to this country years ago when he was a child. I can't imagine America without him. He now has an MFA from UCLA and is a well-respected writer and producer. I thought about how if he'd been deported, our country would've lost a valuable citizen and resource. We have a generation of young consumers and taxpayers that we are exiling and forcing to live in the shadows.

This is now the national debate that I'm seeing played out locally. I'm seeing it in my own home. Why am I affected so much when I'm a so-called legal Latino? Maybe because of that very reason. I'm Latino.

Eventually immigration in America will be resolved, because the price of doing nothing will finally be too high. I may see illegals detained at the border, but I don't see them far from me. I see them as distant relatives, an extension of my Latino experience. Of my human experience. I empathize with them, and it's hard for non-Latinos to understand why. But I do. The fundamental question for Latinos in America is, "Do we have a right to be here?" And we do.

It's not just because this land I live in was once Mexico. No, I'm not saying I want it to be Mexico again. What I'm saying is, I have a right to be here more than a guy named Tony from New York. Many Latinos, myself included, consider this our big issue. The question we Latinos must ask is, are we part of this country or are we invading this country? Are we invited to this party or are we the so-called help? It's a matter of self-worth and history.

My personal history and the history of my people tells me that we belong. So, I'm not waiting to be invited. No one has ever been invited to America. Our immigrant nation is the result of choice. That's our fundamental strength. We're the hopes and dreams of the new world. And we're all here building the "New Jerusalem" together. We're a nation built on diversity. But now I look at my friend, the woman who protects my children like her own, and she needs my help. She is legal, she has the papers to prove it. I am legal. But those she loves, these good tax-paying productive non-citizens don't have papers—so they are not legal.

I only could offer her the day off. "Go home. Do you need anything?" And she just said, "No, I should work. It will take my mind off this." So, she'll work like all the immigrants that come to this country, and we all will keep our minds off this tragedy. And still there will be no immigration reform. We'll all work hard to pretend that it'll all go away. I drink my coffee that she hands me and think, *Yes, it's a small world after all.*

WHO CONTROLS
THE STORY?

"It's expensive to live."

I've been out of the hospital for around six months. I'm getting well and sadly, from time to time, I forget about my stay in the hospital. I'm offered a chance to speak in Miami. I speak around the country, but Susie begs me not to get on any more planes. She begs me to rest. And for the first time in a long time, I do. I'm trusting and letting go. I trust another job will come along if I refuse this one. So, this time I agree with Susie and turn the job down. This is a first. I've never turned down a job before. This time I'm being forced to put my health first. And this time I do.

At the same time, six months into my recovery, I'm paying a myriad of bills to a bunch of doctors for my time spent in the ICU. Health care is expensive, and luckily I have my Writer's Guild of America health insurance. Hopefully, one day I'll also have their retirement benefits. Altogether my WGA producers health plan has paid out around $300,000 in medical bills. If I'd have known how much how much it would cost to repair me, I might have had a "Do Not Resuscitate" sign on me after I hit the $15,000 mark. I'm so lucky that I have health care. I feel for those who don't. It's expensive to live.

I hike every day and I've lost pounds and stress. My wife Susie still worries about me. If I don't call her, she imagines the worst. I'm getting well, but I still have some residual problems. Loss of memory is one. Susie says I've always had a bad memory.

179

Now I'm working on other projects. Life doesn't slow down after a life-changing experience. I'm sure Lazarus, about a week after being raised from the dead, still had to milk the goat and pay Caesar Augustus his taxes. I'm sure he'd go to the local coffee shop and bore people with all his "dead guy" stories. The memory of those bills remind me of what happened, but I'm better, that's for sure. And I thank God for my union. It paid for a good portion of those medical expenses. Cha-ching!

Speaking of unions, I remember being on a picket line during a Writers Guild strike. I was outside in front of CBS. During the strike, Nia Vardalos, the writer and star of *My Big Fat Greek Wedding,* drove up and brought everyone gourmet pizza and Starbucks coffee. I was on the picket line with mostly rich white guys, a few women, and one black guy.

Where's Jimmy Hoffa when you need him? I wondered. *If there were more minorities, this wouldn't be a gentle strike.* It was pretty civilized. If the Teamsters were on strike with starving families behind them, that would be a real rabble-rousing event; heads would be broken and scabs beaten. Not so in a picket line of predominantly white writers walking in an orderly fashion, pleasantly greeting TV executives as they drove by.

My unions have been good to me—SAG, AFTRA, WGA, and Equity. We need unions to ensure that someone has our best interest in mind. As Latinos, are we management or labor? But when it comes to politics, who's looking out for our best interest? Traditionally, Latinos have been on the side of labor. That's why most Latinos aren't Republican. The Republican Party seems like upper management. Upper management doesn't look out for Latinos; upper management looks out for profits. The ratio for Latino-leaning Democrats is two to one. Personally, I believe we need a strong two-party system. I think Latinos should join each political party and change that system from within. Get politicians involved in Latino issues because, in the end, Latinos are America's future. However, memo to the Republican party: Marco Rubio is not the Latino answer.

Most Latinos believe that Marco Rubio was a planned, insincere attempt to reach out to them. Marco Rubio is a Cuban. That doesn't automatically equal understanding of Latino politics. It's not that Mexican-Americans don't like Cubans. They just don't like that particular Cuban.

They don't respect him. His family didn't flee poverty or political oppression. Not a single raft built of tires was involved. The Rubios flew to America after getting a visa from the American embassy.

That the Rubios' family fled Cuba and Castro's regime is a myth. Marco Rubio is more myth than history. I'm not putting Marco Rubio down; I'm turning the spotlight on him. His family came to the U.S. in 1956, before Castro was in power, to find work. There's nothing wrong with that, but to many Mexican-Americans, he seems like an immigrant coming to make a profit off the immigrants who are already here.

Marco Rubio looks more like a politician who was created to calm the fears of older white Republican men. He looks like those Indian scouts and guides who traveled with the army to catch other Indians. Latinos imagine that Marco Rubio was brought out at Republican rallies to calm white America's fear of the brown tide.

"Calm down, gentlemen. Do not fear. We have our own Latino—Marco Rubio," they say. "He's one of the 'good ones.' He's one of ours." Then Marco sings a few bars of "La Bamba," puts on a red valet jacket, and fetches their cars. Afterward, the old white Republican men go home and dream of the America they used to own.

Latinos, myself included, are becoming more and more political. Both sides of the political left and right will have to seriously woo our votes. We won't blindly vote for a political party because a white person on Univision says "Vote for me" in Spanish, or *"Sí se puede"* ("Yes we can").

The only hope for the Republican Party is to recruit more Latinos, because the last time I checked, they'd lost their African-American members. According to the Gallup survey, 79 percent of African-Americans identify with Democrats. In my opinion, the 21 percent who favor the Republican Party are lying. Republicans need to compromise in policy and find a ground plan that more moderate Americans can agree on. And those moderate Americans will be Latino.

The Republican Party needs to court first-time Latino home buyers who build our neighborhoods. According to the National Association of Hispanic Realtor Professionals (NAHREP), Latinos filled 1.4 million, or 60 percent, of the 2.3 million jobs added to the economy in 2011, and they are expected to account for 40 percent of the estimated 12 million new households over the next ten years. Their collective purchasing power is expected to jump 50 percent by 2016, just three short years from now.

Latino home ownership grew by 288,000 units in the third quarter of 2011, accounting for more than half of the total growth in owner-occupant home ownership in the United States. Latino real estate leaders maintain that, while this is just a short-term indicator, it's an example of what's to come as Latinos move from renting to home ownership.

The Republican Party may have to quiet their radical side. Tea Party members and "birthers" are those who believe Obama forged his birth certificate so he could be a native-born citizen, a requirement to be President. It's like an episode of *The X-Files*. "Is this case about a crafty plan instigated by extraterrestrials?" Mulder asks, excited. "No, Mulder," Scully replies with a serious tone. "This case we're investigating is about a Kenyan foreign exchange student. This student created a false birth certificate for his foreign-born son in order for him to one day become President." Mulder looks at Scully, dumbfounded. "You've got to be shitting me. Who would be dumb enough to believe that story?"

Scully rolls her eyes. "The birthers, Mulder. To the birthers, President Obama is the black bogeyman designed to scare white America. He's the conservative Republicans' worst nightmare. They fear this president, not the illegal aliens, although I prefer the term 'undocumented worker.'" And as of April 2, 2013, the venerable AP, the Associated Press news service, the largest news-gathering outlet in the world, will no longer use the term "illegal immigrant." The world turns. It's ironic that "undocumented workers" don't fear Obama, even though he has deported more Latinos in recent years than past Presidents did.

The bogeyman to conservative Republicans is the fear of an illegal President in the White House. I think the underlying reason for their fear is . . . hold up. . . RACISM. Obama doesn't look like any one of their ideas about what an American citizen looks like. Even his name, Barack Hussein Obama, sounds just too alien for a natural-born citizen. Ironically, these are the same people wanting to get rid of the clause that says birth in this country equals automatic citizenship. That clause should never be changed. It's like the rule of real estate: location, location, location. Location is everything. Some people want to close the borders and keep all the foreigners out. Well, I'm sure the Native Americans felt they should have been the first ones to do that. All this is really about a class system and more and more the class divide between the rich and the poor is widening. The media is only fueling the propaganda machine that is helping to cement the distortion.

I'm always traveling on a plane to somewhere to entertain. I remember the flight I took two years ago to Diego Garcia, an island in the middle of the Indian Ocean to lift the spirits of our troops.

In the air, there are two worlds—first class and economy—with a definite border between them: the curtain. On one side, it's fresh-baked cookies, free alcohol, and comfortable thrones. On the other side, it's bad food you pay for, a cash bar and smaller seats. First class. Economy. Border curtain. I think that's how life is.

I've traveled in first class as well as economy. On this particular trip, I was traveling in economy, sitting in a sea of Asian humanity wearing surgical masks on their faces. The Japanese have a fascination with germs and plagues. Looking at them, I felt paranoid that I might be a sort of carrier.

I'm not wearing a surgical mask. The Japanese passengers are scared of me. I walk down the aisle and they clutch their children and point at me like I'm Godzilla with a contagious disease, sneezing on Tokyo. I carry the Western plague: fast food, entertainment on demand, obesity, and bad credit. On the plane, I'm a Westerner, not a Mexican-American. I feel very tall among the Japanese. I'm huge compared to them, a giant. It's difficult, being so big in a little seat on a plane for 12 hours.

We would be flying over the Bering Strait, crossing from Alaska over the coldest waters in the world to Japan, then to the middle of the Indian Ocean to Diego Garcia. There's a U.S. naval base there where they fuel huge B-1 bombers and troops wait to be deployed to Afghanistan. I'm on a tour to Asia to entertain the troops, which is kind of ironic since my father also went to Vietnam to work. He was a civil servant during the war, and here I am almost 50 years later doing the same thing.

On the miniature screen embedded in the seat in front of me, I watch the movie *The King's Speech* for fun. I change the channels on the headset and hear the various languages—Japanese, German, English, and Spanish. In the Japanese version the king has a deep voice, even when he stutters. Geoffrey Rush, the king's speech therapist, has a squeaky voice because he's a servant. On the German track, the king who stutters sounds ill and weak. Geoffrey Rush's speech therapist voice is deep, teeming with authority. Germans don't like teachers sounding weak. And the Japanese don't like kings to sound weak. Or servants to sound stronger. On the Spanish track, the king sounds suave and sexy, but wounded.

I hear the cultural differences. *The King's Speech* is a wonderful film about a man overcoming a great misfortune. He's a stutterer. He's a king. He's human. And he's flawed; that's what makes him real. It was the best picture of the year 2010, according to the Academy of Motion Picture Arts and Sciences, aka the organization behind the Oscars.

It's ironic that the actors are so white. They are British. It looks like a Harry Potter reunion. Many of the pictures nominated in 2012 were not ethnic in any way. *True Grit,* an American classic, is minority light. There is one Native American that barely utters a word before being hanged. But the best of all images in *True Grit* is a stableboy. A friendly, happy black stableboy. If they would've put him on a lawn in a jockey uniform holding a lamp in one hand and a slice of watermelon in the other with a menthol cigarette dangling from his lips it wouldn't have been less stereotypical.

I also saw *The Fighter.* That film is filled with poor white people, a few Cambodians, and an Asian woman that becomes a hooker. At one point, she's just a crackhead. Then she gets a promotion and becomes a crack whore. I think it was because she has ambition and a head for business. The only black people in the film are a few boxers and the real Sugar Ray Leonard. How do you do a film about boxers and leave out Latinos?

The media is plagued with the cultures. The winner is whoever is in control of the story and how it's told. Every conquering army writes the history of the people they conquer. The first thing that the Spanish conquerors did in Mexico was burn the writings of the Aztecs. I often wonder what they wrote down. Maybe it was just trashy novels or *How to Rip Out a Human Heart for Dummies.* We'll never know for sure.

When I saw *The King's Speech,* I recognized in it the humanity that unites us all. I recalled Shakespeare's brilliant prose. I remembered why I became an actor. But when I'm in Hollywood I see the direct opposite. Time and time again, I see the casting and the networks that strive to homogenize our country and keep us from true greatness. I see a battle being fought where groups like the Tea Party claim to want to "take America back," and I think, from who? From the poor and the middle classes? The African-Americans, Native Americans, and Latinos? That's right, take America back from all those poor and huddled masses yearning to breathe free.

I see right-wing fear mongers trying to push back a tide of immigration that began under the sea below me on a land bridge crossing the Bering Strait. Yet the networks and Hollywood are doing everything to keep our TVs white. In the words of one of my casting director friends, "Rick, they don't give a damn about diversity." Maybe she's right.

I spent a week observing and shadowing a director on a show called . . . well, I won't say. It's set in New York City, and on that New York set, there were no Dominicans or Puerto Ricans acting in the show. Only one black, blue-collar worker who was hired for one day, and he only had three lines. It gets worse. The writers were almost all white, and I was one of maybe two Latinos on that set. It might as well have been apartheid. The director was white as well. Luckily, the director was a woman, so they scored a point. But I want everyone to win; we need to think that way in order for America as a whole to win.

Fast-forward to 2013. The Best Picture winner at the Oscars is *Argo,* a story about Tony Mendez, a CIA extraction expert who gets six Americans safely out of Iran. Is it only me? I think CIA extraction expert sounds a lot like a "coyote," which is slang for a "travel agent" for "undocumented workers." The CIA got a Mexican, Tony Mendez, to get six people across a border. Tony's a Mexican-American. Of course it will work. However, Ben Affleck plays him. And then there's *The Impossible,* a true story originally about a Latino family (Spanish). The two leads are English actors, Naomi Watts and Ewan McGregor. Hollywood takes our stories and recasts us as white. Latinos buy tickets to movies, but we are in them less than any other ethnic group. I believe the predominantly white male Academy forgets Latinos. Not out of malice, but out of ignorance.

I remember one time I was working with a white writer on an HBO pilot. I wrote a scene with a white female jogging through Central Park in NYC. She runs by a *conguero* (a conga player) playing in the park, and as many Puerto Rican *congueros* will do, he flirts with her. As she runs by he yells, "Don't run from love, baby." My white cowriter stopped me. "Rick, we can't have a Puerto Rican yell at a white woman in Central Park. It would be very frightening for her." What? "Saul," I said, "she's not alone. It's not late at night. It's broad daylight. It's an innocent flirtation. He won't run after her with his conga in hand. He's not chasing her down in the middle of Central Park." He relented. "Okay, I see your point. You're a great writer, Rick." I asked him point-blank, "Saul, have you ever worked with a Latino professional before?" And without hesitation he said, "Oh, yes. My maid, Maria."

Reality check: The influential people in Hollywood don't have the experience of working with creative Latino professionals. They're only experience with Latinos is as the hired help. And that's usually how we're cast.

Of course, being Latino and naturally polite, I observe more than I complain. Latinos never complain. The last time we complained was in the '60s. That's when we were called Chicano and marched to protest the Vietnam War and the high number of Latinos who were killed.

Cough, cough . . . wheeeeze . . . wheeeeze . . . cough. It sounded like a death rattle.

A Japanese man coughing next to me interrupted my thoughts. He looked bad, like a human petri dish of disease, and he was sitting right next to me, almost in my lap. He's Patient X. I'm almost sure he was in contact with a sick farm animal.

I think bird flu. I'd only worry more if he were holding a chicken. I'm positive he's a carrier of some cross-species virus. I'm positive, he's positive. I want to ask him if he was in contact with farm animals, but it's rude to ask.

He wasn't wearing a surgical mask. Now I was worried. Luckily, we were on an international flight with hundreds of movie selections and access to liquor, so while I might get infected, I'll be entertained and drunk as hell and I won't care.

This international flight only reminds me of my life back home. Separated by a curtain and a border in Hollywood, or banished to Spanish television, separated by a language that I don't even speak that well, I'm Latino. We're left out. We're locked. I think about that for a moment, 30,000 feet over a cold ocean. I don't like borders. Borders are barriers. I smile as I think about the indisputable fact that nobody can cross a border like my people can.

I AM 38

"He who opens a school door, closes a prison."
—Victor Hugo

Election day—November 6, 2012. I'm hiking a mountain trail with Edward James Olmos, almost eight months after I was in the ICU, fighting for my life. President Obama is trying to keep his job; Mitt Romney is trying to take it. This election year, whether I like it or not, I'm involved in California politics, fighting for Proposition 38.

Proposition 38 was originally called the Munger Initiative, named after its author and creator, Molly Munger. I became a part of Prop 38 a few months after my accident. I was looking for a reason to live. I'd been released from the ICU and wasn't quite sure what to do with myself.

To my fellow actors, I always seemed to be a leader. I'd mentored and become a father figure to many in my industry. I'm amazed by how many Latino actors know of my work and have performed my monologues and sketches and plays.

Most of the theater world chooses the works of playwrights they feel audiences can relate to. When word had spread about my coma, people were shocked to discover that I was human. I've always projected the illusion of being invincible, and the reports surrounding my time in the ICU were dreadful.

I knew I'd survived a miraculous near-death experience, and I was slowly inching back to my former self, but I was still experiencing moments of downheartedness. I was preoccupied with trying to understand why I survived. If there were no coincidences, why was I still here? The answer came to me unexpectedly through a phone call.

I listened to a voice mail message on my phone. "Hey, *Primo*. It's your cousin, Mike. I need your help. Call me back."

I was buoyed up, because my cousin was treating me like a man who could help, not like a man who needed help. I returned his call, left my own voice mail, and waited.

He called me back. Mike Najera, my tall, New Mexican, Mexican cousin. He and his wife Betty have always been good friends. They're an example of a great team. Mike's family is the side of my family that married into Cesar Chavez's family. Chavez was the great union organizer who founded the United Farm Workers (UFW) in the '60s. In or around 1992, I emceed an event with him and several Hollywood celebrities. It was one of my favorite moments. I have a picture of Cesar Chavez and me together; I treasure that photo.

"Hey, Primo, it's Mike. Listen, cuz, I need your help." Then he started talking about Molly Munger, a civil rights attorney who raised millions for California schools in legal action, making it possible for schools in poor neighborhoods to get the same monies as those in rich neighborhoods. She was all about fairness. She received a Martin Luther King, Jr. Award that she shares with her law partner, Connie Rice.

He explained that Connie Rice is Condoleezza Rice's cousin, as if to warn me. "Rick, Molly's the daughter of Charles Munger, one of the richest men in the world. He's partners with Warren Buffett of the Berkshire Hathaway fund. And Molly's biggest cause is education."

Education, I thought to myself. *Aside from immigration, education (or lack of it) is the biggest issue Latinos face today.* Education (or lack of it) will decide our future. But, in California, there has been a prison boom since 1977, when then governor Jerry Brown signed a law that made it tough for judges to reduce or change sentencing. With that and the "Three Strikes" law, along with a war on drugs, you have a prison explosion.

In fact, when Jerry Brown took office there were 44,000 prisoners; now there are 44,000 prison guards. Thirty new prisons were built, but only one state college and university were built during the same time. In 2011, during Jerry Brown's second term as governor of California, he was ordered by the Supreme Court to move his prisoners out of crowded prisons; he opted to move them to county jails. He needed money to do that, so he came up with a so-called "education" bill that partially paid for it. He claimed it was his way of getting monies into the school system and to help with "public safety," but in reality, he was moving a chunk of those monies into the prison system.

According to a survey by Hills + Knowlton, 80 percent of all Americans think that Latinos are criminals. There's a lot of people that think I must have been in the mob. I must have done something. The truth is, it's harder for them to believe that I'm a good, upstanding citizen. It's easier to think I was at one time part of a criminal syndicate.

Some of the classic gangster movies are rooted in Latino culture. But Al Pacino—who is Italian—plays two Latinos, and they both were Mafia guys. Al Pacino playing these two consummate, top-of-the-mountain gangsters in American culture–defining movies has had a big impact. To many people, these movies are more real than real life. That's what people don't realize. Society gets built on this kind of propaganda. So do prisons.

The impact of those images of Latinos as criminals on American culture is incalculable, and it gets compounded daily. People don't realize that, because we have no consistent alternative images of Latinos that are being seen.

You know, Joseph Goebbels, the propaganda minister in Nazi Germany, had a PhD in theater, which makes me kind of glad I never got a PhD. Think about it—who better to give Nazi propaganda than a man who has a PhD in theater? A man who understands the power of images constantly being replayed in your head? A man who revels in the fact that a picture is worth a thousand words? Propaganda is no joke.

Kaiser Permanente did a media-consumption study that revealed that in contemporary culture, children and young adults now spend 77 minutes more on the Internet and video entertainment than they did five years ago. Seventy-seven minutes. We have 77 more minutes of images and distortions. Citizens don't want to give a minute of prayer in school or silence or meditation or some moment to give praise, but as our educational system is falling apart these kids are being exposed to 77 minutes more of images that distort reality and contribute to the perception that all Latinos are criminals because Al Pacino's and others' skewed portrayals of Latinos are the only images that they see.

The impact of these images on culture, compounded daily, is criminal. What people don't realize is that there are no alternative images to the ones that the media perpetuates. Why do we think immigration reform can't be passed? I think it's because of propaganda. That's right, propaganda. The images being sold to the American people are of criminal illegals crossing our porous borders and stealing our jobs.

That's why when you choose to be a member of your tribe, you also have to choose which positive images you're going to support, nurture, and sustain, and which negative and destructive images you're going to call out, protest, and defeat.

Veteran Latino comedian Willie Barcena nailed people who promote fear of a brown America when he addressed the issue of job loss to a so-called illegal immigrant in his routine this way:

"If some guy with no language skills, no education, has no money, totally poor, comes to your job, and takes your job? You're an idiot! . . . Oh, I took your job? You no longer work here? I crossed the border. I can barely speak English. I come to your office. They made me vice president! I can't imagine!" Only in America. That's the ridiculousness of it.

My cousin Mike called me back. "Hey, Primo," he asked, "do you know Edward James Olmos?" "Yes," I replied. He lives a few blocks from me, and in 1997 he did one of my monologues for the Latino Laugh Festival in San Antonio. I remember one night Ed, Erik Estrada, Cheech Marin, and I grabbed a limo and took it for a joyride.

"Rick," my cousin Mike continued, "we have an education proposition, Prop 38, and we need Ed's help to get it passed." I love anything dealing with education, so I agreed to meet with Bonifacio Garcia (aka Bonny), a big Stanford-Law-trained Chicano attorney who wanted to meet me.

I met him at a wine bar he co-owned. What's ironic to me is that in the '70s, Cesar Chavez boycotted grapes; now Chicanos are turning those grapes into profit. I met Bonny, and he talked to me about getting Edward James Olmos involved in the campaign. I know Edward James

Olmos cares about education; he received an Academy Award nomination for his work in *Stand and Deliver* portraying Jaime Escalante, the East Los Angeles math teacher. It seemed like an idea worth discussing, so I call Eddie and asked him to have a meeting with me.

Cut to: A restaurant in Encino, California. Edward James Olmos, after hiking in the Valley, meets me for breakfast. He shows up sweaty and hungry. "I heard what happened to you," Eddie said. "You gave us all a real scare." He sounded like a scolding father, and I accepted it; I knew he was doing it with love. I told Eddie when I came out of my coma that I wondered what I should do with my life. I believed that working on Prop 38 was something that I could do to make a critical difference for our kids.

It was a bold move, putting on a ballot a proposition that raises $10 billion a year for schools and keeps it away from the politicians. The money would go directly to the schools. "What's the downside?" Eddie asked. "The governor's proposition raises money, too, but not all of it would go to the schools," I replied.

"Okay," Eddie said, his interest piqued. "The governor is against Prop 38," I added. "What else?" he pressed. "The money is coming from a wealthy civil rights attorney—Molly Munger," I said. Eddie paused, thinking it over.

"Eddie, over fifty percent of the children in California schools are Latino. This should be our cause, and if a rich white woman from Pasadena cares more for our children than I do, then shame on me." Eddie nodded in agreement. "What do I have to do?" he asked. "Sign the ballot statement and be the Latino chairman," I said. "How bad will it get?" he asked. I hesitated. "Very bad," I admitted. "The governor will most likely win, but I think we have a chance to shake up politics."

Eddie looked at me with his intense Edward James Olmos stare. "I'm in," he said.

I called my cousin Mike and told him that Edward James Olmos was on board. I drove to Pasadena to tell Bonny that we had a genuine celebrity who really cared about education on our side. I've seen Eddie give his own money to causes he champions. When he's in, he's in all the way. Bonny is overjoyed.

Suddenly, in walks Molly Munger, a woman who gave up her career in law after the California riots to aid the poor. I'm hoping she's as good as everyone says she is. We hit it off, and compared the California we grew up in to the current New California, ranked 47th in school funding. This is a state where we have cut over $20 billion from education in the last three years and laid off more than 40,000 teachers. This has affected nearly three million Latino schoolchildren. What a coincidence that as Latino enrollment increased, funding decreased.

Later, I coined a quote for the campaign: "Education is a civil right." I even suggested we use the Victor Hugo quote: "He who opens a school door, closes a prison." I actually told Molly I wanted to meet the woman who wanted to fight for our children and was about to blow millions on a failed campaign. She smiled and laughed and I was hooked. Was this the reason I survived my coma? To support Prop 38—the impossible dream?

The governor of California was a very shrewd politician who needed the money his ballot initiative would provide. But I thought the children should get the money; it should go directly to schools. It was definitely a revolutionary idea. Money going directly to schools, not to the politicians in Sacramento. People, parents, and students would decide their own future. I knew we would most likely lose, but I decided it was better to fight for the right cause than not fight at all.

I thought that our plan should be to get the Latino vote, and having Edward James Olmos on board was a good start. He was loved in our community and he loved the community back. He'd never backed a political proposition before and he chose to champion this one.

I decided to get younger Latinos involved, too. Tyler Posey was a young actor from MTV's *Teen Wolf*. His father was a respected screenwriter. Tyler brought a young demographic to the campaign. Marco Antonio Regil, a Spanish-language star from the MundoFOX version of *Minute to Win It*, brought yet another demographic to the campaign. He'd grown up in Tijuana, Mexico. I'd grown up in San Diego, California. We were friends and both children of the border. They all came aboard. I began to build a website and presence. I also organized a comedy tour.

Here comes the hard part. I told Bonny I wasn't going to lose like the

legendary San Patricios. The San Patricios were a brigade of Irish soldiers who, during the Mexican-American War, were conscripted to fight
against the Mexicans. When they saw the Catholic churches being fired
upon, they revolted and switched sides, joining the Mexicans in their
fight against the Americans. They joined a losing battle and nearly won,
but lost in the end because they ran out of ammunition. They fought
bravely and are celebrated and remembered in Mexico to this day.

With the San Patricios in mind, I told Bonny, "Don't leave me without
ammunition to fight this fight." So, the Prop 38 campaign put a few
thousand into my bank account and told me to "Run, Forrest! Run!"
And I did—a comedy tour, a website populated with testimonials, television and radio commercials starring Edward James Olmos.

Then came disaster. The governor got political. His campaign began to
paint the Prop 38 initiative as disruptive: if the two campaigns battled
it out, both would be in danger of losing, and education would be hurt
in California. The governor began to spread fear—he threatened budget
cuts if his prop didn't pass. Huge signs and billboards proclaimed disaster
if his bill, known as Proposition 30, wasn't passed. The opposition also
created confusion and misdirection by adopting our Prop 38 ads and
also claiming "Money to schools, not to politicians." I called their tactics
"weapons of education destruction." I felt Prop 38 was a better solution
that put students first. Proposition 30 fixed the budget and the jails.

The full force of California politics was put on Molly Munger. Prop
30 even had major senators begging her not to attack the governor's
initiative or make comparisons to it. I was in crazy land. How can you
show the differences between the two propositions without comparing
them side by side? The PTA members who supported Molly were scared
to attack the governor's proposition even though it was flawed. If Prop
30 passed, it would put an additional estimated $5 billion a year into
the general fund, whereas Prop 38 would put the money into a fund
that politicians could only use for education; it would be a felony if the
money was used for anything else.

So, the Prop 30 campaign began to attack Molly Munger for putting
her millions into getting the public to vote for Prop 38. Our problem
was that the Prop 38 proponents didn't want to attack the governor or

the system. It was an unfair fight, because our hands were tied. Even Molly's most trusted advisors told her to play nice. And in politics, if you play nice, you lose. I was frustrated, but proud of the fact I was giving the campaign my all. I learned early in life it's bad to fight, but if you do fight, then fight to win.

I wrote several comedy sketches because I thought it was necessary to attack the opposition with humor. All of them were about prisoners in their cells talking about how the governor was using the money in his proposition for prison realignment. So, I called Johnny Sanchez, an actor who starred in Fox's MADtv, and George Perez, a comic who'd served time in prison.

SKETCH #1:

I AM 38—SCHOOL BELLS VS. JAIL CELLS

CLOSE-UP on Johnny's face.

JOHNNY

I like to read. I spend a lot of time reading. I don't know why.

WE PULL BACK to reveal Johnny is in prison. George is in the background doing push-ups.

GEORGE

You know why, fool! You had a bad lawyer. Now you're studying to be one. So, I was reading *The Economist* the other day, and it said that California's 33 prisons and associated camps are the reason for the state's recurring budget crisis. (He stands.) It's also the reason for the decline in school and university funding.

(George goes back to working out.)

JOHNNY

Last year, California spent $179,000 per incarcerated youth versus approximately $7,500 per youth for K–12 education. And to keep us adults here, it costs about $50,000 a year per adult.

GEORGE

That math doesn't add up.

(George goes back to working out.)

JOHNNY

If we could vote, we'd vote for Prop 38.

GEORGE

But we can't vote because we're felons!

(CLOSE-UP on tattoo: DON'T VOTE NOW CRY LATER)

JOHNNY

And anybody who tries to redirect the money Prop 38 raises for the children becomes a felon, too.

GEORGE

Vote on that, homeboy!

(CLOSE-UP on George's neck tattoo: I AM 38)

Sketch #2 went like this:

I AM 38—SCHOOL BELLS VS. JAIL CELLS

(George hangs out by the bars as Johnny reads a book in the background.)

GEORGE

During Jerry Brown's first administration, there were 44,000 people in prison. Today, there are 44,000 prison guards.

(Johnny pops his head up.)

JOHNNY
In the past 30 years, California built 22 new prisons versus only one new university and one Cal State school.

(Johnny goes back to reading.)

CHOLO
I'm not putting down the politicians. They're tough on crime, but they're even tougher on education. The politicians are threatening "Trigger Cuts." That sounds like extortion. That's what I used to do.

JOHNNY
That's how he ended up in here.

CONVICT
Prop 38 doesn't threaten anybody. It just guarantees to use California tax money to educate our children.

JOHNNY
And that's not a threat. That's a promise.

(We zoom in on his neck tattoo: DON'T VOTE NOW CRY LATER)

And Sketch #3:
I AM 38—SCHOOL BELLS VS. JAIL CELLS

(Johnny is leaning against his cell.)

JOHNNY
I learned a lot in here.

GEORGE

Like if someone gives you a dessert, don't take it. It's not necessarily for free.

JOHNNY

Recently, I learned that California currently spends nearly as much money on prisons as it does on all of higher education.

(George walks up.)

GEORGE

California spends $50,000 a year to house me, and all I did was steal a pizza three times.

JOHNNY

Our prisons are crowded. Very crowded. But you know what else is crowded? Our K–12 public schools.

GEORGE

What are you talking about? We rank 47 out of 50 in the nation. We're in first place!

JOHNNY

No. That means we're almost dead last.

GEORGE

Well, how was I supposed to know? I was educated in California. We're 47th out of 50, remember?

JOHNNY

Perhaps if we spent more money on children's education, we would end up spending less money on us.

GEORGE

That's what's up.

(ZOOM IN on George's neck tattoo: I AM 38)

FADE OUT

Those were my sketches using comedy against the system that incarcerated minorities instead of educating them. I loved it. I had a crew ready and actors cast when I got a phone call from Molly apologizing to me that her advisors were against the sketch idea and we shouldn't shoot them.

"Why?" I asked. "Three out of four prisoners are non-white, so statistically, the majority of prisoners are Latino. In other words, Latinos are in prison." If it passed, Prop 38 would bring in millions for preschool and K–12 education. Considering the majority of Californians are Latino, education (or lack of it) increases the prison population. I don't know if I can prove that, but most Latinos in prison are undereducated. I hated the math. It costs over $50,000 to house a prisoner and only $7,000 to educate a child.

Education increases the chance kids won't end up in prison. Victor Hugo was right. *He who opens a school door, closes a prison.* But the main Prop 38 campaign didn't want my sketches out there. They worried that my comedy tour would "derail the campaign." They imagined angry Mexican comedians tired of the Three Strikes law and mandatory sentencing who might get angry and say something off-color or wrong.

Since it was her money, they asked Molly to call me and cancel the project. I did. At that moment, I knew we would lose the battle. I believed in Molly, and felt if we didn't win, it would mean that I let her down. More importantly, it would mean that I let Latinos down. I was taking the campaign fight personally. I cared too much.

Cut to: Edward James Olmos and I are on a morning hike.

It's November 6, 2012. Election day. It's been an interesting contest— Mitt Romney versus Barack Obama. Prop 38 versus the governor's Prop 30, with millions spent by each side. Latinos had been asked more than ever to get out and vote.

Heading down the mountain, Eddie and I round a bend and run into a

200

man heading up the trail. He looks at Eddie. My campaign ads with him asking people to support education have been airing. I directed the last one, and I'm proud of my 30-second spot that tells the truth.

We all stop, and the man says to Eddie, "Hey, you're you." Eddie nodded and smiled. "I'm me," he said. "I saw your ads," the man said. "God bless you for trying to help our kids." Eddie looked at the man and pointed to me. "That's him," he said. "Thank you both for giving a damn," the man said, and he continued on his way up the trail. It was a sweet and profound moment. Eddie, always the optimist, said, "Rick, we might win after all." Me, Mr. Pessimistic, smiled at him. "We tried, Eddie. That's what counts."

That night we went to dinner with Molly and most of the campaign. We lost the fight. It hurt. Prop 30 won, and won big. I knew the governor's plan wouldn't radically change education like Prop 38 would have. What was worse, I saw a wonderful woman attacked by the media and painted as a meddling rich bitch with "an agenda." Her only agenda was the children.

As for myself, I wondered why I fought hard for a proposition that from the beginning I knew would lose. I truly believe there are no accidents, but I couldn't see the greater plan. I thought, *I came back from a coma for this?* I was depressed, but then I realized that I'd directed commercials and produced them, hired crew and staff, and got people to think about education.

For some reason, I remembered when I was in the ICU and Scott Montoya, a producer at Showtime, visited me. He said, "Rick, you need to get out of bed and walk. Walk to that mirror." I did. Hooked to IVs, with a catheter inside me, I got out of bed and struggled to the mirror. "Rick," Scott said, "you have a choice. You see that man in the mirror? Do you see anything good in that reflection? You're at a crossroads, and you should decide where you'll walk in your future." I cynically checked my Vicodin, thinking he was going to take it, but I looked in the mirror.

I saw a man with a bruised and battered face staring back at me. I said to myself, "I have to change." At that moment, I realized why I survived. I knew there were still important things for me to accomplish. Keep moving forward. Life is a journey, and mine wasn't over yet.

CHIHUAHUA CALLING

"This is where my DNA was formed."

After the election in November, I wanted answers. What was the point of my resurrection to life if I was going to lose? I'm a writer, and I need completion.

So I took a trip to Chihuahua, Mexico, to visit the city where my grandfather was born; the government of Chihuahua wanted me to take a tour. My grandfather was born in San Andrés in Chihuahua, nearly a hundred years ago. I know it's changed since the days of Pancho Villa. I decided to bring my producer Rafael Agustin and my director Francisco Ordonez to film the trip. We had come to investigate my origins. This is where my DNA was formed—in the deserts of Mexico. Certain strands were no doubt formed earlier in Spain, but Mexico was my real DNA birthplace. I was curious to see where my grandfather was born.

History, especially personal history, should give you a better perspective on yourself. I was in Chihuahua to observe and report and be positive. Mexico needs good news; it's been enmeshed in a horrific war on drugs. A war oddly fueled by the United States' love of drugs and all things addictive. Ironically, the original colonies were started to promote and capitalize on tobacco. Slavery came next, and cotton helped fuel slavery. Slavery was a cancerous growth on humanity until finally, after 620,000 American soldiers were killed in the Civil War, slavery was abolished. America went cold turkey off of slavery. As a result, slavery evolved to the deadly virus of Jim Crow prejudice and legalized discrimination.

Like every addict, America has its withdrawal symptoms—Mitt Romney and Barack Obama immediately have a polarizing effect on people. Thousands wanted to secede from the Union after President Obama's election. Chihuahua had many civil wars and conflicts with Mexicans fighting Indians, and Indians fighting Mexicans, and hacienda owners fighting the serfs who worked the fields, and everyone fighting in the Chihuahuan desert. Chihuahua has large deposits of gold and minerals, and ranches with some of the best meat and cheese. In fact, the pizza I had was made with cheese that the Mennonite farmers made. Pizza in Chihuahua? Yes, pizza is alive and well in Chihuahua. It's baked daily. The Mennonites were a religious group who came to Chihuahua to settle. Their preserves and jams are incredible. It's strange all the contrast you find in Chihuahua.

My guide met me. He explained why Chihuahua seemed a bit violent, but told me it was peaceful now. He assured me the drug war was over. "There is a new president in Mexico. This new Mexican president is going to be sworn in and things will get better." The drug war "es over," he said. There were 60,000 lives lost, 26,000 missing, and a generation of people left with little to show for the struggle. Oddly, in the past, Mexicans seldom used drugs; drugs were for the rich. However, after drug lord Joaquín "El Chapo" Guzmán introduced crystal meth and cheap drugs, the lower class began to get addicted. The rich could already afford drugs; now, so could the poor. The Chihuahua tourist board wanted me to see only the good. But I was also willing to see the bad as well.

First, I was taken to where Father Hidalgo began the Mexican revolution and where he was executed by the Spanish. There's an eternal flame and huge statue in a white marble room. Then they took me to a large cathedral dating back to 1725, located in the middle of the town. It's a baroque-style cathedral, and is one of the best in Mexico.

That night, my guide took me to a great restaurant that served incredible steaks. I had Mennonite cheese and thought to myself, *Did my family dine on steak like this? Did they have this kind of diet?* I come from big, Northern Mexico men—men with moustaches and attitudes. Maybe the fact that those men mixed with the indigenous population—tough Tarahumara Indians renowned for running and for surviving in the harsh, mountainous climate—is why there are big, Northern Mexico men. The Tarahumara Indians lived in the Copper Canyon, five times the size of the Grand Canyon. Tarahumara Indians are tough.

The next day I'm supposed to take a train to the Copper Canyon. There were armed guards with machine guns patrolling it. At the station I asked my guide, "Why all the armed guards?" He quickly said, "Oh, just for safety. Maybe it will make some bandits think twice about robbing the train." I thought he might be right. It made me think twice about getting on the train.

Later, we traveled through apple orchards and cattle fields, and slowly moved into the mountains. I saw some Tarahumara Indians below the train. They were dressed in beautiful dresses and colorful clothes. Before I got on the train, I'd seen an Indian woman selling trinkets. I bought a gift for my son, Julian. It was a carved ball made of wood. The Indians run, kicking one of these balls before them. Their children play for hours with this wooden soccer ball of torture. My son Julian loves his computer games and gets bored quickly. What a contrast.

One of my travel buddies asks me, "Rick, do you know there's a state department warning about travel to Chihuahua?" I say, "It's been amended. Many cities are off the list." My friends look at me. "Yes, that's true," he says. "Except Chihuahua and the Copper Canyon area."

As I went farther and farther into Copper Canyon, I felt I was on my own voyage of darkness. I looked for anyone who might be related to me by blood. I didn't see my grandfather's eyes in the eyes of other natives. My grandfather had steel-blue eyes. He was serious and quiet and said very little. But when he did speak, what he said meant a lot.

I got off the train and took a ride up to the lip of the canyon. The canyon is deep, and looks much bigger than the Grand Canyon because it is. You can fit three Grand Canyons in Copper Canyon. I took a sky trolley across. I have a deep fear of heights, and I was thousands of feet above a huge canyon. I saw little human trails under the trolley and Tarahumara villages down below. On the other side, on top of this mountain thousands of feet above the canyon, I saw a Tarahumara Indian woman with a baby on her back and a young child next to her. It must have taken her hours to climb up to the mountain peak. She was selling trinkets. I looked at the carved wooden soccer balls she was selling and I thought, *How poetic. The ball is as hard as life in this canyon.*

Mexico is a land of deep contrast, between living history and modern history side by side. I think I bring up history so much because you must understand your history in order to gain perspective on where you are; history is a compass. As I continued to tour the Copper Canyon, I noticed a man and woman walking behind me. They looked like tourists. As my guide described the canyon, I noticed the couple getting closer and closer. I assumed they were listening in to my tour guide. Then I noticed that the man was armed. He had a holster on his hip. I thought he might have another gun on his ankle. Then he was standing next to me.

I asked him quietly in Spanish, "What do you do?" He said, "I'm your bodyguard. I've been near you this whole trip." I noticed five police cars near the tram when we returned. My bodyguard called the police so they would be there for my protection when I returned from the tram. Then I remembered the travel warning. I moved to a waiting car. The bodyguard spoke with my guide in Spanish. I was too far away to hear what they were saying. The bodyguard moved off a bit and I asked my guide what he had said. My guide told me, "He had his feet held over the fire." I found out later that he'd been kidnapped by narcos and held for many hours. I didn't know if that meant he was symbolically under some kind of pressure, or he literally had his feet held over a fire.

Later that night in the city of Creel, I decided to go for a walk. I brought my bodyguard with me. A car passed by, slowly at first, but then it turned around and passed by us again. My bodyguard casually said, "Let's go back to the hotel." So, we did. Later in the hotel around a nice fire, eating delicious pizza made by the local Mennonite community, he told me his story.

I noticed he had a machine gun with him. He was heavily armed, in contrast to his wife, the woman who traveled along with us. They looked like a nice couple on vacation. But in Mexico, so many things are multilayered. He began to speak.

"I was kidnapped by narcos. I'd been to this town many times, but this time was different. I was surrounded by 20 men. I was captured and placed in a house. There were more men outside. I was nervous. The men who captured me never spoke. I wasn't sure who was in charge. My captors weren't, either. They couldn't kill me without permission." His wife chimed in. "I was told he was captured and I began to pray." I imagined the extreme pressure he must have been under. He laughed and said, "I began to grow gray hair after the experience. Before then, I had jet-black hair. Now look. I have gray in my hair." I remember thinking that was a small price to pay for your life.

His captors told the local press that he was dead, and the evening news reported that he had been killed. His wife added, "I knew in my heart he wasn't dead, but most of the family believed he was." And then he said just as quickly, "I was released." The fireplace crackled behind him. "Why do you think they released you?" I asked. "I don't know," he said. "You never get an answer to why or why not. It was just not my time."

I remember an old saying in Mexico that goes like this: "In Mexico, nothing ever happens. But if something happens, remember nothing ever happened." It's the Mexico I know.

I thought about filming in Mexico. A year earlier, I had filmed a web series there with Eric Roberts, a great actor who had starred in such films as *The Pope of Greenwich Village* and *Runaway Train* with Jon Voight. We took a private jet to film at a resort and spa called Hacienda Tres Rios in Riviera Maya. It was a great experience. I have so many good memories of Mexico.

The next day my guide took me to San Andrés where my grandfather was born. I had a copy of his birth certificate with me. It was sunset. A family circus was happening near the church. It was old village *vaqueros;* men on horseback rode through the streets as they would have during my grandfather's time. They were tall men with cowboy swaggers. They filled the plaza. They were having a fair that day and everyone was dressed in their best clothing.

I began to see my grandfather's face in so many of the vaqueros. I saw his blue eyes. I saw Tarahumara women who wore bright, colorful dresses. In these women's faces I saw my grandmother's face, strong and stubborn. She was a hard woman. She was dark like these women.

She was the same kind of woman that joined Pancho Villa as he rode and fought in Chihuahua. I realized my grandmother and grandfather symbolized Mexico—the European mixed with the native to create a new beginning. They were Mexico. My wife and I similarly mixed, creating children who were the new America.

As I walked through the plaza with my bodyguard close by, I found a plaque that read, "To the people of San Andrés who fought and died in the revolution." It also had the year my family had left for the United States.

I wanted to put an addendum next to the plaque that read, ". . . except for the Najeras, who missed out on all of the fun because they left before the revolution. Thanks a lot." I laughed to myself and thought how it must have been strange for my great-grandfather and his infant son to leave Mexico. I wondered if he thought he would ever return.

Nearly a hundred years later, I had returned. I walked alone and went into the church where Pancho Villa was married to his bride. It was estimated that Pancho Villa had 37 wives, but only one who was recognized by having a church wedding. He had married her in this church. Later, I would visit Pancho Villa's wife's home. There's an old Chinese saying: "Don't look too much to the past. You might end up going in that direction."

I like my future in the States and I'm thankful for my past. Now, looking at the same places my family lived, I realized how grateful I was to come from a family that dared to change.

It was September and I was ready to leave, to go back to Hollywood and get back to work. I was going to do the *CBS Diversity Showcase*. It had been almost a year since my time in the ICU. Would I still be funny? Did I have the stamina to direct and write a comedy show with other writers and actors and still have the strength and vision to win, if not for me, at least for them?

THE CBS
DIVERSITY
SHOWCASE

"Diversity is the best defense against adversity."

Every year for the past eight years, I've received a call from Fern Orenstein, the vice president of casting for CBS. It's like clockwork. It's almost like the swallows of San Juan Capistrano that come back to nest. She calls me with that Fern voice, which is very sweet. "Hello, doll, how you doing?" She's a very good and loving woman. "Well, it's that time again. How will we ever top last year?"

Fern came to the hospital the moment she found out about my accident. She was with my wife and was worried about seeing me in the ICU with tubes attached to every part of my body. She was traumatized by it enough to go to the same place I went to afterward, the Optimum Health Institute. I couldn't imagine her organic and wheat-grassed out, but she went. I think we are in each other's lives to challenge each other. The image of me in the hospital was so powerful; she vowed to live healthier. This was after she had bagels, lox, and cream cheese delivered to the people in the waiting room there to see me. When I was down, she was honestly scared she might lose me. It had been almost a year since I last took Fern's call.

She told me she wanted to start the *CBS Diversity Showcase* again. My body went slightly into shock, and I flashed back to last year. At that time, I noticed I was tired and feeling really run-down. I went home after teaching an acting class and remembered how I couldn't breathe very well. I asked my housekeeper to feel my head. She said I had a fever. I walked into the bathroom and threw up. "Are you all right, Mr. Rick?" she asked. I told her to go home. I needed to rest.

I was told later that she called my wife, who was in San Diego with the kids. She went home and Susie began calling me. She couldn't get ahold of me and began to worry. Then sometime during the day, my fever raged so high, that I had a seizure, blacked out, hit my head, and ended up hooked to a life support machine, where I fought for my life. That was March 3, 2012. It's now been a year and I'm recovered. I remember the day I left the hospital. Those memories are still fresh. And now Fern wants me to direct the show again. I wonder if I still can handle it.

For years, CBS had done showcases individually featuring diverse people of color—African-Americans, Latinos, performers with disabilities, Asians, Native Americans. They were live performances that put great new talent on display for the industry. But no one had ever done a showcase putting all of these groups together. I wanted to be the first to do it. CBS agreed and the *CBS Diversity Showcase* was born.

At first, it wasn't easy. Most performers going into the showcase were skeptical. They couldn't believe there was a forum to show off people of color. It's not surprising that most performers just want to be recognized as actors first, not as actors with hyphens. They want to be just actors, not as African-American actors, or Asian-American actors, or Minority-Actors.

I understand their feelings. I think the underlying problem is the roles written for actors are not written by people of color for people of color. Years before I had learned that lesson when I wrote with Whoopi Goldberg, and when I wrote my first one-man show, *The Pain of the Macho*, and when I wrote for *In Living Color*.

Write your story truthfully and honestly, and the laughter will be there. Laughter comes out of pain. Laughter comes out of truth. Comedy is a way of saying what others may not.

The *CBS Diversity Showcase* would be done the same way. Thousands auditioned for this show, and Fern and I would choose around 20–25 to be in it. I demanded the discipline of the stage. I called it a "show," not a showcase. I was bothered by the fact that there had to be a diversity showcase at all. But still, I applauded CBS for allowing me to create the best one.

When I watch a show that is set in New York and the cast is white and the only person of color is the man delivering a TV, I know why I do the diversity showcase every year. I think we are better together than apart, and diversity is the best defense against adversity. I devote three months of my life out of the year to this show. I see Fern's devotion as well as the devotion of many others at CBS. I know there's no showcase quite like it. I know of no other showcase that has a Who's Who of Hollywood in attendance. It's because of the professional directing, acting, casting, producing, and writing and the commitment of the actors involved that everyone in Hollywood goes to this show. Fern and I and all those involved treat it like a network TV show. Every year people ask, "Why isn't this on TV?" I don't know, but I'll keep doing it until it is.

The program has proven successful throughout the years. After participating in the CBS program, Kate McKinnon joined the cast of *Saturday Night Live* as did Nasim Pedrad. In fact, many network stars have come from this program; at least 16 showcase actors have gone on to become TV series regulars.

The program takes unknown actors and showcases them to hundreds of industry professionals. This year, after eight years, we added an additional night at the El Portal Theatre. Thousands of people came to see it. Every major studio sent executives.

Doing the showcase would be my last test to prove I was healed. CBS added more writers and I had to give a master course in writing, so the pressure was even greater in 2013. But I had learned my lessons; I had limited my workload and trusted that I didn't have to take every job I was offered. I'd begun hiking regularly and had lost weight. I changed my diet. I added more greens and cut out red meat altogether, and prayed the same group of cattlemen who had sued Oprah wouldn't sue me.

A Hollywood career, for the most part, is a series of nos, rejection, and criticism punctuated by a few rare moments of success. There is so little success; you need to truly enjoy it every time it comes along. I try to always enjoy the happy moments. There are many, but they're rarely what most people might think they are. Walking out of my office at CBS Studios one night, I looked at my parking space and saw my name. There it was, R NAJERA, stenciled in my space. I remembered years ago I was at CBS pitching a TV pilot. Now I had an office there. But I live in a world where I know I could lose my office and that parking space in a heartbeat. So I simply reveled in that little moment.

I taught this group of 50 actors and writers all the lessons I had learned in my careers in Hollywood and in comedy—from my days on *In Living Color* and with Whoopi Goldberg, to the alumni of Second City, to Broadway, and the 15 years coaching and working with over 150 actors in *Latinologues*. Everything I had learned in my life in comedy was being passed down to these students. I always tell the actors, "You'll get back what you put into the show." And it's true. I rehearsed the final cut of actors for three months. As always, it's a journey.

I remember as a child my father could talk to anyone with ease. He had a way of making people comfortable. One day, I asked him why he would talk to anyone. Why he would engage in conversations with such ease. As a child, I was very shy. My father simply replied, "Because I want to know everyone's story, and everybody wants their story to be told."

Through comedy, the *Diversity Showcase* could tell stories that needed to be told. It's not easy, directing such a huge ensemble. Mostly because of attitudes of the students themselves. They will argue and fight the process because for many, being directed is a new experience. Working in an ensemble is a new experience. I have to remember that these are young performers who see this showcase as their big break. One actress told me, 'I'm sorry, Rick, but I don't handle stress well." I told her, "Well you're in the wrong business. Stress is the cauldron that forges comedy. Comedy never comes from relaxation."

The showcase is like the TV show *Fame,* but on steroids and with a diet of desperation. The first month of the process is creating material and sketches and ideas to put into the one-hour show. Normally, hundreds of sketches are created in that time. I run it as any network sketch show—pitches and first drafts of sketches and rewrites with my notes.

Then Fern steps in with the harsh reality of the industry with her loud, "It's not funny."

I remember at one point a cast member put a scene I did in the movie *Red Surf* 20 years earlier on YouTube to mock me. It had become their Internet joke—"Look at our director playing a drug lord!" Even when I see the scene, I think, *How ridiculous.*

After the second month, I'm in rewrites and the group is becoming a cohesive ensemble. Acting is taught mostly to remove old bad habits. My main goal is to create actors, not comedians. Comedy comes from truth; not indicating an emotion, but being an emotion that goes through your soul. My second goal is to create an ensemble, a unit of actors who live in the same reality. I want acting skills, not performance skills. There's a difference. It's subtle, but there is a difference. A performer is someone you watch and who amazes you. An actor is someone you feel for and through.

I want an actor first and a performer second, because when you merge those skill sets, it's a hard combination to beat. Bad sketch comedians are after laughs, not truth. An actor is after the truth; that's when the laughs come. I had one of these bad sketch performers tell me, "I'll trust your direction, but if I feel it's not working, I'm going for the laughter." An actor's job is to trust that as long as he or she follows the path of playing the reality of the situation, laughter will be an outcome of that work. There's an old acting adage that's true—"If an actor cries less, the audience will cry more." Many actors will work hard for the audience's emotion when they really don't need to.

By the third month in the program, there's more rehearsal and writing. This year we created 600 sketches and chose 24 for the show. I was told by one executive that the CEO of CBS was coming, and to knock three sketches out of the show. Imagine telling actors that their sketch might be taken out after they've spent three months working on it. This is "a professional show, not a showcase," I tell the actors. I could never fight to keep a sketch of mine on *MADtv* or *In Living Color* or *Townsend TV* because I wanted my showcase moment. Acting is a profession that has a discipline like an army. Ironically, in the end, it's not about ego; it's about time. Each show is timed to the second. And by the time I'm in the theater, the stakes grow bigger, because now the clock is ticking and we're paying huge money for the theater rental and manpower. Each one of these actors must give up weeks of their time for free just for a chance to be seen. And they do it. The pressure is incredible, and it's that pressure that laid me up in the ICU.

Many young actors' attitude about the diversity showcase today is, "Hey, I'm out to get myself a job." I see that as a problem, because they don't recognize the struggles other people had to endure to get them on this stage. Every generation must sooner or later look back to see the sacrifices made that future generations fail to acknowledge. When Americans talk about the Greatest Generation, they're referring to World War II; a time when everyone jointly sacrificed through larger-than-life events so we could all be here today.

When I consider the diverse actors in the showcase, I think to myself, *They have no idea what went on before they arrived.* Many of them are very cavalier. Because of my conversations with people like Sidney Poitier and Lupe Ontiveros and my relatives who were involved in political and civil rights struggles, I am personally connected to this history.

I have seen the pain in people's faces, and I realize the deep sacrifices people have made. I want this new generation of talent to stop deluding themselves that they have nothing to do with our culture, or with people of color and all of these different life issues. They "just want to work!" I understand that completely! No one wants to be a token. But you can't just work without realizing what got you your work, how that actually happened.

Part of the problem with entertainers is that we are self-centered and not self-centered at the same time. The whole world revolves around us, but most artists also want to help the world. I don't want them to lose that. I want them to feel all the work and everything that went into this; not just this year but also every year before, and the struggles and challenges of every single person to make it.

And yes, I want them to laugh at the YouTube clip of me playing a drug lord. "Oh, look what Rick did! He played some ridiculous drug lord." And it's funny to them, but at the time, that reality wasn't very funny at all. It was tragic because there were no other options. And that's what I wanted them to understand.

The younger generation is very skilled in rapidly tuning out and say-ing, "Well, that has nothing to do with me." But even the ones who get the jobs and land a show don't really understand that if that show doesn't work they may not get another audition for two or three years. They don't understand that the innate racism and the control of the medium means that if they don't understand the bigger context, they're not going to be able to be gainfully employed as actors.

These pervasive inequities are the reason for having a diversity show-case. Even white professionals realize that the situation is unfair. They recognize that something needs to change. They look at the statistics.

Part of our cultural evolution means we have to know where we're headed and why. But the first step, strangely enough, is honestly ac-knowledging that there's a problem. And if you don't understand that there's a problem, then you're a like a frog swimming in a pot of warm water until it slowly comes to a boil; you don't even realize that you're dying.

If you don't realize there's a problem, you can never become the so-lution. But when you recognize the problem and commit to solving it along the way with like-minded others, that's how we all move forward. If there's anything I'm teaching it's that it's not just about the showcase, it's about all of us.

In the *Diversity Showcase,* our niche is dealing with ethnicity. But a lot of our charges don't understand why they're not getting jobs or why there isn't a call for them. They'll understand it when they go to an audition and the casting call is for someone who's "ethnically ambigu-ous." That's an actual casting term. It means, *Ethnic, but we're not sure which ethnic group.* So, it's an odd thing, but those casting terms are very racially coded.

When the breakdown goes out, it might say, "We're looking for a La-tino male, 40," or they might say "an Antonio Banderas, good-looking guy." You know, okay, Latin lover. They might describe it a little bit more, but overall, it's age and ethnicity. All those things come out in the breakdown. Then you go out for the audition.

But if there are mostly white people writing those roles, they may not include anyone like you. And so it takes a studio or someone else to intervene, because the studio's worried about keeping an audience. Now that Tyler Perry has done really well, some producer or director or casting agent might suggest, "We should have a black lead in it." Or they should have "another black role in it," or something else, to "draw the Tyler Perry crowd." And then, as the economics start to move them, they start adding more roles.

Most of the networks have very little ethnic representation. The recently merged Screen Actors Guild (SAG) and the American Federation of Television and Radio Artists (AFTRA) have openly commented about this. Everyone's trying to figure out how to get more diversity within the industry, but there is no real mandate, no push. So, the mandate has to come through economics, like, *Hey, do you realize if you have a Latino in the role you're going to get a Latino audience that will come out for them?*

You can name off all the reasons why it's wrong, but if there's no law, no mandate, or no one saying to move forward, nothing happens. It's kind of like a gentlemen's agreement—*Look, we agree that there's a problem and we see that it needs to be fixed. But we don't know how. We don't want any real regulations. We don't want any of those kinds of things, but we do all agree that there's a problem.*

A lot of the younger talents breaking into the business are really making it all about them. They don't see a bigger picture. I want them to see that bigger picture, which is not, *Oh, I'm going to be seen by a bunch of casting directors and agents and it's going to be really great for my career.* That may be true, but I'd also like them to understand that their success is going to be a great way to solve a problem that affects everybody. And that's what they don't see.

I have one last night to make the show a success. Tempers are flaring. I have to get the show up. The actors are desperate to show an invited audience our three months of work. My goal is a perfect standing ovation, and to get that from this tough audience, everything must be perfect.

Now our stage manager is about to call "places" at the El Portal Theatre, and I bring the actors together for one last lesson. The crowd is filling the theater. Edward James Olmos is there, and so is nearly every major management firm and Hollywood executive. I offer the actors and writers assembled in the green room one final speech.

Look, I'm done directing and teaching you. My work is over. I have been tough on all of you because you beat out thousands to be here tonight. You are being given a gift that all those other talented actors did not get. A lot of talented actors auditioned for Fern and me—2,500 to be exact—and you took their spot. Now all I ask of you is to earn your place here.

Most of you saw me in the film Red Surf, *and it may be a huge laugh to a few of you, but let me put it in perspective. Two decades ago, those were the only roles written for Latino actors. After I played that role there were no other auditions. They were not looking for any Latino types. But the same white actors in that film had many auditions lined up.*

I spent eight years and CBS money to give you this night, and you will go out there as diverse performers and I want this audience to be ashamed that you are being sent out as diverse actors. And not just actors. I want them to be ashamed that we live in a world where there are categories such as diversity, ashamed we live in a world where racial groups still have invisible hyphens that restrict opportunities.

But after tonight they will see your hard work and they will see your discipline and your talents and you will be simply professionals—professional artists and comedians that demand to work because you earned it.

I played a Cuban drug lord in Red Surf *after completing a master's program in acting, followed by working in nearly every major theater in the nation, so that you could be here. I played a stereotype not written by me. But after that film I swore I would write my story and would help others to do the same.*

I have given every person I played dignity and professionalism. I did that so you could have this night. A lot of performers played ridiculous stereotypes so you could have this night. I want you to be professional and give your work dignity, for all the actors who came before you. The Hattie McDaniels. The Sammy Davis, Jrs. The Lupe Ontiveroses.

Tonight you will join many performers of color who came to Hollywood to work. As minorities, we not only have to act, but we also have to change Hollywood. So, when you step out there tonight let your work speak for itself; let your hard work show that you deserve to be seen. Show why you deserve to work—not because you're a minority or you're diverse or you fit a category.

You deserve to work because you've earned it. I'm proud of you all because maybe the jobs you get will balance our society that much more, and with your art you will create some justice.

The cast looked at me, some indifferent, some more concerned about their makeup, and some genuinely moved. But they went out on that stage and earned a standing ovation. The day after, three actors were cast and many more received offers.

Les Moonves, the CEO of CBS, came to the show, and a week later, a deal was made to film it and create a pilot. Adam Small, Fern Orenstein, and I at this time were tapped as executive producers. It took eight years for that Hollywood success story. Hollywood is slow, for sure, but if you knock on enough doors, sooner or later you'll find someone who opens one and says "Yes."

REBEL LATINOS

"I put the weight of Latinos on my shoulders because I saw very few opportunities to shine a bright light on who we really are."

After the diversity showcase one year, the producers asked, "Would you do a show for children and teens?" "Kids are great," I said. "What they love, what they tie into—they're incredible. I'm in!"

One of the first exercises I gave my young students was to tell me a monologue about themselves. To say, "Hi, my name is _____,"and then explain themselves. "Hi, my name is _____, and I'm this." "Hi, my name is _____, and I'm this."

This one girl, a sweet and shy 13-year-old, was very quiet when we started talking, then she finally agreed to try her monologue.

"Hi, my name is Cassidy Mack, and I'm a survivor."

That was her opening line—*I'm Cassidy Mack, and I'm a survivor.* Wow! "Well, what did you survive?"

"I survived the foster care system. I was in the foster care until I was six years old. I have a biological family but I couldn't go to live with them. I'm going to lose my mother. But after spending years in foster care, I was finally adopted and got my forever family."

I was blown away. "You know, Cassidy, that's a beautiful monologue. Write your story down." She was very hesitant at first. "No, I shouldn't. I really shouldn't." She had been afraid to tell her story because she had been teased and bullied and felt that people misunderstood what it meant to be in foster care. She felt that people looked at her as damaged goods.

"You're not damaged goods, you know. Write that story. Tell me that monologue." And so, she got it together, and this was right before I went into the ICU. When I got out, I got this nice little note from Cassidy. She said she'd been praying for me the whole time, and I'd changed her life because I gave her a voice. She said that she had performed her monologue at the showcase that I unfortunately missed when I was in the ICU, and that people had actually listened and appreciated her honesty and was cast in a film as a result of her performance. She started to understand herself and to feel good about herself. Because of the positive response, she realized that she had the ability to change lives for other foster youth, and decided to start her own Foundation called Love Gives Chances. Her motto is "Take a Chance to Give a Chance."

Next, Disney wanted to do a story on her. And after that, she was asked to give a speech at a conference for foster care parents and children. When I congratulated her on her achievements, she said, "You're the one who did this for me. You gave me a voice."

I had encouraged Cassidy to find her voice and to tell her story—but her voice was just waiting to be heard. And now telling her story is changing other people's lives. And that's the beauty of finding your voice, of discovering who you are. And she's just 13 years old.

I saw Cassidy recently as she was preparing for a big speech in Arizona. And as her mentor, I reminded her, "I know you totally feel a special responsibility to foster care kids, Cassidy, but I want you to remember that you're a 13-year-old girl. You've done more in your little 13-year life span than most humans ever do. You survived the foster care system, have gone on to become a professional actress, and started a foundation—at your age, that's simply extraordinary! I understand that you're tempted to put the whole weight of all the foster children on your shoulders, but remember that you don't have to do that."

Later, when I started thinking about Cassidy, I understood what was driving her. I, too, put the whole weight of Latinos on my shoulders because I saw so very few chances and opportunities to shine a bright light on who we are. So, for people like Cassidy and me, our success is thrown down from the roof to share with others like our Laguna Indian brethren. But not everyone is hardwired this way.

Other people reading this book may be focused on a simple question like "Am I funny?" or things like that. I not only want to be funny, I also want to be socially relevant, honest, and aware that I'm one of the few voices at the mike right now who can do what I do. That means my life is filled with different kinds of questions. As I thought of Cassidy and all of the pressure she was under, I realized how blessed she was because she empowered herself and she has something in life worth fighting for at such a young age.

I'm sitting at home with my son, Julian. It's nearly the one-year anniversary of my time in the ICU. I'm home. It's Sunday. All is quiet in my world. It's my favorite time. Sunday is always the lull before the Monday storm, and as I surf the channels on television, I see an old British film called *Cromwell* starring Richard Harris and Sir Alec Guinness. I stop. I'm brought back to my childhood, about the same age as Julian is now.

Julian recognizes Sir Alec Guinness from the film *Star Wars*; he was Obi-Wan Kenobi. We're both glued to the TV, watching the movie. My little girls are baking in the kitchen. The house smells of good food. My wife is getting ready for a trip to Mexico. Her blog, The Mexico Report, is her passion. It's about positive stories in Mexico. I love the fact that she's positive; I think that's why I married her. She's courageous, compassionate, and creative.

Before the weekend, I had a meeting with George Lopez about an animated series based on one of my characters from *Latinologues*. George has signed on to star in the pilot. My lawyer, Bonny (Bonifacio) Garcia from the Prop 38 campaign, along with Evolution Studios, will negotiate. CBS is calling me about doing a sketch pilot. They want me to work on a budget. So, after eight years, CBS may give me a shot. Like many in Hollywood, they want diversity. They may not know quite how to achieve it, but they are trying.

I don't know how the shows I'm working on will work out. I know it's a process. After knocking on many doors and hearing a lot of nos, I just heard two yeses. That's a step in the right direction. Of course, I'm suspicious of happy endings.

But this weekend I'm watching Alec Guinness play the king of England, Charles I. It's the same film I watched with my father when I was around Julian's age. There is a great ending monologue spoken by Richard Harris in *Cromwell*. The monologue comes after Cromwell breaks into the Parliament and sees what his revolution has brought. He is disgusted by the politicians, who are fighting only for their own ego and ambition. Cromwell sees what his civil war has brought and sees how Parliament is unable to act. He is sickened by the corruption and lack of leadership in his politics, and I relate now having been in California politics for Proposition 38. I was disgusted by the political apparatus that I saw on both sides—people more worried about politics than solutions. Politics is a slow beast that wears its rider out. And as I sit next to my child, we watch together.

Cromwell is the supreme leader of the army. He's a man full of power, but he is disillusioned by all that has happened since the civil war and the execution of King Charles. He drives the corrupt bureaucratic politicians from the Parliament, just like Jesus did when he kicked the moneylenders out of the temple.

Cromwell takes over the Parliament, throws down the gauntlet, and declares a new revolution, where college and universities and education and justice reign supreme. He declares a human revolution of sorts, where all men are created equal.

It's the same philosophy Abraham Lincoln adheres to in Steven Spielberg's *Lincoln*. I had taken my son to see that film as well. Watching *Cromwell* on television with Julian, we both absorb the dramatic speech, as he proclaims, *"I'm declaring a land governed by laws fair and just."*

The symphony rumbles and blares and swells to a rousing conclusion, and I see how my son is transfixed by the screen, inspired just as I was, sitting next to my father and dreaming that I would accomplish great things and lead men like Cromwell did.

A lifetime ago, my father leaned over to me and said, "I would be very proud if you could speak like that," and that's what spurred me to read and study Shakespeare over and over again. *Cromwell* inspired a Mexican-American boy to find a voice and try to get the world to listen. And now, watching my son, I realized life had come around full circle.

Julian looks at me. "Dad, where were the women?" It's a good question. "The women in Parliament?" I ask. He was right to notice. I look at my son. "There were no women then." His eyes widen. "Women hadn't been invented?" he asks innocently. I laugh and he looks embarrassed.

My wife comes in the room. "Rick, don't make fun of Julian. And this better not end up in some TV special or your comedy show," she warns. "Of course not," I reply. "Unless it's funny. If it's funny and true, all bets are off."

Julian looks at me. "Dad, I know there were women back then, but why were there no women in that place?" He waits for me to answer. "I'm sorry," I correct myself. "I meant to say there were no women in Parliament."

"Really?" Julian pauses for a moment. "No women in Parliament?"

I shake my head. "No. At that time, there were no women in politics."

Julian pauses again. "No women in politics? Oh, well that's not fair. There should be women there, too."

My son learned a lesson that day. And so did I. Julian knew about fairness and justice, but the movie had prompted him to ask a seemingly simple, but important question: Where are the women?

When I see Hollywood films, I ask, Where are the minorities? Where is the justice? Where is the fairness? The inclusion of my community? Of my world? Where is the truth?

Cromwell inspired my son to ask those questions. I knew why. Art has a way of making us all dream and hope for a better world. Art is the light beyond politics that has moved man out of darkness. Good art inspires us and prompts us to ask hard questions, and I know that there are answers.

I was proud of Julian. And I was proud of all our shared humanity. "Where are the women?" my son asked. "Where is the fairness and justice, and where are the minorities?" I ask. But I need not ask where the vision is.

I hope Julian keeps asking those questions. I hope he will see when something is out of place or wrong. I hope he asks where all the members of our communities are at the table. I pray Julian will always see who's missing, and dare to right the wrongs until no one is ever missing again.

THE CAMPFIRE

*"We tell our stories to say
we are alive and we are here."*

My love for my family made me a performer at home, entertaining my father. Making him laugh, filling him with pride and hope. My love for my community made me a performer on stage. Knowing I was knitting a community together one live performance at a time, creating a gathering place where my community could meet, share ideas, and be entertained was a rare gift.

It was love for Latino stories that led me to become a writer and it was the lack of Latinos in the media that made me become a director and producer. It was the love of my family and the need to give them stability that made me an executive. In truth, it has been my Latino culture that has shaped my life and career at every stage.

Latino life is built on an incredible sense of community rooted in our strong belief in family. Latinos believe in sacrificing for their families. Many make enormous sacrifices to come to this country. They leave everything behind. I think of my father and my mother. They worked five different jobs, sacrificing without complaint. Why do Latinos sacrifice? It's simple. We do it for our families. We're willing to sacrifice because to us, to work and sacrifice and care for your family is a noble thing. Our love of family is one of the things I treasure most about Latino culture.

A big part of the reason that Susie and I got together was not that I wanted to marry an Anglo—I think you fall in love with who you fall in love with. But Susie shared the same sense of family that I did. She possessed the same kind of "family first" values that, in many respects, are Latino values. Latinos are very bonded to family, God, and country.

Latinos' love of family is almost primal. When young Latinos go to college, it's often hard because they don't want to leave their families to go to school. And there's a good deal of pressure to stay, because the family realizes that they're not always going to be together and that these days of our lives are precious. You're going to go away four years or seven years—away from your family? For a lot of Latinos, that's very hard to understand.

Traditionally, in most Latino homes, you don't move out of the house until you're married. The thought is, "Why would you move out? You're with your mother and father and all your family." Your lives are intertwined. "Why are you going to go away? Why are you going to break up your family?"

I once had a psychologist friend tell me, "You are totally enmeshed in your family." I was confused because I did not see that as a bad thing. But according to him, a family where members are involved in each other's lives limits healthy-functioning individual autonomy. Latinos don't think of independence as a virtue, as typical Westerners do. Many believe in our interdependency. We're dependent on each other. We're part of each other. We're in the community of each other. We're all interrelated and we're all part of each other's lives. So, we are guilty as charged, we are an enmeshed people.

In *Nothing Like the Holidays,* a Latino family film I wrote, Debra Messing's Anglo character gets confused by all the chatter of her Latino husband's family at the dinner table. She thinks they are arguing, but John Leguizamo's character tells her: "No, they are merely talking." I had another Latino character tell her with a thick accent, "I'm not arguing with chew—I'm just discussing." We as Latinos are totally enmeshed in family culture. And I love that. We value family and our community, and we will sacrifice for that community even with our lives. Maybe that's why there are so many Medal of Honor winners among Latinos.

In my culture to be independent is a bad thing. To be banished is a bad thing—and to be outside of the circle is a bad thing. You want to warm yourself next to the tribal fire, to travel as part of the community, to face life together. A producer friend told me that a family can hurt your career, but to me what's a career for except to provide for your family?

If I had been born Anglo or Black or Asian, I would have had a different life, moved in a different direction and no doubt had a different cause. But Latinos believe you're born who you are to serve a greater purpose, to serve your family and in turn your community.

My purpose is to be on the front lines to protect the Latino community, my family. I can do this by fighting ignorance, presenting a clear point of view, and offering entry into a world that most people don't ever see. This commitment and willingness to educate people at a local and global level comes with responsibility and a certain degree of solitude. You may never see the men and women that you're working for and yet we're all connected.

I make that connection. I am a bridge. I honestly like people, and I think when they read my work or see my plays, films, or TV, or whatever I create, they recognize that this is a guy who doesn't have a grudge against humanity—who actually celebrates our humanity.

The Mayans had a term, *In La'kech,* which means, "I Am Another Yourself!" In other words, you are me and I'm you. You know, "Love your neighbor as you love yourself." See yourself in your neighbor. So, although I am indisputably Latino, at the same time I can respect the other cultures within the wider community, be myself, and know that I am advocating for us all when I advocate for my community.

If I were a real cultural propagandist, I'd say, "Latinos! We're the best! We're the greatest!" But I've never said that. I've said, "Latinos are an amazing people!" And I want people around the globe to recognize that fact not for my own cultural horn blowing, but rather because of what I think people will miss if they don't know Latinos.

If we say, "I'm Latino, I'm proud," then the next question must be "Okay, Latino. Why are you proud? And how will acceptance of yourself and Latino culture help you accept other people and allow you to make a contribution to your community and the world?"

Latinos have rapidly become America's majority minority, and with that comes a major responsibility to advance the greater good. Just like we now turn to the Anglo culture and say, "There are more of you. So you need to even be more responsible for justice and kindness, because the world expects you to lead," the same will be true for Latinos. One of the challenges of being Latino is advocating for the advancement of the group while honoring one's own individuality. It's a balancing act that everyone has to address. You may want to preserve certain traditions or rules in your family and yet inevitably some may change. None of us can escape cultural evolution.

Yet even as we all move forward, there will be those who are determined to take us backward.

They say: "Oh my God—you're Latino?"

"Well, yeah, I'm Latino."

"Oh, you must be *part* Latino."

"No, I'm full Latino, you know, my people go back hundreds of years in Mexican history and culture. I am pure, unadulterated Mexican. But it seems that I'm not your image of what a Mexican is, and if that's the case, then, maybe your image is wrong or false."

These conversations are far too common. I've even had people say to me, "You're a credit to your race!" It's amazing. I once had a professor tell me that. At first I thought: not really; there are plenty Latinos that are better than me—that are far more of a "credit" than I am. But when you say, "You're a credit to your race," what does that mean? Do you not think my race is full of people that are, you know, wonderful and special and great? Am I a unique individual in that somehow I've risen above the horrible people that I come from? In reality, I'm not a credit to my race; I'm part of a tribe and history bonded by love and family. I'm an individual with a shared culture. I'm no "credit to my race," I'm simply one member of my race. Tell me that I'm a credit to the human race—now there's a compliment.

Sometimes I feel like there's a huge attempt to domesticate my people into a new homogenized brand of Latinos, the good Latinos. It reminds me of the Catholic Church bringing little indigenous kids out to sing at a Mass. Too often it felt like, "Look what we've done. We've civilized the natives. We've made them like us." To me, that was horribly humiliating, like saying, "See my dog, I dress him up like a human. Isn't he cute?"

What is it in human nature that makes the majority want to turn the so-called minority into people just like themselves? Perhaps it makes them feel more comfortable. There's no room for dissent, no space to say, "Hey, wait a minute, that individual is different from us and that's a good thing, that enriches all of us. Our battle should not be to make everyone be just like us. That's a waste of energy. How about seeing other people's cultures and their individuality and accepting it, enjoying it, and celebrating it along with our own?" Wouldn't you prefer having an authentic human being as your ally in making the world a better place—instead of a bad reproduction of yourself?

Every great idea is a really simple idea, you know. Love your neighbor as yourself. Okay! Pretty simple! How do you love yourself? By taking good care of yourself and your family, making a contribution to your community, preserving your health, getting a good education for yourself and your children, and helping your neighbor achieve the same thing because that neighbor is you. So, let's end the culture wars that boil down to the dominant culture saying, "You must be like me." Mixing doesn't automatically mean having to match.

Since I don't fit the stereotype of a stereotypical Latino—in other words, I'm not the dark, short Latino—I get to be the fly on the wall in worlds that a lot of Latinos don't have access to. Often, I get to hear the deeply felt convictions of non-Latinos arguing about Latinos. I hear at least a few sentences or paragraphs and occasionally a full-blown rant before I interject, "Before you go on, you ought to know I'm Latino." Then people turn bright colors or turn around to defend their positions, saying, "Oh, but you're not one of those Latinos." Then I have to set the record straight: "Yes, I am. I'm one of those Latinos. We're all one of 'those Latinos.' It's not 'selective Latino.'"

Ironically, sometimes I've got my own people looking at me saying, "Hey, Rick had it easy!" I really laugh at that because the worst part of being almost white is that you get to see both cultures. If I was purely a thick-accented, very brown gardener, I wouldn't be noticed and diversity wouldn't be my issue. My priority would be putting food on the table and that would be it. I wouldn't even think about what it means to be Latino.

229

So when members of my tribe say, "Rick, you just don't know what it's like, how it really is," I interrupt them to say, "Yes, I do. I actually know how it really is more than you do."

Being "almost white" has sentenced me to a kind of dual identity as someone who walks between both worlds. I see and hear what people are really thinking and feeling in the master's house without censorship. I experience real levels of racism, discrimination, and prejudice that are often hidden. I am exposed to the unfiltered stereotypes that white people really hold about Latinos. Yet my presence ultimately flies in the face of this disinformation once people find out that I'm Latino myself. Like it or not, my ability to "pass" often puts me on the front lines of segregation and assimilation in America.

A new colleague once subjected me to a cultural interrogation. "Rick," he demanded. "Do you like being Latino? What's it like? Would you rather be something else?"

I thought he was hilarious. Do I like being Latino? How could I ever be anything other than Latino? It would not be me. I believe that there's a reason for everything; there's a plan for me and that's a Latino plan. Latino culture values love, warmth, sacrifice, and family. We have a huge belief in spirituality and God. We built pyramids, cathedrals and altars—sometimes we even have altars in our homes. We have ceremonial rituals, like the Day of the Dead, to remember to express our love for our ancestors and our family members, and no one could ever take that away—not even Disney.

Love is also treasured in the Latino world. Perhaps we celebrate love and romance more than we should. You can see it plainly in our Quinceañera celebrations, where an adolescent girl has an unofficial rehearsal for her wedding. I love the love of Latino culture. I'm not saying other cultures don't have love, but we do it in our own way, and if you share those values you can join us and be Latino—because we are a welcoming culture.

One of the very last things Desi Arnaz did in his life was a phone call with Lucille Ball, and he just kept saying to her (and she kept saying to him), "I love you. I love you. I love you." Those were some of the last moments they had with each other. If saying "I love you" in the last minutes you have on earth reflects anything of who you are, then it is clear that Desi loved passionately; it is clear that he was Latino.

Telling Latino stories says to the world: "We belong here, in this world, in this time; we are valued, we are important." When early man left paintings on the walls of their caves, some say it was to conjure power over the animals that they would hunt. I think it was a way to tell a story, to bear witness to what they had done, what they had seen, what they had experienced, and to share that story with future generations. That's human nature and it's also very much Latino. We build to be remembered by our families and to leave them a legacy. We tell our stories to say we are alive and we are here.

It was around ancient campfires that culture was first born. Around those fires families huddled together to share that warmth, to hear those stories. That's where culture was slowly knit—and one of those cultures became mine. In the modern era we have thousands of channels and devices to tell those stories, from movie screens to TV screens to computer screens to telephone screens. The screens in our lives have gotten ever smaller and more portable and easier to access, but our stories remain the same.

Once my father told me a story about when he was just 17, at war in the Pacific, and how on an island with natives one night he shared their campfire. He said, "Rick, I was as far away from home as I could be, but that night around that fire I began to see my family in those natives' faces. I began to see and recognize my family, my mother's smile, my father's laughter, my brothers' and sisters' faces in theirs, and I wasn't alone that night. I felt I was home."

That was my father connecting to others, joining in community with others who were not Latinos. My community has a great desire to share and belong. That is why the greatest insult to us, after having built, fought, and died for this country, is to be feared and not allowed to belong. I believe if you knew us you could not fear us.

When Latinos story see their story through the eyes of the media, they notice their absence. They understand that they don't count. And that's the bigger lesson that Latinos are constantly fed: "You're not important. You're not even worth reflecting in the media." We don't need to see you. You're not in the conversation. You're not in the game.

A lot of Latinos seem to accept this situation. "Well, you know," they defend, "that's okay. At least they're not showing bad images of us." Well, not being shown in the media is like being adopted into a family and looking at the family album only to discover that you never appear in a single picture. You don't exist. You have been purposely cut out, removed from the family history.

That's why being aware of the images that are being promoted about Latinos on every media platform is so important. That's why the lack of positive images becomes of the very greatest importance to our survival.

The way to keep American culture honest is to have a very strong media anti-propaganda machine that pushes back against the way Latino culture is being defined by what's broadcast. Today, the "third screen" is an increasingly dominant force in America's media consumption. Children are watching 77 minutes more media every day than they were five years ago. What could those 77 third-screen minutes mean if they were spent on education? If we're not watching the media and what they're putting out there and what *we're* putting out there as an antidote to the poison, then we're going to inherit decidedly worse and worse images of ourselves. Think about this: the unspoken problem with Mexico and the narco war is not only that 50,000 people have been killed. The problem is there's a generation of people on both sides of the border who have been fed those images, and those people take that witness into the next generation.

I'm convinced that in many ways Latinos are genuinely surprised and bewildered when we encounter prejudice. That's why when faced with discrimination, we are often more ashamed than angry. We think, "How could anyone be against us when we know how much Latinos love, give, and sacrifice for this country?"

Our innocence gives us a false sense that we, too, are part of mainstream American culture. How could we not believe this? We work and die for our country. We share the same land. We share much of the same history. And in many instances, we practice the same Christian religions. Latino culture is a welcoming culture. We welcomed Anglos to Texas and the Southwest when it was part of Mexico. We invited American settlers to join us because we knew there was enough for all of us to build a life here.

Latinos are too often made to feel like the uninvited guest at the wedding. We're tolerated, yet uneasy and unsure of our status. We hope no one asks for our invitation because we are not sure that we have one. We are ashamed of the prejudice against us and the lack of inclusion promoted by the mainstream media.

I think sometimes Latinos feel more shame then anger because we know who we are. Thus, we are ashamed that anyone could hate us or discriminate against us, or portray us as unworthy.

After my time in the ICU, I woke up angry at how we are seen. But we need to get angry. Anger draws a line in the sand. It is an emotion that fuels real change. Latinos need to banish shame and replace it with anger. It's time to stop allowing ourselves to be cast as victims.

Being the majority minority puts you in the position where you can really take a stand for the power of images in our society and what images are going to prevail in the future. When you are the majority minority, you must demand your place at the table instead of serving as the perpetual waiter at America's banquet. And the historical implications of having Latinos at America's table are huge. Latinos aren't coming to America and saying, "Please let us join the party." We're already here. The media's failure to recognize this is a major problem.

Unfortunately, it puts me on the battleground in the first wave of any talk on diversity and ethnicity in America, because I worry that people will miss out on a wonderful, vibrant culture that's changing the shape of the United States, as it has for hundreds of years. Latinos need to be seen as part of the solution, not the problem. We need to be recognized as the group that is already here doing the hard work and the heavy lifting of an American culture that makes our world better. It's time to recognize that Latinos have been at the campfire a long, long time. At last it is time for Latinos to share our stories.

EPILOGUE:
MARCH 3

*"Make sure you watch for the little miracles as I do
—because those miracles are here."*

March 3 is an important date for me. It's my new birthday. It marks the day of my second chance. March 3, 2012, is the day I ended up in the ICU hooked up to an array of tubes and breathing apparatuses. On March 3, 2012, I was more machine than a man. Now I barely have a scar. Exactly one year after my stint in the ICU—and a lifetime later—my story is still not finished. While I'm never certain about my future, I do know there is a plan. If I don't win this battle, my children will. And I see like-minded others who are willing to take a stand in this fight.

I've joined the board of Latino Rebels Foundation with Julio Ricardo Varela and Charles P. García, and other women and men who believe passionately in our culture. They want to fight to change our image in the media and raise money for scholarships to change newsrooms on the East Coast and writers' rooms in Hollywood with more of our people to balance the images with truth.

I look at my life with all of its contradictions and ironies and complexities and history that make me who I am today, and I know that after coming close to death, I'm more determined now than ever to live. And like my father, I will do it all the same way, just a little slower. I'll watch for the little miracles. And I'll expect them. I'll continue to work in the media for my family, my community, and my nation.

I remember after my time in the ICU, I got a call from Internet sensation Ray William Johnson, the incomparable video blogger, producer, and actor. I had directed Ray at CBS, and now he offered me a job working with him on his show. Ray was the first to hire me after the ICU. I was a little shaky, to say the least, but I was grateful and humbled. I was humbled because the tables had turned: once I had believed in him when I cast him in the diversity showcase and now he believed in me.

I was especially grateful because Ray showed me the future. His Internet show *Equals Three* has over 8.5 million subscribers and over 2 billion video views. Ray never waited for a network to discover him—he discovered himself. Ray represents the future that I know is possible for Latinos when we take charge of our own destiny. And with the Internet we can. The Internet is our new campfire to tell our stories around—new, vibrant, and unheard stories ready to entertain and enlighten on those cold, dark nights.

Recently I've been in Silicon Valley working with investors who share my vision. I've ask them to invest in Latino stories and they've asked me to invest in Latino ingenuity. It's working. I'm starting to see change, and I'll expect a lot more to come. I have a lot more faith now. I know there are no coincidences. Change is coming. Our stories will be told and our images will be seen but this time they must be told by us.

ACKNOWLEDGMENTS

I'd like to thank all the great people who have contributed and helped to make this book a reality, especially Mary Najera, Edward Najera, and Tavis Smiley, who believed in me. Muchas gracias to Denise Pines, Jeremy Berry, my primo Rafael Agustin, Edward James Olmos, Lynda King, Molly Munger, Steve English, Bonny Garcia, Fern Orenstein, Gary Blumsack, my primos in San Diego, and Pastor Rustin and the Bethel Lutheran Church.

There are no words big enough to express my gratitude to my incredible wife, Susie, who never fails to encourage me or stay up late to work by my side. Special thanks to the talented Anne Barthel and my wonderful editor, the brilliant Cheryl Woodruff, who gave me her knowledge and guidance.

Above all, I want to thank those who ended up in these pages one way or another—forgive me if I did not get it right, but this is how I remember it.

ABOUT THE AUTHOR

Known as the Latino Tyler Perry, Rick Najera is an award-winning actor-writer-director-producer and literary pioneer who has captured the warmth, humor, pain, and triumph of the Latino experience for over two decades.

With extensive credentials in film, television, and theater, Najera is the celebrated creator of the award-winning play *Latinologues,* which has toured the nation to sold-out houses and standing ovations for more than 15 years, making it the longest-running showcase of its kind and crowning Najera as one of three Latinos in the history of Broadway to write and star in his own theatrical production.

In addition to being one of the most sought-after comedic talents in the industry, Najera is also a tireless advocate for the Latino voice in Hollywood and has directed the groundbreaking *CBS Diversity Showcase* for seven years. This ALMA Award winner and Writer's Guild of America nominee has also been twice honored by *Hispanic Business* magazine as one of the "100 Most Influential Latinos" in America.

Rick and his wife, Susie, are the proud parents of three beautiful children and live in the heart of Los Angeles.

SmileyBooks Titles
of Related Interest

THE RICH AND THE REST OF US:
A Poverty Manifesto
by Tavis Smiley and Cornel West

HEALTH FIRST:
The Black Women's Wellness Guide
by Eleanor Hinton Hoytt and Hilary Beard

PEACE FROM BROKEN PIECES:
How to Get Through What You're Going Through
by Iyanla Vanzant

TOO IMPORTANT TO FAIL:
Saving America's Boys
by Tavis Smiley Reports

BRAINWASHED:
Challenging the Myth of Black Inferiority
by Tom Burrell

HOPE ON A TIGHTROPE
Words & Wisdom
by Cornel West

BLACK BUSINESS SECRETS:
500 Tips, Strategies and Resources for
African American Entrepreneurs
by Dante Lee

All of the above are available at your local or online bookstore, or
may be ordered online through Hay House, at www.hayhouse.com®

• • •

We hoped you enjoyed this SmileyBooks publication.
If you would like to receive additional information, please contact:

SMILEYBOOKS

Distributed by:
Hay House, Inc.
P.O. Box 5100
Carlsbad, CA 92018-5100
(760) 431-7695 or (800) 654-5126
(760) 431-6948 (fax) or (800) 650-5115 (fax)
www.hayhouse.com® • www.hayfoundation.org

• • •

Published and distributed in Australia by:
Hay House Australia Pty. Ltd. • 18/36 Ralph St. • Alexandria NSW 2015
Phone: 612-9669-4299 • *Fax:* 612-9669-4144 • www.hayhouse.com.au

Published and distributed in the United Kingdom by:
Hay House UK, Ltd., Astley House, 33 Notting Hill Gate, London W11 3JQ
Phone: 44-20-3675-2450 • *Fax:* 44-20-3675-2451 • www.hayhouse.co.uk

Published and distributed in the Republic of South Africa by:
Hay House SA (Pty), Ltd. • P.O. Box 990, Witkoppen 2068
Phone/Fax: 27-11-467-8904 • www.hayhouse.co.za

Published and distributed in India by:
Hay House Publishers India
Muskaan Complex, Plot No. 3, B-2, Vasant Kunj, New Delhi 110 070
Phone: 91-11-4176-1620 • *Fax:* 91-11-4176-1630 • www.hayhouse.co.in

Distributed in Canada by:
Raincoast • 9050 Shaughnessy St., Vancouver, B.C. V6P 6E5
Phone: (604) 323-7100 • *Fax:* (604) 323-2600 • www.raincoast.com
• • •